Summer 2003
ISSN: 0276-0045

M000286249

THE REVIEW OF CONTEMPORARY FICTION

Editor
JOHN O'BRIEN
Illinois State University

Senior Editor
ROBERT L. MCLAUGHLIN
Illinois State University

Book Review Editor
TIM FEENEY

Silas Flannery Casebook Editor
ZACHARY HAMMERMAN

Production & Design
N. J. FURL

Editorial Assistants
DANIELLE CASTELLI, ADAM JONES

Cover Illustration
SAMUEL BERKES

www.centerforbookculture.org
www.dalkeyarchive.com

The Review of Contemporary Fiction is published three times a year (January, June, September) by the Center for Book Culture, a nonprofit organization located at ISU Campus Box 8905, Normal, IL 61790-8905. ISSN 0276-0045. Subscription prices are as follows:

Single volume (three issues):
Individuals: $17.00; foreign, add $3.50;
Institutions: $26.00; foreign, add $3.50.

DISTRIBUTION. Bookstores should send orders to:

Review of Contemporary Fiction, ISU Campus Box 8905, Normal, IL 61790-8905. Phone 309-438-7555; fax 309-438-7422.

This issue is partially supported by a grant from the Illinois Arts Council, a state agency.

Indexed in *American Humanities Index, International Bibliography of Periodical Literature, International Bibliography of Book Reviews, MLA Bibliography,* and *Book Review Index.* Abstracted in *Abstracts of English Studies.*

The Review of Contemporary Fiction is also available on 16mm microfilm, 35mm microfilm, and 105mm microfiche from University Microfilms International, 300 North Zeeb Road, Ann Arbor, MI 48106-1346.

www.centerforbookculture.org

THE REVIEW OF CONTEMPORARY FICTION

BACK ISSUES AVAILABLE

Back issues are still available for the following numbers of the *Review of Contemporary Fiction* ($8 each unless otherwise noted):

NOVELIST AS CRITIC: Essays by Garrett, Barth, Sorrentino, Wallace, Ollier, Brooke-Rose, Creeley, Mathews, Kelly, Abbott, West, McCourt, McGonigle, and McCarthy

NEW FINNISH FICTION: Fiction by Eskelinen, Jäntti, Kontio, Krohn, Paltto, Sairanen, Selo, Siekkinen, Sund, Valkeapää

NEW ITALIAN FICTION: Interviews and fiction by Malerba, Tabucchi, Zanotto, Ferrucci, Busi, Corti, Rasy, Cherchi, Balduino, Ceresa, Capriolo, Carrera, Valesio, and Gramigna

GROVE PRESS NUMBER: Contributions by Allen, Beckett, Corso, Ferlinghetti, Jordan, McClure, Rechy, Rosset, Selby, Sorrentino, and others

NEW DANISH FICTION: Fiction by Brøgger, Høeg, Andersen, Grøndahl, Holst, Jensen, Thorup, Michael, Sibast, Ryum, Lynggaard, Grønfeldt, Willumsen, and Holm

THE FUTURE OF FICTION: Essays by Birkerts, Caponegro, Franzen, Galloway, Maso, Morrow, Vollmann, White, and others

NEW JAPANESE FICTION: Interviews and fiction by Ohara, Shimada, Shono, Takahashi, Tsutsui, McCaffery, Gregory, Kotani, Tatsumi, Koshikawa, and others

Individuals receive a 10% discount on orders of one issue and a 20% discount on orders of two or more issues. To place an order, use the form on the last page of this issue.

www.centerforbookculture.org/review

The *Review of Contemporary Fiction* is seeking contributors to write overview essays on the following writers:

Felipe Alfau, Chandler Brossard, Gabrielle Burton, Michel Butor, Julieta Campos, Jerome Charyn, Emily Coleman, Stanley Crawford, Eva Figes, William H. Gass, Karen Elizabeth Gordon, Carol De Chellis Hill, Violette Leduc, Olive Moore, Julián Ríos, Esther Tusquets.

The essays must:

- be 50 double-spaced pages;
- cover the subject's biography;
- summarize the critical reception of the subject's works;
- discuss the course of the subject's career, including each major work;
- provide interpretive strategies for new readers to apply to the subject's work;
- provide a bibliographic checklist of each of the subject's works (initial and latest printings);
- be written for a general, intelligent reader, who does not know the subject's work;
- avoid jargon, theoretical digressions, and excessive endnotes;
- be intelligent, interesting, and readable;
- be documented in MLA style.

Authors will be paid $250.00 when the essay is published. All essays will be subject to editorial review, and the editors reserve the right to request revisions and to reject unacceptable essays.

Applicants should send a CV and a brief writing sample. In your cover letter, be sure to address your qualifications.

Send applications to:

Robert L. McLaughlin
Dalkey Archive Press, Illinois State University, Campus Box 8905, Normal, IL 61790-8905

Inquiries: rmclaugh@ilstu.edu

Contents

SLS
Summer Literary Seminars

Nairobi
KENYA
December 7 - 20, 2003

A 2-week session

Seminars in Fiction, Poetry, Nonfiction, Kenyan Literature and Culture, and Swahili.

Faculty: Cornelius Eady, Arthur Flowers, Stanley Gazemba, Peter Kimani, Andia Kissya, Phillip Lopate, Evan Mwangi, Josip Novakovich, Yvonne Owuor, Binyavanga Wainaina, Colson Whitehead, and others TBA

For further information on Summer Literary Seminars, Inc. and all its programs, write: Summer Literary Seminars, PO Box 1358, Schnectady NY 12301; call (888) 882-0949; (518) 388-6041; FAX (518) 388-6462; or email: iosselm@union.edu. For the most up-to-date information see our website at http://www.sumlitsem.org.

Rick Moody

Joseph Dewey

I want to be an American writer.
—Rick Moody

What have I but my style?
—Vladimir Nabokov,
a favorite Moody quote

It might seem odd, even perverse, to hold a writer accountable for apprentice work that, by his own admission, he abandoned as unworkable. And when the writer in question has produced in little over a decade (while still in his thirties yet) a considerable body of work notable not only for its daring prose line but for its audacious willingness to skew genres and upset formal expectations, even mentioning apprentice work can seem a bit unfair, rather like waving about a spouse's long-ago prom photo or taking delight in circulating an older sibling's baby-in-the-bathtub picture. Yet the novel that a young Rick Moody started only to abandon can provide a telling entrance into the dominant influences of his aesthetic sensibility. In that unpublished work, a teenager yearns to be vice president and, to accomplish the charade of maturity, outfits himself with a cumbersome set of self-designed prosthetic devices that actually convinces voters that he is an adult. Long after abandoning this techno-futuristic idea as unworkable, Moody held onto the notebook in which he first fashioned the storyline: ten pages of notes otherwise decorated with the elaborate noodlings that marked a mind struggling with creativity.

Here, even in an abandoned work, is telling evidence of Moody's signatory influences: the unlikely troika of Don DeLillo, Nathaniel Hawthorne, and Samuel Beckett. From DeLillo, there is the young character's struggle to define the self, to construct (literally) a self within and for a collective, within a public context, extending the privilege of the self by maintaining the widest possible conversation via a dynamic interaction with its cultural moment, the political, social, economic dimension of self-definition. From Hawthorne, there is the creepy parable-esque quality, a threshold adolescent masquerading as something he is not, indulging a preposterous deception, and willingly burying as secret whatever reality has come to define his self, beginning a life necessarily committed to deception and to the heavy manipulation of appearances, the cloaking of the true self within immeasurable shadow. And from Beckett, the fascination with, indeed the addiction to, the medium itself, the preservation of the notebook-qua-talisman, itself a rococo exhibition of doodles and phrases and sentences, not only a held thing but a held-onto thing that testifies to the human fascination with the system of understanding experience into words, of deploying arbitrary signs as units of expression, an object that as the formal manifestation of the thought process represents the signature effort of the species: the desire to encode into a sequence of squiggles and spaces the elaborate conjurings of the imagination, the fetish for the *objet d'écriture* itself.

But what is perhaps far more interesting than whatever thematic foreshadowing such an effort offers is the fact that this was actually the second novel Moody started—*by age eleven.* That—more than the inchoate echoes of writers that the young Moody of course did not even know yet—may be far more salient, and far more telling.

Two books begun by the sixth grade.

Although it is surely no critical leap to suggest a writer's career has been spent within the company of words, it is perhaps more accurate to suggest that Moody's *life* has been spent amid such cool company, a life bound from its earliest moments to language: first consuming books as a lonely child, relishing their giving company, then studying them through the postgraduate level; and then, before turning to writing them full time, working for a time in bookstores and for publishing houses, selling them, evaluating them, marketing them; and then, after finding his initial success as writer, teaching them, in a number of both composition and creative-writing programs, thus instructing fledgling writers in the how-to's of producing even more texts. It has been a life essentially defined against and amid the industrial expressions of the technology of language.

A Life Story

> Vladimir: *What do [the leaves] say?*
> Estragon: *They talk about their lives.*
> Vladimir: *To have lived is not enough*
> *for them.*
> Estragon: *They have to talk about it.*
> —*Waiting for Godot*

> *That's the story, all right, and if you have a few more nights to spare I've got a thousand more just like it, because I'm a desperate guy and like all the anonymous I have the urge to talk.*
> —"The James Dean Garage Band," Rick Moody

Moody's life has agreeably, even conveniently, followed the familiar contours of a *Künstlerroman*. Moody was the clichéd lonely, often inexplicably sad, middle child, left-handed, ungifted in athletic endeavors, chubby, and by his own admission a slow learner and a painfully shy kid (even saddled with an impossibly ponderous moniker, Hiram Frederick Moody III) given over early on to the companionship of books (fiction, he has often said, was his earliest narcotic). Born 18 October 1961 in New York City but soon relocated to the affluence of the comfortable Connecticut suburbs, Moody, happily for this life story, grew up in a family enthralled by narratives: tale-tellers (his maternal grandfather, a masterful raconteur, was full of Yankee lore and family legends; his mother wrote for her own pleasure) and readers (his father was an American literature major who opted for the far more lucrative promise of a career in banking and finance, but who at every Thanksgiving dinner read—and this is apparently no joke—the terrifying chapter from *Moby-Dick* about the doomed Bulkington). As is the especial privilege of the upper class, his family collected books, reverenced the value of the clean physical artifact itself—"I came to want to write because the first thing I loved was books, the texture of them, their physicality, and then later came what was contained in them" (qtd. in Goldstein 1). Moody's sterling New England pedigree included a prominent Manhattan newspaper publisher as well as several notable poets, academics, theologians, essayists, and lecturers: a veritable genealogical foundation of wordsmiths. During an adolescence given over to voluminous reading (including a fondness for speculative fiction and a serious love of comics) while attending private boarding school at New Hampshire's prestigious St. Paul's Academy, Moody essayed his first original stories; by his senior year, with the unalloyed endorsement of both parents, he was certain that he would be a writer, just socially angular enough to relish the act of writing rather than the uncertain art of talking.

Although he toyed with the notion of attending seminary, he earned an English degree (with an emphasis in creative writing) in 1983 from Brown University, studying most notably under novelists John Hawkes and Robert Coover who both encouraged Moody to investigate how experience is brought into coherence using language as a system of understanding. During his college years, playing guitar for a rock band, Forty-Five Houses (the name taken from a smart-assy answer to a question posed in André Breton's *Manifestoes of Surrealism*, "What's your name?"), he began to drink heavily and to experiment with the campus drug scene (habits he had actually begun much earlier, partly in response to his parents' 1970 divorce). After taking a year off following graduation, spent largely in San Francisco where he worked for a time as an art-museum guide, Moody returned to New York and enrolled in the prestigious

Master's writing program at Columbia, completing that program in 1986, submitting a story-cycle (still unpublished) that occasioned one advisor, novelist Russell Banks, to caution that such a talent would take some time to find an appreciative audience. Whatever success Moody found in school, however, was significantly tempered by a careening private life in which the recreational drinking and drug experimentation of his college years had begun to overtake his life.

Apart from brief stints in the clichéd work of college students (house painting, restaurant work, store clerk), Moody has worked his entire life within the world of words: his initial postgraduate employment came in 1986 as editorial assistant first at Simon & Schuster and later as assistant line-editor at Farrar, Straus & Giroux, jobs in which he would read manuscripts and draft rejection notes to would-be writers, a job phylum he would soon join. In 1985, in his second year at Columbia, his drinking becoming more of an issue, he was evicted from university housing for not paying his rent. Unwilling to use the resources of his family, he moved across the Hudson to Hoboken, New Jersey, in an effort to save money and there began to gather materials for what would prove to be his first novel. Begun in 1987, that first manuscript, a stark minimalist narrative that focused on the desperate and disconnected loves and dysfunctional family lives of New Jersey teenagers struggling into adulthood in Reagan's America, made the rounds within the New York publishing community but found no interest, publishers seeing little commercial promise in a manuscript so singularly depressing. Moody had become that most *Künstle*-romantic cliché: the struggling writer, the passionate artist with serious intentions, aprowl amid the urban philistines, unemployed with a battered (and unwanted) manuscript under his arm. Unable to find a publisher, he applied for and was turned down for doctoral study by no fewer than five universities. It was, by his own assessment, the darkest time of his young life, struggling with profound questioning over his choice of a commitment to serious fiction, doubts over his talent for writing, and the dubious expectations of ever making it work as a career, all complicated by bouts of depression and anxiety attacks and by his ongoing struggle with drug and alcohol addiction even after he voluntarily committed himself for one-month rehab in 1987.

Then would come that most clichéd of *Künstlerroman* clichés: the big break.

When in 1990 a small-press editor happened to read the manuscript of *Garden State,* he forwarded it for consideration for that year's Pushcart Press Editor's Choice Award, annually awarded to draw attention to an outstanding work of fiction unfairly ignored by the Manhattan publishing community. When the manuscript won, part of the 1991 award was its publication—and since then Moody has lived from his writings, a steady production of novels, experimental short stories, enthralling book reviews, spacious website commentaries on literary interests including John Cheever, Thomas Hardy, and comic novelist Stanley Elkin, and loosely structured meditations on pop-cultural topics ranging from rock's enigmatic techno-producer Brian Eno to Japanese cinema monsters to the September 11 terrorist attacks. When, increasingly out of step with the editorial taste of Farrar, Straus & Giroux, Moody was let go in 1991, he explored teaching, accepting a part-time position in creative writing at Vermont's Bennington College and, finding an agreeable affinity for classroom instruction, has maintained academic appointments steadily since at, among other places, SUNY-Purchase, the Fine Work Centre in Providencetown (MA), and most recently at New York's New School for Social Research. He is in constant demand as judge for prestigious literary awards, a function of his celebrity that he performs with relish. Gifted with Hollywood good looks and an enthralling performance style and dressed often in his signature black, he executes with grace the grueling demands of reading tours and public appearances. And, of course, he writes . . . a lot. In a little over a decade, in addition to publishing three novels, two short-story collections, and his 2002 experimental memoir, he wrote for a six-month stint on a conceptual comic book; he edited a collection of strikingly original essays on the relevance of the New Testament; and he even experimented with found poetry, the playful hip-hop art of fashioning collage verse by randomly cutting and pasting the unpromising phrases from already published documents (one, for instance, that appeared in the 5 October 1998 *New Yorker,* fuses lines from the *Starr Report* investigating Bill Clinton's Whitewater investments with bits of Whitman and Cotton Mather).

In short, Moody is fascinated by words, sustained by language, by the writing process itself, by the inordinate demands and responsibilities of text production. Consummately bound by a reverence for the sheer reach of his profession, when he isn't writing, Moody is talking about writing. In his copious interviews, Moody, schooled in high-eighties Lacanian semiotics, philosophizes comfortably, even enthusiastically on the often dense arguments of contemporary language theory and specifically on the heartbreaking difference between what we can imagine and what we can conjure with words, between what we experience and what we encode; he expounds on his own wide-ranging reading interests; and he even dispassionately ruminates on the drearies of publishing: the obligatory promotional tours, marketing strategies, the estimation of first-edition units, the role of agents, the scale of advances, and even script optionings. Named in 1999 among the *New Yorker*'s most promising talents under forty and a 2000 Guggenheim Fellowship winner, Moody has emerged as a young talent poised to help set the direction of post-Pynchon American fiction.

Compassionate Postmodernism/Voyeur Realism

I am a citizen of somewhere else.
—The Surveyor, "The Custom-House"

To me, the greatest job a person could ever have is being an usher at a movie theater.
—Quentin Tarantino, film director

What is remarkable about Moody's fiction is not his much-vaunted experimentation with the prose line, with pushing sentences and paragraphs to their maximum weight-bearing load, but rather the disparity, even the tension, between the life Moody has lived and the works that he has written. Seldom has Moody drawn from his own considerable life story, and when he has it has been carefully manipulated. For instance, *The Ice Storm,* his second novel and—largely because of Ang Lee's stylish 1997 Oscar-nominated rendering of it—his most recognized work, investigates the ennui, alcoholic excess, empty sexual escapades, and wounded families of the contemporary affluent suburban world of Connecticut by juxtaposing two families bound by adultery whose spiritual vacuity comes into focus one terrifying weekend in 1973 during a fierce Thanksgiving ice storm, a sort of lost-weekend-in-one-night that culminates in the electrocution of a one son by downed power lines—a compelling narrative, of course, demonstrably cinematic, but drawn little from the difficult shattering of Moody's own Connecticut family. His other fictions dramatically re-create narratives of, among others, bored working-class Jersey slackers; a retiring nuclear engineer held accountable for a plant catastrophe; a stammering middle-aged entertainment promoter who nurses a bedridden mother with a death-wish; an assortment of prostitutes, AIDS-ravaged street addicts, petty criminals, sexual deviants, and S & M connoisseurs in Hell's Kitchen; an insecure husband convinced his wife is cheating; a hapless ostrich rancher in Ohio; disaffected members of a California high-school garage grunge band; a terror-stricken mother and daughter pinned in the random crossfire of a crazed gunman at a Los Angeles McDonald's—none, of course, drawn directly from Moody's own life narrative. And when Moody does set out most forthrightly to explore his experiences (as in his poignant Pushcart and O. Henry Prize-winning short story "Demonology," ostensibly about his older sister's sudden death, and his 2002 "memoir" *The Black Veil,* ostensibly about his addiction recovery), he is careful to skew the premise of revelation, to tease the reader with the promise of confession only to dismiss the presumption of such intimacy between reader and writer, to stall such a shatteringly invasive moment even as he manipulates the confessional mode. Interestingly, in that conceptual comic storyboard that Moody produced for *Details* magazine in 1995, a fictional Rick Moody, distracted by the obligations of an approaching book promotional tour, hires an actor to impersonate him. As the story unfolds with a vintage *Twilight-Zone* flavor, it becomes impossible to distinguish the impersonator from the real thing, a strategy that allows the fictional Moody to exist (un)easily within the intriguing paradox of revelation and concealment.

Although Moody's critical assessment is confined at this point to on-line critiques and periodical reviews, he is clearly being positioned—along with other forty-something children of the postmodern era, a generation of schooled novelists raised within the free range of university seminar rooms (among them Donald Antrim, Michael Chabon, Richard Powers, Jeffrey Eugenides, Jonathan Frazen)—as part of a new movement in American fiction that has reanimated a hipper sort of realistic novel, turning narrative away from the absorbing experiments in tale-telling that defined the postmodern heyday of the midcentury and returning it to recognizable characters in a recognizable landscape (often, reflecting these writers' backgrounds, university towns or affluent suburbs) who are caught within the anxious haunts of the everyday. Call these writers compassionate postmodernists who have returned to narrative reliables: dilemma, psychology, tension, resolution.

Or call them perhaps voyeur-realists. Moody's fictions testify to a most problematic sort of "return" to a most problematic sort of realism. It is as if he cannot decide whether to be a really hip Raymond Carver or a really square William S. Burroughs. Yes, Moody writes stunningly realistic narratives—but in ways that recall, say, the films of Quentin Tarantino (a contemporary whose work can help assess Moody's), they are about lives that their creator has never actually lived, has never directly experienced—which rather significantly alters the contract between reader and writer and ultimately between writer and text. They are each (like Tarantino's films) an amalgamation, an uncanny simulation of realistic fiction, "real-enough-ism," a nervy combine of brash invention, recycled clichés, skewed genre components, attentive (if neutral) observation, meticulous research, and the splendid shadow-show projections of a self-enclosed, self-sustaining imagination. And (like Tarantino's films) they are audacious celebrations of their medium, elaborate (and potentially overbearing) reconceptions of the form that relieve the artist entirely of the responsibility (even the expectation) of establishing any authentic self.

Make no mistake. Moody's life would make a most profitable rendering. It has been shaped by the deep pressure of three pivotal traumatic events, any one of which could sustain a shelf of narrative exploration: his parents' sudden divorce when he was ten, his cool estrangement from his father, and the beginning of a difficult adolescence shuttling back and forth between parents' residences and coping with the multiplication of stepfamilies; his subsequent harrowing slide into an addiction to alcohol and drugs that culminated in a month-long voluntary commitment in 1987 as an in-patient at a Queens psychiatric hospital; and the unexpected death in 1995 of his vibrant older sister, Meredith, a photographer and busy single mother of two, of complications from a cardiac seizure after a minor car accident. What is interesting is that such tectonic events have seldom shadowed the narratives Moody has written. Not to enforce fascistically the tired bromide of freshman comp ("write what you know about"), but such wide and deliberate veering from experience demands reexamining the premise of mimetic realism. Schooled in language theory and narrative de/reconstruction, encouraged to consider with deliberate self-consciousness the process of converting experience into the arbitrary signs of words, Moody has never been content simply to restage dramas of doomed love, too hip to simply replay the crushing evidence of a capricious nature and the chilling reality of inevitable death: those basic contours, after all, have been fundamental to American literary expression since Hawthorne's *The Scarlet Letter,* American literature's first exploration of love's anticipation, expectation, detonation, and inevitable disappointment; the first exploration of the deep vulnerability of the heart to loss and pain; the first rendering of the intrusive quietus of death. But, perhaps taking his cue from that text (he has often cited Hawthorne's massive influence and his deep love of that particular work), Moody intuits that the only fulfillment within such a dark tale belongs to the Surveyor, the framer of the tale, happily expelled early on from the public arena, fired, as he tells us in the extraordinary introductory sketch, from his dead-end ledger-bound position in the Salem Custom-House, to settle before a comfortable fire there to spin a tale, the man with the imagination audacious enough to pose a dilemma in which the town minister and the town whore share the same secret, content not to solve the dilemma, but rather to embroider its implications in his own splendid language-chord, the magnificat of his ornate prose line. Hawthorne's Surveyor, once introduced into the narrative, demands acknowledgment; he is implied, indeed foregrounded—the defiant Hester, the cowering Dimmesdale, the cuckholded Chillingworth, indeed that entire milling gray-suited throng outside the rusted doors of the Salem prison, they are all the expressions of the Surveyor's liberated fancy. It becomes an infolded text that concedes the traditional elements of character/plot/action to create a lexical space, to endepth only the narrating presence but, paradoxically, to defer as irrelevant any direct authorial revelation—we learn little directly about the Surveyor, he lives only within the story he tells. Storytelling, then, is not revelation, but rather the simulation of revelation, a structured space that is to be admired exactly for what it is: a structure that reveals even as it conceals.

Moody's Fiction: An Overview

> *Even yet . . . [the tale] wears, to my eye, a stern and somber aspect; too much ungladdened by genial sunshine; too little relieved by the tender and familiar influences which soften almost every scene of nature and real life. . . . It is no indication, however, of a lack of cheerfulness in the writer's mind; for he was happier, while straying through the gloom of these sunless fantasies, than any time since he had quitted the Old Manse.*
> —The Surveyor, "The Custom-House"

Moody (and his generation of post-Pynchon post-postmodernists) illuminates a new and potentially intriguing relationship between the aesthetic enterprise and the life lived, between narrative and experience. Their response falls into neither of the warring camps whose open hostility generated f(r)iction that sustained a battle of the books across the closing decades of the last century. Moody's generation is neither realist nor postmodernist. They are not intrigued by the evident complexity of experience, its stubborn resistance to order, yet its occasional glints of nobility and magnificence; they are not eager to recover, by dint of careful observation and generous recording of its very artlessness, some fragmentary sense of purpose: that compelled the imaginative engine of the midcentury realism from Cheever to Carver. Nor are they amused/terrorized by its sloppiness, its sheer shapelessness, how ordinary experience is actually long droughts of boredom occasionally spiked by the intrusion of blind chance; they are not, in turn, drawn to the protective shelters of imaginative constructs, private linguistic worlds happily divorced from anchorage to that imperfect and messy reality, toy-world constructs that are curiously self-sustaining and exuberantly self-justifying and that exhibit a bold control so sadly lacking within nature's freewheeling, if clumsy processes: that compelled the familiar midcentury argument of postmodernists from Burroughs to Pynchon.

Neither intrigued nor terrorized nor amused by experience, Moody's generation, book-fed and theory-fat, are ultimately casual to its impact—the pass of pain, the cut of disappointment, the inevitable shadow-cross of mortality—unimpressed by the argument of experience, but stunned by the premise of narrating it, engrossed with the production of remarkable simulations of real life done within the overarching reassurance of a larger narrative presence that is always insinuated, at least in Moody's fictions, by a recurring sort of cinematic voice-over, a contemporary update (a cover, if you will) of Hawthorne's Surveyor vehicle, a reassuring projector who ultimately packages into a stunning prose line the chaos into which Moody's characters are so casually pitched. The narrative voice-over—telling tales of characters whose invented lives are so often crushed by the hammer-fist of random accident—provides cool shape, clear form, and careful logic, along with the comfort (and the verbal music) of a voice to listen to.

Moody's narratives, then, are either hand-me-downs—second-hand testimonials, traditional framed tales—or they are riveting stream-of-consciousness constructions where the voice itself compels, the manipulation of words, phrases, the pitch-perfect re-creation of a voice, the novelist-qua-master ventriloquist. It is difficult to locate a sustained character in Moody's fiction: they exist as voices, we hear them, we read them into vitality. Their assorted neuroses will not sustain too much exploration, too many "whys." Indeed they are most often melodramatic caricatures (like Hawthorne's Puritans and like the comic-book figures of Moody's own childhood love). It is fiction as the art of recording disclosures, the art of recording epiphanies—the actual substance of the epiphany is secondary. Voice itself emerges as a theme of sufficient consequence. Even the most captivating moments in Moody's fictions, those narrative moments when characters confront the brutal pain and sheer waste of contemporary life, are always more about the language Moody deploys. Moody has often recounted his own struggle early in his career with the construction of plots, with the premeditated scheduling of a rigid sequence of believable dramatic events, the manipulation of suspense, the tight, calculated movement toward satisfying closure. With an epiphanic jolt while writing *The Ice Storm,* however, he intuited a far different mission: the management of language, the manipulation of pace, breaks, silences, and sounds, that would present traditional dilemmas of fictional characters as a wholly original aural and sonic event. "Any dramatic situation, rendered in language that's new and spontaneous, is plenty to drive a narrative," Moody has said (qtd. in Gordon 39). Moody's prose has become his signature: elaborate and elongated sentences, lyrical and intense; a playful indulgence of a high-caloric vocabulary; litanic cataloging; the free use of fragments that can build momentum across pages; punctuation gimmicks such as forsaking quotation marks; odd syntactical arrangements that work best when read aloud; and a rich reservoir of allusions to literary and pop-culture referents. With Moody, then, we can never forget or even minimize the (f)act of reading. Indeed, as Moody's career progressed, his pages have come to be often unbroken, intimidating planes of language, jazzy riffs that exuberantly renegotiate the rules of conventional syntax (sentences can go on for pages) and paragraph design. Not surprising, when Moody describes his prose, he borrows metaphors most heavily from his considerable background in music: "I come at a lot of what I do as a frustrated musician" (qtd. in Gordon 40). Indeed, once the narrative line is established, rereading begins the process of hearing the intricate music of the prose, Moody's careful balance of sounds, his attention to the syllable beat of his sentences, to the harmonics of how a word cooperates with the sounds around it. We must be aware we are holding a made-thing in our hand—for instance, Moody's trademark deployment of italics at random moments compels the reader to be aware of the complex reality of typeface itself by creating a veritable second register of prose by the simplest manipulation of typography.

Even his characters obsess over language: they are inveterate readers with a massive range of allusions at their command; they are writers struggling with unfinished manuscripts, students completing brilliant if unconventional term papers, lovers groping to find just the right love letter phrasing; a civil engineer laboring over the text of a deposition on an accident claim; a fifty-seven-year-old feeling suddenly the need, Scheherazade-like, to tell of his days long ago in a garage band. Or they are talkers—or those unable to talk. Some indulge with ease the noncommunication of parlor chit-chat, circulate in rooms heavy with weather factoids, office gossip, impromptu movie reviews, and investment tips. Others struggle against the sheer impossibility of executing even the simplest speech acts, laconic by nature or hampered by merciless stammers, by thick rows of canker sores, by debilitating neurological disorders that short-circuit speech, or by painful shyness. Such characters come dramatically to the pressure point when language finally happens: they open up, like dormant geysers suddenly convulsing to life, in an explosive, multipage declamation that has the feel of orgasmic release.

Indeed, whatever critical objections have been expressed over Moody's emerging oeuvre have centered on this auteur sense of prose itself, tour-de-forced writing that is pure performance. His prose, critics lament, is distracting, too gimmicky, too cerebral in its play, too conventional in its rejection of conventional grammar and syntax. They are tricks, divertissements that threaten to infect the heart of Moody's fiction, the lurking presumption that he should rather be about the business of traditional realism with its assumptions of transparent prose. Yet prose itself *is* the heart of Moody's fiction. Although it is chic, because his narratives often center on the banal experiences of love and death, work and family that compel traditional realistic narratology, to argue that Moody is a postmodernist with a heart, Moody's fiction is perhaps more profitably approached as a masquerade, a staged performance that manipulates experience into language systems that themselves—not the characters—stay most immediate. It is the sort of fiction that a generation of writers who *studied* writing would invariably produce. Like kids raised in a theme park, they are distracted by mundane experience and are far more fascinated not by the imagination but rather by what it can construct, determined to pull off believable simulations, to get an audience to applaud what are essentially wire contraptions, audio-animatronic facsimiles. If their postmodern parents demanded their audience also tour backstage and see the technology that made the illusions possible, a strategy that led inevitably to the wearisome self-reflexive navel-staring that alienated a generation of important fiction from any audience larger than the university, this generation, raised within the considerable pressure of Disney and Spielberg, Nintendo and Lucas, wants the audience to stay riveted, to stay convinced that those banjo-strumming country bears and that adorable encephalitic alien hiding amid the stuffed animals, those plucky Italian plumbers rescuing the princess and those intergalactic star fighters are breathtakingly real, or at least real enough. Artifice is the only theme left, language the only valid exercise in a world that Moody—and his generation—consigns to a darkening chaos that Hawthorne himself, the Ur-Imagineer, intuited more than a century and half ago even as his Surveyor settled comfortably before a roaring fire to hide behind, within, and above a most believable tale.

Within Moody's fictional treatments, the reader is necessarily one step removed from experience. We are engaged within a tight fuselage-world of the rendered text, an intricate and highly original language system wherein lurks characters sustained by the exertion of words, like the music sustained by the exertion of piano keys. Indeed, Moody's characters are like word-chords whose considerable tribulations and emotional woundings are never the central fact of the text, but rather convincing casings, occasions to press ink on paper. Voices emerge—language projections that ignite from plot moments, from brutal experience set to the available music of language, characters finally as sonic events who inhabit a geography of print.

The Thematic Argument

What I have written, I have written.
—Pontius Pilate (The Gospel of John),
a favorite Moody quote

Thematically, Moody recalls the often unforgiving, brooding sensibility of midcentury realists who initially explored the dark heart of the postwar prosperity and the late-century minimalists who anatomized the debilitating effects of the pain, blood, and waste of Vietnam, the morass of Watergate, and the malaise of the Carter era. It is, on the whole, a familiar vision. In Moody nature is a dysfunctional force, apparently cruel in its sheer haphazardness, but actually just poorly fashioned, clumsy. Despite his own fascination with the spiritual impulse and the hunger for such validation, his characters engage a universe that is stubbornly horizontal in its argument, redemption inaccessible, even ironic. Deprived of the grand purpose and inscrutable benevolence of a creator, the world within Moody's narratives is regularly, casually upended by the curiously inexplicable cut of chance, the intrusive jolt of contingency, the irruption of spontaneity. Although characters struggle to shatter the self, to love (more often finding the pull of the heart entrance to paralysis and disappointment and sex itself a jizzless friction that produces scant heat), the primary relational unit for Moody is the shattered family so unanchored to any inherited notion of authority or traditional sense of moral imperative, so riven by pointless adulteries and adrift within unfathomable boredom that its very viability appears in question. Within such a bleak world, where isolation and loneliness are inevitable, Moody's characters find solace in the cool interactive company of aesthetic artifacts—films, books, recordings, television—or more often turn to the dead-end excess of drugs, alcohol, or promiscuity and, when such addictions prove unfulfilling, to weigh the heavy pull of suicide. Indeed, death haunts Moody's characters, inevitable, ever approaching, its prolonged absence only serving to lay waste, or at least render ironic, the curious need they (and we) have on occasion to feel significant.

Despair would be all too easy while reading such narratives. Yet Moody never inhabits such a world—he creates it, like some theme-park imagineer. As readers, we forsake the drama and pressures of the characters—that is, we void the standard contract of mimetic realism. We do not read about it; we simply read, stunned by Moody's verbal dexterity, his willingness to push language into the musical register. We do not merely read sentences; we track them, listen to them, follow their ornate unfolding. Here, the "story" itself creates an unexpectedly viable space, the drama of nouns and verbs strung into elaborate sense, the pressure to find the right words, to press that forbidding sense of experience into a mesmerizing form. Amid characters who must negotiate the oppressive muscle of catastrophe, heartbreak, and accident, even as they roil about their narratives starkly vulnerable, Moody sustains a viable, sturdy rendering of such a condition that, despite its apparent jazzy improv feel, is in its pitch-perfect execution and attention to its own structure all about confidence, control, and order. It is not the tiresome self-reflexive guerilla fictions of the postmodernists—language that leads only to itself, the empty thrill of exposing the sorry sham of words. Moody respects the reach of language. Indeed Moody boldly reverses the axiom of realism: where once story led to style, here style leads to story. The prose—not the story—is the initial encounter. It is intimacy not with characters or with their predicaments, but rather with the sentences constructed, the words deployed to convey those dilemmas. Within the expectations of the mimetic tradition, initial reading traditionally introduced plot, thematic concerns, character psychology, the multilayered symbol or two, and only rereading revealed the care and polish of what appears to be a transparent prose line. Moody's prose is anything but transparent—it demands notice—only in rereading do his troubling thematic concerns, his attention to character psychology, and his introduction of multilayered symbols emerge.

The deepest mystery then in Moody's fiction is not love or family or God, but rather the desire to express those mysteries. The point of writing, Moody argues, is the writing. As with all fiction, Cheever *and* Burroughs, Updike *and* Beckett, there are only two characters in Moody's narratives—the reader and the writer—and only one tension—the struggle between language and silence. The question foregrounded by Moody's fictions is far more complicated than why love is empty or why families are unhappy, why death is always premature or why work is unfulfilling, the quotidian dilemmas that haunt his creations. Why, Moody asks (as all writers do directly or indirectly), does language happen amid such ache? Why do we encode such dilemmas within such a system? Like other compassionate postmodernists/voyeur realists, Moody is caught in a distinctly contemporary quandary: intoxicated by the possibility of language, snagged early as a nerdy child within the enveloping comfort of conjured worlds, but taught as he moved through the stages of education to distrust the capacity of language to capture the essentials of experience, left then with a disturbing sense that for all we talk, we speak very little of what needs to be said. This creates a most fascinating dissonance in his narrative work, a trope of indirection, a cool indulgence of storytelling that manages nevertheless to suggest evasion, equivocation, and suppression. Do we speak, Moody asks, because we have a mouth or because others have ears? In the one case, we conjure to sustain imagined company amid unbreakable isolation; in the other, we struggle inexplicably to complete the mysterious loop called communication. Which ultimately defines the act of writing itself? Within the uncompromising guerilla fictions of Rick Moody, language both boldly reveals its relevancy, unapologetically demands notice, confidently asserts its continued viability despite a media-saturated era of images that has for a more than a generation now threatened to make quaintly nostalgic the notion of its workability AND reveals itself as a clumsy charade, a cheap shape-making trick, an elaborate evasive crabwalk, a shallow, self-sustaining dodge, a desperate lexical game of (a)voiding the terrifying hiss of silence and the reality of our irrelevance: the sheer joy of writing braided to the bleak certainty of its uselessness.

Garden State (1991)

"Drizzle coated Haledon, N.J., with a sad, ruinous sheen."

So begins Moody's first novel, a sentence that is a euphonious complex of languorous rolling vowels, narcotic sibilants, and soft-hissing consonants, an indulgent luxury of slow-dripping sound that is cut nevertheless by a stabbing counterpoint of dissonance—the reader cannot avoid rending the sentence's even flow midway through with the inevitably intrusive (comma-split) harsh slash-chops of EN JAY. It is thus a sentence in conflict with itself, in lexical tension between harmonics and cacophony, a struggle echoed in the fragmented lives of the three north Jersey twenty-somethings that Moody's narrative will track through one liminal spring. Alice Smail, at twenty-three, is jobless, still living at home with a mother who is herself deeply depressed over a life of routine hardship and a daughter unable to grow up. Alice, a woman-child, struggles with the gnawing sense that whatever sweetness life might have offered is somehow gone already; a brief stint playing rhythm guitar with a high-school garage band may have signaled her glory days ("one summer with the band, and since then everything's fucked up" (79)). Her boyfriend Dennis, a union plumber, who romantically dreams of someday painting her, offers in fact a far more pedestrian sort of love. As his occupation suggests, their sex is stripped and mechanic and less than incendiary—"Fucking was nothing that would change the world" (11)—and promises to lead to nothing grander than itself. The novel's intriguing, enigmatic center is Dennis's half-brother Lane, whose life after his father had been institutionalized had oddly lost whatever momentum it had had. As the novel opens, Lane is returning to Haledon after a disastrous, inexplicably unbearable attempt at college in the city. He now spends an enormous amount of the day in bed, sustained by four-times-a-week counseling, a complex of prescription painkillers, and alcohol that leaves him nauseous and largely immobile, unable to read or even watch television.

It will prove a most ironic springtime in the Garden State. Each of the three characters interdicts whatever feelings might be stirred by nature's careless rush to resurrection by the ruinous indulgence of alcohol, television, pot, or bored promiscuity. It is, Lane argues, a culture of addiction, "Addictions, blossoming in personalities like parasites. All over Haledon, kids were coming apart. They bounced back for a while and then they stopped bouncing back, and surrendered to the whisper of their cells" (54). Played out against Moody's stark mood-picture of Jersey (a Springsteenesque landscape-in-ruins: gritty train yards, shallow rivers thick with chemical spills, utility plants belching carcinogenic smoke, triple-X drive-ins, creepy abandoned factories, all sopped by a nearly steady rain) and struck in a plainsong prose line that is as flat and depthless as the characters themselves, the plot centers on the tension that evolves as Alice sorts through her growing feelings for Lane. In a resonant moment as she and Dennis make decidedly inglorious love along a railroad track, she sees the brooding Lane saunter slowly by, watching. The troubled Lane then undergoes a psychotic episode (a clumsy suicide attempt, appropriately enough, at an April Fool's Day Party, a fall, induced by tranquilizers and beer, from a rain-slicked roof). During a brief hospitalization, Lane will come to accept as irrevocable the absence of his father and to understand that the self needs to be shared. In a scene that will come to be something of a signature in Moody's fiction, a nervous Lane phones Alice from the hospital and, feelings so long bottled up, explodes in a fifteen-minute language torrent that is as poignant as it is therapeutic:

> Alice didn't say anything. Lane breathed. . . . Then he just started talking. All these decisions came about as though they were made somewhere else, not in his own head. It was like taking dictation. He told her about where he was, about how there was this day the second week there when he had suddenly known he would survive, about how everything cleared in that moment. Like some long, involved fugue coming to its resolution. Lane told Alice about women. He told her his crimes — not even knowing if she was listening. . . . There was no way to start all the conversations he owed. He didn't even know where to begin. . . . He told her everything that had gone wrong, everything he had lost, everyone who had hurt him, and then he told her about his father. (180-81)

Although Alice and Lane end up together — after he is discharged, they share a bus ride into the city on a heat-blasted Memorial Day weekend — Moody can affirm only what they cling to: desperately to the precarious now and loosely to each other (Lane decides as they step out of the bus terminal to let go of the past as a suffocating accumulation of ironies even as he briefly holds Alice). The ending cannot sustain an up-tempo feel (indeed, Lane is dressed in black), the toxic world hardly encourages tenderness (suggested by the terminal's magazine racks of hard porn, by the oppressive humid morning, and by the reports of a man who had dived-bombed a private plane into a stadium during a track and field event and of bookies in Atlantic City taking bets on when and where an errant government satellite would fall). Indeed, it is only at this point in the narrative that Moody reveals the full story of Mike Maas, whose death had been the subject of cryptic remarks throughout the narrative. A top student, a singer in the school chorus, an athlete, Mike had dated steadily a friend of Alice. Alice had apparently suggested to the girl that she should sleep with someone else just out of curiosity. When the girl actually does, a distraught Mike immolates himself on a stretch of highway.

It is on the whole a terribly bleak picture of kids in their early twenties, kids already nostalgic, left to play out inauthentic lives that inexplicably spiral into leaden ennui and who must struggle against the relentless pull of the logic of casual self-destruction. They struggle just to matter. Moody dispenses with entirely convincing causality — divorce, mental illness, a vague quiet sort of desperation are offered — and focuses more on recording the effects: pregrunge X'ers wasting lives stripped clean of depth, kids who hunger only for some sense of resonance, some sense of consequence to what appears to be the inevitable unspooling of passionless years ahead; they are kids who dream of mall jobs. Locked within such an unpromising premise, the kids seek the only solace Moody permits: the vital release of their angry garage band music, that sonic assault a defiant urgent release of passion—all now past. As Lane and Alice head out of the terminal (away, metaphorically, from fixed and certain ending), the closing pages offer Moody's slender promise of purpose, a promise as romantic as it is cinematic: a hand to hold onto, a some other one to hear what you say, to cut into the loneliness.

To paraphrase Hemingway, it would be pretty to think so.

Like a fugue, this freshman effort is written in two contrasting styles, two different registers: for most of the narrative, Moody's prose is clinically descriptive, his sentences clipped and barren of ornamentation, a Hemingwayesque deadpan delivery that records with subject-verb-direct object monotony each pointless movement of the characters as they conduct the dull colloquial pound of their slacker conversations. Whatever psychological depth his characters possess—and life has traumatized them to the point where denial and escapism are the preferred strategies for day-to-day survival— must be inferred from hard surfaces. Unrelieved by stylistic flourish or emotional exclamation, the sentences happen up against each other without elaborate transition or flow, like rusted train cars simply shouldered one to the next.

Until the closing. The only thing that actually blooms in the *Garden State* is language itself, a sudden florescence of sentences and paragraphs in the closing pages that signals the slim hope that Moody can tender. On the bus ride into town, for instance, we are told:

> When the bus came down from the bridge, onto the cloverleaf, it circled around and around a rubble of shattered glass and abandoned automobiles. City of narcolepsy, city of machinations, city of public executions and prerecorded accompaniments and prenuptial agreements, city of basis points and in vitro fertilizations and squatter's rights and electroconvulsive therapy and dreamlessness and aberrations of need. The bus took a right turn at the university and headed down along the river. (210)

Where does that second sentence come from? The faintest throb of original verve and improv, that incantatory jazz-riff of a second sentence that comes out of nowhere, is tightly bound between the status quo, bloodless and tepid descriptions within cookie-cutter constructions. Thus the true epiphany belongs to the reader, not so much to Lane and Alice. In the closing pages the prose line dramatically stirs, expands as Moody captures the possibility of spring-resurrection with sentences that suddenly experiment with imbedded constructions, create emphasis by varying length, shake up the prose line with sinewy catalogs that bust around punctuation and suggest a revival from enervation. Paragraphs suddenly are stouter and fuller, sentences suddenly alert with adjectives and adverbs, with color and sound, heat and depth: the formal equivalent of an awakening to possibility to match Lane's own hospitalization and recovery. It cannot be about the tenuous healing of the characters or the spare affirmation of love in a difficult and unyielding landscape—it is more about the recovery of language, a robust affirmation of the power of language in a dead landscape, itself able to record with originality the most banal and diminished lives.

The Ice Storm (1995)

Like the fragile coating of ice on a wintertime branch, the surface in Moody's second novel is deceptive and unstable, entrancing but ultimately insubstantial. Story is not left to itself; we are rather in the hands of a Surveyor-figure who, unlike Moody positioned above the narrative actions of *Garden State* like the surveillance camera that watches over Alice and Lane in the bus terminal, this time actually insinuates himself periodically in the text, a presence that moves adeptly from the consciousness of one character to the next, calls attention to his own storytelling abilities, undercuts with studied flippancy the unfolding family soap opera that moves with such (melo)dramatic Greek-tragedy intensity (Moody maintains a tight temporal unity: the action takes place on the weekend of the tenth anniversary of the JFK assassination), and—most significantly—establishes that the imagination and its manifestation in the act of narrative production are the sole antidote to the anxious late-century loneliness that appears in Moody's fiction to be all but inescapable.

Absent the narrator's presence, Moody's sophomore effort is a suburban Gothic—imagine Cheever channeling Poe, the calm, lovely homes and pretty families of the suburbs masking profound, disquieting horrors. It is a brooding tale of two dysfunctional affluent families (the Hoods and the Williams) plagued by casual adulteries, the significant consumption of alcohol, unfulfilling employment, and an anesthetic sense of ennui and midlife emptiness, all set in the tony Connecticut suburbs against and amid the grievous moral compromises and national betrayals of Nixon's America (the book is meticulously embroidered with the cheesiest period details, from Pet Rocks to Tang, from *Jonathan Livingston Seagull* to *Jesus Christ Superstar*). Ben Hood, a securities analyst who specializes in media and entertainment stocks, a forty-something alcoholic with eyes the "color of antifreeze" (6), whose career has just begun to tank (he had unforgivably missed the profit potential of both *Billy Jack* and *The Exorcist*) and whose wife, Elena, has emotionally departed their marriage ("when she saw his penis now . . . she felt no more for it than she felt for any plucked and headless game bird" (54)) to pursue life-purpose via a regimen of trendy self-help manuals and pop psychobabble, is conducting a dispassionate affair with neighbor Janey Williams, an office widow (married to a man who wisely invested in packing curlicues, suggesting their life of comfort has been made possible by a faith in insulation), as a way to try to ignite some sort of feeling, to introduce even the possibility of depth to his life. But it is difficult as Janey permits little emotional chat and keeps the relationship coolly casual and nonchalantly physical. In the novel's opening scene, Janey abruptly departs their late-afternoon tryst in the Williams' own guest room, leaving Ben to wander about her house, his erection slowly withering, until he happens upon one of her garter belts in the laundry basket, whereupon he desultorily masturbates. Then, he stumbles on his seventh-grade daughter, Wendy, and Janey's son, Mikey, in the basement rumpus room, pants down for a stab at an afternoon quickie. Make no mistake. Moody's narrator, like some unforgiving Hawthornesque incarnation, relishes revealing the sludgy moral wake of the 1960s lifestyle, the inevitably devastating effects of self-indulgent free love on family and marriage and particularly on the children of such parents. It is telling that the talking G. I. Joe that belongs to Mikey's younger brother, Sandy, uselessly repeats the same May Day message, a warning here unheeded, indeed annoying.

Given such spiritually desiccated parents, their adolescent children, routinely unattended, unsmiling, and bored already with life, already absorbed by the voyeuristic lifestyle of watching screens, and morally unanchored, come to experiment clumsily with alcohol, drugs, and promiscuity largely as ways to pass time. Paul, the elder Hood offspring away at boarding school, painfully shy and given already to black-light posters, military strategy board games, and getting high, soaks his penis in milk to encourage the housemaster's cat to "have congress with him" (88). Wendy Hood is preternaturally fascinated by sexual acts, exposing her body for cool titillation, bartering sex acts for chewing gum, performing a teasing cunnilingus on a stunned girlfriend at a recent sleepover, and finding her sole orgasm (while Mikey dry-humped her) an "out-of-body experience" (150). When Ben tells Elena about finding Wendy and Mikey in the rumpus room, he cannot think quickly enough of a clear reason why he himself was in the Williams' house and Elena surmises the devastating truth. Nevertheless, with the creepy calm of a woman who never vents anger, never speaks her mind ("silence was a tongue Elena understood" (56)), she nevertheless insists on their attending a neighborhood party that night even as an ice storm of biblical proportions bears down on New England. That party turns into a "key party," a high-seventies suburban swingers' game in which wives blindly select a set of house keys and then agree to go home with that husband for the night. Indeed, it is while the parents are negotiating for their bed-partners and while prepubescent Sandy and Wendy are looting the Williams' vodka and fumbling naked into their waterbed (they do little but heavy petting before they fall asleep) that Mikey, wandering about the stormy countryside, fascinated by the picturesque effects of the snap-freeze, is electrocuted while resting momentarily on a guardrail just as a sputtering downed power line casually brushes against the metal railing. Clearly no one is directly to blame for Mikey's death. Rather, Moody's narrator suggests, he dies because of the moral carelessness and hands-off parenting generated in the 1960s and visited upon the children of the 1970s.

There is, then, a cavernous loneliness at the heart of *The Ice Storm,* characters unable, unwilling, or simply uninterested in unburdening the self. The more sexual activity Moody records, the colder the text becomes even as the menacing rain begins to freeze. The more the characters talk, the less they communicate until ultimately they lapse into self-protective nonconfrontational quiet: Ben is plagued by canker sores that make talking painful; Elena has read herself into the habit of silence. After Ben discovers Wendy and Mikey in the rumpus room, he struggles during the long walk home in the stinging sleet for the slenderest gesture of communication with his troubled daughter, and she for her part suddenly feels the urge for accountability ("Wendy wanted to know why conversation failed and how to teach compassion and why people fell out of love and she wanted to know it all by the time she got back to the house" (50)). Ultimately they both concede and chatter emptily about the approaching harsh weather. The key party itself begins sparkling with lively parlor chat only to chill by evening's end into a difficult and uncomfortable silence as the bowl of house keys is brought out. Paul, who has ventured to New York City that same night to attempt a rendezvous with a particularly stunning classmate, Libbets Casey, is so nervous at the prospect of spending time at her family's fashionable upper-east-side home that when he arrives he encourages both of them (along with a friend who accompanies him) to ingest a combination of beer, pot, and Seconal from the Casey medicine cabinet. Only then does he try to open up to the beautiful girl, to talk to her about his family and its deep problems ("I have stuff I want to tell you" (102)), even teeters on the verge of authentic revelation only to notice that she is too stoned to answer any of his earnest questions, questions that in turn are left dangling. Later, at a dance club, Libbetts will try to explain to Paul that she cares for him only like a brother, but will find herself still too stoned to say it right. On the train back to Connecticut, Paul struggles to start a conversation with a stranger on the train, content finally to imagine a secret, sinister life for the guy. After the devastating discovery of the dead Mikey the following morning, Janey's husband attempts to explain to his remaining son Sandy his own hasty liaison with Elena (she had selected his keys the night before, and after a particularly low-octane quickie in his car she spends the night in a guest room after they skid because of the storm) by using an unconvincing food analogy, the need after years of catsup for some A-1. At the same moment, Ben struggles to make amends with Elena—only to find the attempt at simple conversation aborted as useless.

The Ice Storm then would appear to be an unforgiving, old-fashioned (read Hawthornesque) morality play that disdains the casual ethos of the midcentury sexual revolution, the late-century freefall into unearned ennui by the materially comfortable class, the cultural stagnation of amorality in the wake of the irrelevance of institutional religion, the easy oblivion of pharmaceuticals and alcohol and television, the inability of the contemporary family to sustain the burden of itself without irony—and the inevitable prison house of the self, the inviolable loneliness of contemporary life, underscored by Moody's repeated allusions to Nixon's America, specifically the invasion of Cambodia with its metaphoric argument of spreading infection, spiraling betrayal, and extended madness.

That is until you listen to the voice that tells the tale.

Listen to the odd invitation that opens the novel: "So let me dish you this comedy about a family I knew when I was growing up. There's a part for me in this story, like there always is for a gossip, but more on that later" (3). Comedy? It is surely an impulse Ang Lee denied the film—Tobey Maguire's depthless voice-over, deadpanned as if locked into permanent recoil, certainly complements the air of tragedy that hangs about the forbidding icy wasteland of Me-Decade Connecticut. But the voice that tells the narrative is casually flippant, creatively evasive (he eventually reveals that he is actually Paul, twenty years later), densely allusive, always self-deprecating, always playful, even teasing as he lovingly piles up period references and hip pop-culture referents to the point of parody. Why, then, does Moody bother with this frame at all? Much critical ink was spilled objecting to the narrative presence as intrusive and structurally unsound. But like Hawthorne's Surveyor who also delights into conjuring a dark parable of failed morality and community moral bankruptcy and who also freely invents the interiors of his creations, Paul is clearly relishing this act of re-creating his boyhood era, self-consciously constructing sets loaded with period detritus and appropriate furnishings, and (as Hawthorne did) assembling a cast of cartoonlike, morally challenged exaggerations engaged in extravagant melodramatic actions that lead inevitably to manufactured peril. It is not the story he tells, but that he is telling a story. Like the Surveyor, Paul freely embroiders, indulges the occasional overkill of hyperbolic prose, freely creating details and conversations in which he did not actually participate, decorating the prose line with jarring, entirely ornamental figures of speech and a love of the meticulously imagined scene.

In a narrative where language comes to fail every character, where conversations are maddeningly disjointed and elliptical, where explanations collapse into misunderstanding, and earnest gestures at communication lapse in hapless silence, Paul alone as narrator taps into language's adhesive quality, launches his prose as a bold affront, a strategic invasion (like the Cambodian offensive) designed to shatter his own loneliness by offering him the opportunity to violate the hard exteriors of his characters/family (each chapter shifts its narrative perspective, although the style is consistent, and re-creates a convincing, psychological interior sustained entirely by the manipulation of voice). That daring colonization is the underplayed heroic impulse of the narrative (Paul-as-unsuspected-superhero, he loves comic books)—and the cause of the narrator's joy as, twenty years later, he alone of his creations unloads the self, writes himself into deliberate confederacy with his characters—and into an accidental conspiracy with his unnamable reader. Consider the fusion assumed by the moment of Mikey's electrocution:

> His last thought, a simple, adolescent *oh, no,* was all he had time for; in fact it was exactly simultaneous with his electrocution, because through some strange celestial circuitry, he knew at the moment of his death that it was his death. A jumble of images appeared at once to him, a jumble of dreams and recollections, condensed and displaced. And then Mike said, *oh, no,* subvocalized it. And then his consciousness split from this plane. . . . (214-15, italics Moody's)

Within the narrative act—not within the narrative—fragments cohere, vertiginous chaos is bent to form, disconnected bits create a connected storyline, random event becomes foreshadowing, the simplest trifling becomes loaded with symbolic resonance (it suddenly matters, for instance, that Wendy and Mikey make out to the hokey sci-fi flick *When Worlds Collide*). In a narrative where characters are damned because they cannot listen, we are always aware that we are listening to a story—Paul steps in regularly, God-like, he tells us (he rings the narrative closed with the mock-imperial *FINIS*), to put (often with a mock-cringe) the appropriate period furniture into the setting and period costuming on his characters, to put those characters where he needs them, generally to remind readers of the continuing pressure of his narrative muscle. It is cause for whatever celebration Moody's grim second novel can sustain. Paul's voice has survived the moral rubble. Like the comic books he so loves (indeed, he compares his family to the Fantastic Four and claims he sees a faint number 4 in the morning clouds at narrative's end, à la the Surveyor and the sky-borne A in *The Scarlet Letter*), no matter how absorbing the action, the patently contrived thing we read will never let us forget that we are holding a made thing with characters boldly drawn to teach a too-tidy moral lesson. To disregard the narrator in favor of the story he tells denies Moody's narrative its sole triumph: the sheer verbal suction of the storytelling act in a world hopelessly given over to brutality, accident, and loneliness.

"The Ring of Brightest Angels around Heaven" (1996)

It is not altogether surprising that Moody finds the short story the optimum genre for executing his more radical formal experiments; their brevity, their conciseness, allows for intensity of effect and the opportunity to void formal conventions and excuses from consideration the normative expectations of any longer narrative: character development, suspense and plot intricacy, and tidy resolution. They are what he has frequently and happily termed his "weird shit." The stories are each discrete experiments in upsetting conventions, re-imagining formal boundaries; they deliberately push to an extreme an "idea" rather than rest content to simply tell a story. Thus in his first published collection he offers, among other laboratory experiments, an unbroken ten-page free-flowing stream of language that ostensibly recounts the negotiations for a screenplay ("Treatment"), but that turns ultimately into a sort of screen treatment itself; "The Grid" wildly bends time and space with the (in)elegance of chaos theory as it works a freewheeling riff on the vulnerability, the elaborate emotional negotiations, and even the mechanics of a first kiss set within a context of a vast city-matrix of other first-time kisses simultaneously seeking out love within a violent urban setting, all played out amid a shifting and precarious sense of the thin viability of that magic moment before it slips into the inevitable sour of pastness; "The Apocalypse Commentary of Bob Paisner" is a final draft of a bizarre term paper, written in the overnight press of a missed deadline, on the Book of Revelation by a misfit bookworm Temple University sophomore, a rambling commentary that ultimately reads his own lonely life of Quaaludes and masturbation using the rich symbolism of John the Divine until we sense we are perhaps reading a suicide note; "Primary Sources," a skewed autobiographical fragment, offers a glimpse into Moody's own life, although typically recounted as an annotated bibliography of works—fiction, nonfiction, and even recordings—that he sees as critical to understanding him. That strategy, apparently inviting yet oddly distant, is key to the larger sense as you move story to story of a certain forbidding coolness, a willing detachment from the material in exchange for the chance to come up with a startling way to write about it.

Consider the title story, a novella first published in the *Paris Review* and in many ways a defining text of this collection. It is on its surface a complex multistrand narrative that tracks how a disparate gathering of the street life of Manhattan's notorious east side comes to be waiting in the same line outside a bakery that fronts for heroin production and distribution. It offers on the surface an uncompromising and familiarly Hawthornesque moral vision that chronicles desolate lives ruined by addiction to sexual excess, criminal activity, and a range of alcohol and pharmaceuticals. These characters unironically suffer—they are the urban lost, the wasted, the living dead, the marginalized, the lonely. Jorge Ruiz, a hustler and veteran of the sex clubs and peep shows along Times Square, relishes the itch of pornography and the thrill of living each day according to the dangerous ad lib of the streets and following his cellular craving for crack. "Go ahead, dive," his motto for the casual recklessness of his lifestyle, cannot mask the dangers he lightly engages: he is robbed by a transvestite he picks up for quick money. There is the lesbian affair between the needful Doris and the dominant, tough-talking black call girl Marlene, an intense relationship that will come to involve the standard equipment of the underground S & M lifestyle—clamps, bonds, chaps, threesomes, chains, elaborate strap-ons, whips—but not love, although Doris falls in love with Marlene who cannot return the emotion, her heart calloused over by a lifestyle where emotions are defined by the exchange of pleasure and pain. After too much abuse-qua-affection, Doris intrigues with the other member of the threesome and abruptly catches a plane to New Orleans (a brutal act of betrayal, appropriately done while Marlene is enjoying *Lear* at a performance of Shakespeare in the Park). Doris even has her things boxed up and removed, to appear as if the apartment had been robbed. A suddenly devastated Marlene, worried over where Doris might be, is driven to hang herself. There are the young hip filmmakers Randy Evans and Yvonne, veteran clubbers and cocaine junkies, who, even after Yvonne becomes pregnant, introduce sex toys into their love life, particularly a device that provides simultaneous electrical stimulation to both genitalia (a facsimile of a Latin American torture device). Even as Randy begins to think of traditional marriage and finds the pregnancy appealing, even arousing, Yvonne craves only the stimulation of pain delivered by the box. Ultimately, finding her film unfinishable, she miscarries and their five-month marriage collapses of its own irony. Months later, Jorge, Doris, Randy, and Yvonne all wait outside the bakery—their lives unpleasant, terrifyingly empty, corroded by vice, and lost beyond even the idea of finding essential validity, at once narcissistic and self-destructive and locked within ever-narrowing options.

Such moral chaos, however, cannot swamp the storyline—indeed, it is not even the story. Moody again fashions a Surveyor, a voice-over, a friend to each of the street-damned, who observes from the fringes rather than participates in their harrowing slide into sleaze, addiction, and viral holocaust. He keeps us once-removed from the experience, engaged in the rendering of it (he tells us, for instance, he is a confidant of Jorge and that he helped Doris box her things and clear them out of the apartment). He perches above the harrowing action like that bus terminal surveillance camera in *Garden State*. He engages in the sole gesture of consolation he can coax: he tells their story, renders the mess and inconsequence of their lives into the stability and sequence of form. He cannot afford the white-hot indictment of some furious latter-day prophet—he does not convert their lives into convenient lessons, such a gesture would be lost in the age of license. Like the Surveyor, apart from and yet a part of the amorality he relates, he as artist pursues the quiet redemption of order found in the aesthetic enterprise. He cannot offer meaning or sympathy or understanding, but rather the passionate intimacy with the technology of recording, the architecture of formal order. He shapes the waste into manageable units, into sentences whose elaborate construction offers more logic and more purpose than any of the lives we watch spin out of control. Consider this breathtaking catalog as Jorge emerges from masturbating at a squalid corner peep show:

> He knew why people went into Peep World. Because they were feeling really good; because they were feeling really bad; because they had had trouble at work; because they were having trouble with their girlfriend; because they had no girlfriend; because they had two girlfriends, or two boyfriends, or a girlfriend and a boyfriend and didn't know how to

choose between them; because they were lonely; because they never got any time alone; because the world was full of hypocrisy; because it was not; because they weren't caring for the people they loved; because they were tired for caring for others; because the skies were blue, or their car had a dent, or their cat was sick, or they'd had an argument on the subway, or they wanted to live in the country and own a trailer, or they hated tuna, or they loved rock and roll; or because they had no money; because they had too much; because they were honest with themselves; or because of chance—Jorge said—*because of chance*. (166)

Such expansive contemplation is clearly the work of the narrator, not the drug-addled Jorge. It is an impressive formal construction that gives and takes with sympathy and generosity and acknowledges without indulgent judgment that vice is innately part of the human condition. It is the voyeur-voice-over that reassures, that gathers up the evidence of these shabby lives and fashions into plot the coincidences that lead them each to the bakery doorstep on Avenue D. It is the narrator who assures us that those street people who have most casually squandered everything are finally "the ring of brightest angels around heaven" (229), an appropriation of wasted lives into the reassuring verbal matrix of a magnificent metaphor, refitting their considerable pain into an elevating conceit that will not bear too much examination. Simply, it sounds good—the artifice of language extending a sort of aural and verbal benediction that such lives seldom brush. The recording, Moody argues, is everything. The story ends with the narrator, resolving (because he can, unlike the street life he has observed) to leave the Village, watching footage from Yvonne's street documentary that records a Christmas party in one of the Village's more infamous sex clubs, footage that captures images of the chaotic drug-compelled nightlife, its casual inanity elevated to the aesthetic by the unblinking eye of the narrative camera (recall the surveillance camera that records Alice and Lane).

Purple America (1997)

Purple America, certainly Moody's most accomplished work to date, forsakes the comfortable, centripetal ordering of a narrating voice-over to challenge language, specifically the sustained and signatory voices of four main characters themselves, to sustain the energy of a plot. That cooperation of voices, voices that never actually speak one to the other and indeed never directly speak to the reader within the faux-intimacy of traditional first person, actually fashions the narrative as each chapter moves easily from one center of consciousness to another. Although Moody has described this audacious formal challenge as operatic in nature, it is closer to prose jazz, verbally rendered riffs that defy conventional structuring and launch into dizzyingly intense prose monologues. Each voice is rendered in a stylized stream-of-consciousness that locks the reader temporarily within each restricted consciousness. Unlike *The Ice Storm* and "The Ring of Brightest Angels around Heaven," where formal technique distanced the reader from the action, here language is used to fuse reader awareness. Style here creates empathy and connection, the sole such gesture in a narrative where the characters stay stubbornly isolated and unable to touch each other authentically or helpfully. This is a language-rich, deliberately wrought text, every page word-soaked: labyrinthine sentences burst grammatical conventions, striking catalogs move with the cadence of incantations, prose and dialogue mingle, paragraphs unspool for uninterrupted pages, out-Faulknering Faulkner in a text audaciously written in a lush, purplish sort of overdrive (the color dominates the narrative and the audacious overdrive of the writing is suggested by the mock-grandiose title) that compels attention (this marks Moody's first extensive use of italics as a way to focus attention on the typed lines themselves) even as it here reveals the psychologies of the four central characters. Without defining author-ity, the reader becomes part of the unfolding action as we move into each character's thoughts, feelings, and recollections, even characters that are not the most appealing. Much as in the gripping opening chapter (an unbroken four-page sentence) when a middle-aged Hex Raitliffe must bathe his invalid mother, we are asked to attend to these afflicted, at times despicable characters—not sympathize (that is easy emotional manipulation that depends on ignoring the evident reality that every human being is a complex of nobility and brutality), but rather to step within their logic, their desperation, their moment.

The plot can seem secondary within such a daunting formal enterprise. It introduces elements familiar to Moody's readers: a fragmented family in an intense moment of emotional crisis, characters plagued by a world of brutal accident in a toxic and bleak contemporary landscape (both Hex's father, a scientist involved with the Los Alamos project, and his stepfather, a nuclear engineer, have been involved in radioactivity-related accidents, indeed all sorts of things leak uncontrollably in the narrative). Characters again struggle to unburden the self, wracked by a heavy ache of guilt and the unshakeable surety of punishment, confronting the inevitability of physical deterioration and the always-approaching stroke of death. The action covers a single November day. Hex, a stammerer (his name is actually Dexter, but as a child he found the hard *d* sound impossible), an overweight alcoholic, an unsuccessful freelance publicist in his late thirties, has been summoned to return to his upscale suburban Connecticut home to attend to his seventy-year-old bed-ridden mother, Billie, who has been slowly wasting away from a degenerative neural disease that has short-circuited her sight, her ability to control her bodily functions, and even her ability to speak, although, in some ghastly ironic twist, her mind is still sharp within such wreckage. What Hex does not know the mother makes clear after he arrives: she wants him to help her die now with some modicum of dignity. His stepfather, Lou, an engineer nearing retirement from the local nuclear plant, had two days earlier decided, even as he changed her disposable diaper, that after fifteen years, the responsibility of caring for the invalid woman was too much and had left a good-bye note on the home computer; because of Billie's poor eyesight, she must hear it recited by the synthetic voice of the computer's electronic communicator (*"Your poverty has tired me out"* (26)). Suddenly thrust into the role of primary caregiver, Hex decides to confront the stepfather, who is involved in an unfolding crisis at the power plant. Ancient cooper cooling pipes have come to be dangerously corroded by the seawater that the plant uses, and radioactive leaks into Long Island Sound and into the ocean have been detected. (Moody gives us pages of convincing engineering-ese, jargon-riddled explanations for the impending catastrophe, language struggling to contain contingency.) To handle the media uproar, utility officials have decided to use Lou, already on his way out, as the scapegoat, citing his decision years earlier to sign off on seawater as part of the cooling system. Lou himself struggles with his responsibility for the accident and the possibility that his actions may eventually poison a large slice of the Connecticut coastline.

When Hex takes his mother to a local restaurant (it proves disastrous—during the meal, she has a seizure and urinates), he runs into an old high-school crush, Jane Ingersoll, a street-wise motorcycle-riding single mom with punkish green hair, who helps Hex clean up Billie. When she agrees to help Hex get Billie back home, Jane is left in charge of Billie while Hex tracks down Lou—but after sharing a poignant moment in which they struggle to communicate about motherhood, she nearly drowns the helpless woman accidentally in a bath. Ultimately, she and Hex share what turns out to be an uncomfortably pathetic sexual interlude largely because of Hex's inexperience: unable to sustain an erection, Hex prefers Jane to be bound while he masturbates; meanwhile Jane comes by herself. They end up a local nightclub, ironically a remodeled Congregational church, where Hex, agitated first over Jane's attentions to a black man and then by a transvestite who attempts to pick him up, accidentally ignites gas leaking from his rental car. After he is released from the hospital, he returns home and decides in a harrowing sequence to help his mother die, trying first pills and then a dry-cleaning bag over her head and then finally a pillow. Desperate, he even tries to shoot her, only to miss at point-blank range. He is as inept at this as he is in everything he attempts—as his nickname suggests, he is hexed. When a repentant Lou unexpectedly returns home, Hex runs from the house and heads toward the bay, ashamed.

As crowded with event as this twenty-four-hour narrative is, it would resist film treatment—much as a high-kinetic Charlie Parker improv would resist scoring. Its theme is bound to its form. *Purple America* must be performed, read, listened to, endured (it can be tedious), experienced as a sonic event. Even as communication fails each character, the language of the narrative enterprise succeeds, shading these characters with emotional complexity. As Hex walks about the aisles of an all-night convenience store, he watches other isolates wandering the clean, well fluorescent-lighted place and seamlessly reveals his own stubborn isolation:

> There were a half-dozen soft, bespectacled, and unshaven guys in sweats preparing their evenings of domestic beer, microwaved hot dogs, potato chips, tattoo magazines, and network programming. This loneliness of convenience stores was also his loneliness. Loneliness was his parking space, his fully furnished studio, loneliness was that apartness that had been a feature of his comings and goings way back into the browned edges of memory, back through his twenties and after-hours drunkenness in NYC; back through the teens; back through the snapshot humiliations of his chubby boyhood; back even unto infancy, loneliness like a foreign tongue, *like an absent dream*. It was the siren call of himself. (142)

The meanest actions are deliberately slowed, details are meticulously recalled—which is to say meticulously invented (the orangey dandruff of Hex's father that shimmer off his head as he collapses helplessly from an aneurysm; the complex demonstration of the laws of physics that define a roundhouse punch delivered to the chin; the rubbery look of an old woman helplessly slipping under bathwater; the mechanics of catheter insertion; the tension and release of an unaccustomed orgasm). We are invited to do what narrators in previous Moody works relish: do the Surveyor-thing and imaginatively occupy a character, indeed here a cast of characters. The language here convinces that such colonization is possible.

But wait. Perhaps language is not quite so empowered. For all the revelations here, these rendered characters cannot stand up to the rigorous probing "why" of traditional psychological realism. Most prominently, we are never entirely sure why Hex is so completely maladjusted. Raised by a doting mother amid affluence and comfort with memories of a loving father dead too-young from an aneurysm and a caring stepfather who nursed his mother for more than fifteen difficult years while Hex himself took off for New York, what has happened to so short-circuit Hex—his stutter? his chubbiness as a child? Unlikely. There is too much Tarantino and too little Cheever here. But perhaps, given Moody's direction after this work, it is exactly his point. Language reveals and conceals simultaneously. Consider the odd ending. After Hex runs off to the ocean, Moody closes with a three-page letter from Hex's father to Billie written just before he leaves the service in 1946. Perhaps, we hope, this may reveal the cause of Hex's neuroses. But we are given a poignant letter that tells of the father's disgust with his work in atomic testing and his decision, after he watches the last underwater atomic test in the South Pacific, to come home, to have a normal life with Billie and to have a child or two. Nothing, in short, prepares for the creepy suburban Gothic that we have watched unfold. Like the atomic test flash that, he says, no one actually sees, but rather can see only its aftermath, life erupts with a ruinous implosive force that cannot finally be squared into logic no matter how generous the dispensation of language. And trying to stare such devastating reality into clarity can prove disastrous—impulsively, Hex's father slips off his goggles to watch the flash, exposure that we suspect may have contributed to his early death. The more we learn, Moody cautions, the less we understand.

"Demonology" (2000)

Coming upon "Demonology" among Moody's fictions can be initially disconcerting, even perplexing, rather like happening upon a unicorn in a zoo. Even in the 2000 collection that closes with this remarkable story, even among those twelve short story experiments, "Demonology" appears out of place. The other stories mark the same bravura willingness to push the "weird shit," to void the conventions and the boundaries of the short-story form, experiments that can come across (depending on the mood of the reader) as brashly exuberant, excessively tedious, indulgently overwrought and cerebral, deliberately campy, or bloodlessly experimental. To sample, "Boys" tracks in the extraordinarily nervy prose of a simulated street rap the otherwise ordinary growth toward maturity of twin boys from birth through the sexual awakenings of puberty and eventually to the funeral of their father after a car accident, that sense of inevitable evolution and bustling energy captured by a kinetic prose line, rhythmic, galloping, unstoppable constructions in which nearly every sentence begins with the phrase "Boys enter the house"; in "Wilkie Fahnstock: *The Boxed Set*," Moody provides the double-columned liner notes for a ten-volume cassette-tape anthology that ostensibly represents what an otherwise unspectacular nobody has listened to on his way to becoming a nobody; "Ineluctable Modality of the Vaginal" is a dead-center satire, delivered in an unbroken sixteen-page comma splice, of grad school/lit crit-ese as a frustrated feminist doctoral candidate, tired of the endless jargon-ridden conversations of her circle of pretentious friends, hops up on a table after a dinner party and, spreading her legs and offering two shoehorns, encourages her bland lover to conduct a pelvic examination, to actually confront the definition of the feminine not covered by academic theory; in "Drawer," a two-page Carveresque divertissement, a spiteful husband methodically destroys his wife's armoire with a crowbar as part of busting her left-behinds, targeting it typically because of a linguistic dispute—he always called it a dresser; the nearly incomprehensible "Pan's Fair Throng" is a fascinating stream of stylized language that may (or may not) be a sort of parody of a Renaissance fairy tale that involves a snobby king, a kidnapped queen, and a menacing giant (maybe—they may all be allegorical figures of the writing process) all framed (surprise!) by a traveling storyteller. Traditional storytelling gives way to Moody's determination to produce spectacle effects, to push conventions, to pose as cunning, smart-assy artificer, the Surveyor-figure gleefully pushing the imagination, the stylistic razzle-dazzle, to its limits.

Until the closing piece. In "Demonology," Moody drops authorial posturings and confronts the reader within uncharacteristic vulnerability: this is the story of his sister's death. There is no voice-over, no framing Surveyor, no reassuring larger authority safely removed from the unfolding experiences recounted in the narrative and free to experiment with the appropriate language technology to deploy. This is Rick Moody relating the last twenty-four hours or so of his sister's life before a cardiac seizure kills her even as her two young children and her boyfriend helplessly watch. This is a writer smarting from the very real experience of the stunning world of random contingency that has so regularly brutalized his characters—he is barely two months past her death. The smart-assy sense of elevated sensibility, the arrogance of the God-like writer, drops; the italics calm; the sentences are cleaner, less demanding, the vocabulary colloquial. As the closing story, it offers a disturbing sense that Moody himself had reached a traumatic point where language can offer little in the face of such stark evidence of nature's untidiness and unintentional malevolence.

Formally, Moody structures the story in bits, block fragments that alter contrapuntally between a series of apparently disjointed recollections, each triggered by a photograph Moody finds as he pages through his sister's vast photo-album archives, and a series of vignettes that replay the apparently irreversible movement toward the sister's fatal seizure, beginning with her organizing her kids' neighborhood trick-or-treating route (it is Halloween) and ending the next evening with the paramedics at the house. It is narrative without epiphany, narrative without revelation. Language here cannot coax these events to cohere into the logic of plot, the swift intrusive stroke of death simply unanticipatable, the reassuring mechanics of foreshadowing suddenly shoddy and unworkable. Instead, Moody piles up description, verbal riffs on a variety of asides—the opening sentence, for instance, a breathtaking seventeen-line take on costumed kids and their accompanying parents on Halloween streets. He will catalog miscellaneous photos in the albums, describe Meredith's church choir practice, her disdain for instant coffee, her tumor-ridden cat prone to seizures, her frenetic ad-lib dancing at their brother's wedding just two weeks before, her odd penchant for keeping copies of intriguing photos sent to her lab for processing—all merely underscore language's impoverishment, its stubborn inability to coax design. Train a careful spotlight, Moody warns, on any life—I dare you to find death anything but intrusive, premature, and frighteningly unexpected. Death is suddenly not a narrative device, a plot twist. The text struggles to assert the expected matrix of meaning, the comfortable fuselage world of narrative form, the sense that any traumatic narrative event comes with an escalating expectation of its shattering moment—after all, there can be no surprises in narrative, perfect author-ity rests with the Surveyor. Perhaps it "means" something that Meredith's children masquerade as the Little Mermaid and a shark, with that intriguing pairing of innocence amid danger-in-the-water and the predatory unexpected nature of death's assault; surely there is some "meaning" in the fact that the sister's death occurs within the suggestive context of Halloween and All Saints' Day; surely there must be something to the photo Moody happens on of his sister, so soon to be so terribly vulnerable, posing on a past Halloween as Supermom. Moody even seeks to deploy repetition, narrative's most traditional reassuring sense of organizing event into plot: he compares the loss of physical control, the body's surrender to free energy, to possession by demons (hence the curious title): he and sister's long-ago drunken antics under the influence of "*demon rum*" (293); her crazy dancing, as if possessed, at their brother's wedding; the frothing fits of her tumorous cat (at such moments, "He was a demon" (295)); and, ultimately, the meticulous detailing of her spastic cardiac seizure in the kitchen.

But we are left with pieces, meaningful bits that cannot find their way to coherence or explanation or even resonance. Her death denies imagination's gift for clarity. Moody himself concedes in a bald closing moment: "I should fictionalize it more, I should conceal myself. I should consider the responsibilities of characterization, I should conflate her two children into one, or reverse their genders, or otherwise alter them, I should make her boyfriend a husband . . . I should make Meredith's death shapely and persuasive, not blunt and disjunctive, I shouldn't have to think the unthinkable, I shouldn't have to suffer . . . I should have a better ending, I shouldn't say her life was short and often sad, I shouldn't say she had her demons, as I do too" (305-06). We have shared a most provocative moment of insight into Moody's experience—the pages detailing so graphically the medical trauma that kills Meredith are unsettling and immediate. Even when we realize that these searching and meticulous re-creations of his sister's last day, his "recollections," are entirely invented—Moody was not an eyewitness—even when we realize that he is conjuring, the Surveyor at full throttle, providing her death with the vivid realizations of language, capturing its devastation in a heart-breaking slow motion that is purely embroidered by a devastated but still very active imagination, we see in a terrifying (and to this point singular) moment within Moody's fictions that such consolation is finally unworkable, that language has its limits, that the heavy press of the real can bury it as simply irrelevant.

The Black Veil: A Memoir with Digressions (2002)

Because Moody, who has long wrestled with spiritual matters, is given to comparing the narrating impulse to the God-like imperative to create, surely, the narrator-God of *Garden State* and *The Ice Storm* and to a lesser extent of *Purple America* is modeled on the familiar Judeo-Christian figure, the confident master—that show-off imagineer of Genesis, the bold orderer amid the otherwise senseless and violent void, able to tidy up the apparently untidiable, the creator-God who reveals himself in his very creation. But the narrators we meet in "Demonology" and in *The Black Veil* are more the God of agnostics and atheists, bedeviling, elusive, infinitely difficult to pin down, the God that hides within his creation. Inevitably the shattering experience recounted in "Demonology" confirms Moody's own evolving determination to test the limits—rather than the reach—of language. Appropriately the first fit subject is the Surveyor himself, long insinuated by his texts, but never fully revealed. Such setting-out is risky, as the Bulkington chapter, which Moody quotes here in its entirety as he details his family's holiday dinner, counsels. Within the memoir genre (the two-tiered subtitle prepares us for exploration and intimacy even as it warns us against such a premise), we will be about the business of excavation (one of Moody's innumerable digressions investigates the New England quarry business), the often dangerous work of unearthing, in this case, some genetic explanation for Moody's lifelong melancholia. By exploring his family, particularly a long-assumed familial tie with one Reverend Joseph Moody (1700-1753), who at eight years old had accidentally shot a friend while they were hunting and then later in life after enduring the premature death of his wife and daughter, had taken to wearing a black veil for the rest of his life (Hawthorne's famous fable is drawn from this Moody ancestor), the contemporary Moody hopes to provide his own life experience with some clarity, a cohesive ordering, a plausible sense of causality.

What Moody constructs, however, is not so much a realistic memoir or a postmodern parodic antimemoir, but rather a sort of simultaneous (anti)memoir, at once earnest and parodic, compassionate and voyeuristic, that reveals the stubborn (im)possibility of revelation. We shuttle, chapter to chapter, among three narratives that each promise revelation: 1) Moody's descent into drug and alcohol addiction in the mid-1980s, his voluntary commitment to a psychiatric hospital, his release, and his determination thereafter to succeed as a writer; 2) a traditional scholarly/critical/historical examination of Hawthorne's compelling allegory of sin and unnamable guilt and that haunted minister who without explanation wears a black veil for years; and 3) the recounting of a one-week trip Moody took with his father in 1998 to Maine to investigate firsthand the family ties to Reverend Moody by examining the village records, the actual burial sites, the real homesteads, even the home churches of the Moody ancestors, a trip that became a chance for the divorced father and estranged son to confront old emotional wounds—a chance ultimately buried in far-easier conversational chitchat. Indeed, here language—once so resilient, so kinetic, so flexible, so connective—deceives, promises, taunts, distances, and ultimately conceals. The more Moody reveals—and his life brims with the sexy stuff of glamorous tell-alls: a difficult relationship with his father, alcohol and cocaine addictions, paralyzing panic attacks, hospitalization in a psychiatric facility, the struggle to hold even a menial job, a girlfriend's abortion, two half-hearted suicide attempts—the more he mimes the traditional contours of the tell-all, self-help inspirational, overcoming-adversities-through-recovery life-guides that so dominate best-seller lists and talk shows, oddly the more distant he appears to even the sympathetic reader. He does not mock the confessional promise of language—yet the more he confesses, the less distinct he becomes. This may be because such narrative revelations are slender moments that come packed within voluminous asides on topics that range from the loosely germane to the grandly irrelevant: the current rash of schoolyard shootings, an assortment of tales of Puritan mayhem and brutality, a handy guide to New England pine trees, a vivid re-creation of William Burroughs's accidental shooting of his wife, a brief treatise on Kafka and his father, a reprinting of the OED history for the words *moody* and *veil*, as well as extensive commentary on Hawthorne's story, as well as tedious commentary on casual pleasantries such as weather and meals. Reading such a memoir, then, is a structural approximation of the father-and-son Maine excursion itself: a long drive in the fog and rain, frequently feeling lost.

Revelation, then, is not Moody's goal, but rather an investigation into the lure of its possibility. By structuring a "memoir" that turns regularly into the protective security of meandering asides, Moody—himself approaching midlife and long beyond the young writer's confident embrace of his medium—reveals what undoubtedly lurks in the darker moments of any writer's honesty: no matter how sincere the effort, we simply cannot talk our way into order, we can never fully share our emotional experience, and ultimately we are essentially alone, mysteries each to the other and, most distressingly, to ourselves. We are left with the self-inflicted ecstasy of loneliness. Language promises exposure—share your pain with a friend, write a letter to a lover, reach out and touch someone, confide to a priest, emote a poem—but it can never near the howling Moody argues rages in even the most ordinary heart. Revelation then becomes another strategy for concealment—they are synonyms rather than antonyms.

Secrets, then, compel the narrative. In the introduction Moody recalls a mysterious figure he kept seeing in the mid-nineties in a New York subway station, a hooded figure (is he homeless? disfigured?) who dances on the subway platform. He becomes a convenient allegorical figure for Moody's own conscience, the burden of sins, petty and grand, and the consequent burden of guilt that he has carried in his heart since childhood, the something hidden in his soul that he wants to bring to light. Of course, the mysterious stranger never actually reveals his face, much less his history. He entices, he lures, he ignites response—but he maintains critical distance, always dances away. We are warned, then, early on that revelation and concealment will be the same dance. Yet Moody wants explanation, a function of language: Why the estrangement from his father? Why the tremendous impact of the divorce? Why the turn to drugs and alcohol? Why the decision to commit himself finally to psychiatric care? Why the struggle to find love? Every explanation brings only mystery until he must eventually relinquish his faith in the very premise of a secret that, like conspiracy paranoia, shapes terrifying contingency into attractive plot. It is no surprise that Moody recalls that as a child he loved to assemble those big box puzzles, then take them apart and reassemble them, the familiar and reassuring game of recovering design. This skewed memoir, however, is like a box of puzzle pieces that comes without the box, without the reassuring picture that forecasts eventual design.

Formally, Moody does this by shifting chapter to chapter among, between, amid unsolvable mysteries. Consider the recounting of the 1986 Christmas Eve family celebration when Moody first experiences the deep panic attacks that will eventually compel him to seek treatment for his addictions. We share the intimacy of the family gathering, the moment-to-moments of light chitchat, the details of the weather, the homey decorations, the family traditions, the gift wrapping, and even the menu. And we follow the tweed-jacketed Moody and his ugly craving for alcohol, the steady drink-by-drink consumption (rum and eggnog, bourbon, then beer, then wine). The next morning (on Christmas, a day rich with epiphanic expectations), he awakens, dry-mouthed and hung over, and endures his first anxiety attack: the escalating panic, the inexplicable sweats, the odd sense that he is made of plastic, an unfathomable paranoia, and ultimately the loss of speech itself, all-too appropriately a failure of language. The writer mute: despite the evident honesty of the narrative description, everything is revealed but nothing is explained. But his own admission, such freakish anxieties always accompanied binges—but he is morning-sober now. Thus we are offered only uneasy adjustment, not resolution: Moody tries to bow out of the annual family caravan to his father's house, there to replay Christmas with his new family, but ends up going anyway and there being offered sufficient alcohol to return him finally to full speech. Then in a single page-turn we are shuttled unironically and without transition from such difficult intimacy into a lengthy chapter that offers a sort of Fodors to the widely divergent critical/interpretative paths that have been taken into Hawthorne's "The Minister's Black Veil"—a text, Moody concludes, that still manages to sing free of such interpretative chains, to remain elusive and inexhaustible and able to sustain scores of contradictory readings. What is the connection to the episode of Moody's first panic attack? Like Melville shifting from the operatic melodrama aboard the shadow-crossed deck of the *Pequod* to the narcotic calm of the sub-sub library of Manhattan where he diligently researches the whale, here Moody reveals the impossibility of revelation, the elaborate conjure of language as it necessarily imposes arbitrary order. Revelation is always plural, meaning is always speculation, the dictionary always ironic, and language the enticing vehicle of revelation/

concealment. Like the Surveyor who invites his readers to embroider their own tale of Hester Prynne, here Moody helpfully appends to his "memoir" the entire text of Hawthorne's story and bibliography of critical sources—an invitation to do your own riff on the text. Here, you see, threads spin veils.

Identity itself, the subject of any memoir, is left haunted by speculations, a manufactured commodity that at any single moment could sustain investigation for consistency and logic but that finally cannot be talked into order. We are content with a sort of first-person obscure. At one point, Moody positions himself paging through Melville's *The Confidence-Man.* At another narrative point (during rehab), he gives us an extensive recollection of his fondness for Elton John that turns into a commentary on that singer's painful double life, his glitzy public persona and his tormented private self (a similar point about manufactured identity that he makes as well in an on-line essay about John Cheever and about Jesus Christ in his introduction to *Joyful Noise,* both of which appeared while he was working on *The Black Veil*). When he begins to probe into his ancestor, a literary agent gives him the actual diaries of the haunted Reverend Moody himself (like a memoir, a genre that promises rich revelation). But it is not quite so simple. Initially, the diaries had been written in a nearly inaccessible private code—but even when Moody reads the translations, he is frustrated to find them largely about the busy-ness of the minister's daily life, the weather, and his frequent indulgences of masturbation: paradoxically revealing and concealing simultaneously.

We are given, then, a narrative that announces its intention to reveal yet offers only evidence of those who hide, those who abandon reality and withdraw into protective isolation, those anti-Bulkingtons who abdicate even the pretense of engagement. The father spends a single summer as a nurse in a psychiatric ward and, finding the experience far too harrowing, accepts the calmer world of high finance. Betty Moody, a Puritan ancestor, fearing an approaching Indian raid, heads to a handy cave and, in hiding, kills her children to protect them. There is Reverend Moody himself with his storied black veil. There is the familiar historical record (which Moody recounts) of Hawthorne's voluntary retreat to his second-floor bedroom for a lifetime of willed seclusion amid his projections. There are the addicts in the wards whose lives are inelegant exercises in escapism: not only their drugs and alcohol, but how they artfully dodge the responsibility of honesty in the day-to-day counseling sessions. There is Moody himself. And not merely his evident escape into his addictions. He recounts his ill-considered experiment in actually wearing a black veil while at a writers' retreat—his shopping at

Wal-Mart for the right materials and his frustration over wearing one even for a brief time, how easily it became parody and an amusing gimmick. It is a narrative haunted by characters who fear the violent intrusion of the real (Moody's dominant anxiety before his commitment is an unshakeable fear that he is about to be raped, a suggestion of forced intrusion and the brutal shattering of privacy).

This, of course, provides Moody with his ultimate credibility as writer: the irony that the sheer inaccessibility of explanation alone makes him finally a writer. We (and Moody himself for that matter) never approach Moody, never account for the melancholia, the addictions, the neuroses—he passes by, an articulated shadow in the fog: ". . . I was still in the dark about my illness, *of what did it consist exactly,* since whenever I seemed to locate it, it vanished" (201). The catharsis here is the absence of catharsis, the release of the heavy obligation for tidiness. The danger in such linguistic excavation (and the danger is apparent when, on a visit to a quarry, Moody is nearly blasted by an unexpected explosion) is not unearthing that heart-of-darkness secret, but rather acknowledging finally the treasure is that there is no treasure. If experience were as neat as self-help books pretend, if revelation were workable and reliable, if sufficient answers could be forged for human behavior, if the universe were so ordered, there would be no need for language, no need for libraries of narratives that struggle with why. We do not write because understanding is possible—we write because it is impossible. Writers, Moody concludes, are not those who work lighthouses (that so confidently provide the great, bold guiding shafts of lucidity and clarity in the darkness), but rather are those who look into the bits of shimmering light (plural) that silver the disturbed wakes of boats passing through such illumination, content with necessarily incomplete, secondhand fragments of feeblest illumination. Indeed, Moody ends by admitting a long list of personal events and defining traits, trivial and significant, that he has not even touched (including monumentally his sister's death—he recounts only that he had petulantly refused to answer his phone that day even as he listened to the increasingly urgent messages from his father, another exercise in dodging reality).

He then closes with an expansive threnody on blackness itself, a clear gloss to Melville's similar cataloging of whiteness in *Moby-Dick.* The unbroken three pages of examples of blackness in nature, in history, in science, in pop culture, assault the reader with an unbearable heaviness of evidence, overwhelming, unstoppable, a sort of linguistic panic attack, a wrenching peroration that concludes ultimately that blackness—mystery, shadows—inevitably locks the heart—"my roots, which are *your roots*" (302). A devastatingly pessimistic assessment until you engage the language itself, the great rolling incantatory prose, the lyrical, strident, pulsing, lively palpitating throb of the galloping sentence, the sheer confidence that language, reinvented by every voice that embraces its potential, is finally the only vehicle capable of revealing its own inability to reveal. It is an injustice to quote it in part—its momentum is so steady and unbreakable. Thank God, Moody argues, we have coined the word *why*—it justifies the rest of the dictionary. *Guilt, blame, self, sin, hate, love, melancholy*—these are luxuries, constructions of language that provide shape to contingency and logic to experience that we know in our darker moments is chimerical. We are light-years from the narrator-as-surveillance-camera in *Garden State* and in "The Ring of Brightest Angels around Heaven" and the narrator-as-colonizer in *The Ice Storm* and *Purple America*. But Moody resists the difficult regret of "Demonology." If "Demonology" reveals language's limits, it is left only to point out that such concealment is, ultimately, a type of revelation and that those very limitations have justified libraries of narratives that collectively, joyfully argue the shortcomings of their own medium.

We are left then with the inscription value of writing itself, the "I" as an editor and arranger of words, where the deepest desire is to express yourself with the certainty that revelation cannot exhaust its own subject. The point of writing finally is writing. The only tension then is between language and silence, the impulse to articulate, the music of prose, the intoxicating discovery of new possibilities of the sentence original with every writer, against the lives that hiss away into the unrecorded. Moody, then, affirms the writer as the last vestige of voice and individuality in the electronic age, the instrument of engaged resistance to the larger cultural pull toward conformity and indifference. Unlike painting, film, music (all endeavors with which Moody has experimented)—each rigid and fixed—narrative accommodates the eccentric movements of a fluid and open universe. And narrative expresses a unique sensibility, the writer consciously shaping the form and executing the carefully tooled prose itself. A narrative, Moody argues, is that rare system that permits, indeed factors in, ambiguity, openness, flux, accepts its own limits and embraces, like the universe itself, the rich suggestivity of mystery. As in the universe, the narrative is fluid architecture where coherence does not mean clarity and patterns do not imply meaning. Thus Moody's best fictions, despite their often intimidating prose eccentricities, succeed by provoking the deepest sort of intimacy, a hot/cool nearness/distance: diligent writer and committed reader, two lonely figures in distant empty rooms who manage nevertheless to engage each other in the sustained imaginative act of reading itself, an interactive process necessarily flawed because it can only be undertaken by those aware of its fragility.

Ultimately, then, even the design implied by this "reading" of Moody is necessarily suspect, a tidying into form of a massive bank of data (consider the cast of intriguing secondary characters ignored, the multiple plotlines within each text roundly dismissed, the experimental short stories and essays left out, the considerable list of themes untouched, the stunning passages left unexplicated), a projection of an engaged ingenuity born of the conviction that design is possible, valuable, tenable even if revelation and concealment ultimately function like the twin-pistons of the same great engine. Design—whether here or in the construction of a narrative—succeeds only by its flexibility, like some contemporary building designed to withstand the tectonic shock of an earthquake wave, its willingness to concede its own vulnerability, its provisional nature, its inevitable amendment. Arrangement and expression do not dispel mystery, do not insist on understanding, but rather provide the infinite reassurance of form itself. Language, Moody ceaselessly reminds, is the sole aesthetic vehicle able to defy the casual contemporary assumptions of alienation amid the brutal contingency of a world beyond our shaping, able to shape mystery without flattening it and thus preserving the radiant awe over our every step into the immediate when the time comes to close up a book and return to its roiling unpredictability.

Works Cited

Goldstein, Bill. "Audio Interview with Rick Moody." Transcript of Web interview conducted 1 Feb. 2001. Available at http://www.nytimes.com/books.

Gordon, Fran Dilustro. "Moody on Dark Humor, Bright Angels, and Quantum Leaps." *Poets & Writers* 27.2 (1997): 37, 39, 40.

Moody, Rick. *The Black Veil: A Memoir with Digressions.* Boston: Little, Brown, 2002.

—. *Demonology: Stories.* Boston: Little, Brown, 2000.

—. *Garden State.* Wainscott, NY: Pushcart Press, 1991.

—. *The Ice Storm.* Boston: Little, Brown, 1994.

—. *Purple America.* Boston: Little, Brown, 1997.

—. *The Ring of Brightest Angels around Heaven: A Novella and Stories.* New York: Warner Books, 1996.

A Rick Moody Checklist

Fiction

Garden State. Wainscott, NY: Pushcart Press, 1991; Boston: Back Bay, 1997.

The Ice Storm. Boston: Little, Brown, 1994; Boston: Back Bay, 2002.

The Ring of Brightest Angels around Heaven: A Novella and Stories. New York: Warner Books, 1996; Boston: Back Bay, 2002.

Purple America. Boston: Little, Brown, 1997; Boston: Back Bay, 1998.

Demonology: Stories. Boston: Little, Brown, 2000; Boston: Back Bay, 2002.

Nonfiction

Judith Schaechter: Heart Attacks. Philadelphia: Institute of Contemporary Art, 1995. Catalog description of an exhibition of the works of a Philadelphia-based stained-glass artist.

"Introduction: The Parable of the Hidden Treasure." *Joyful Noise: The New Testament Revisited.* Ed. Rick Moody and Darcey Steinke. Boston: Little, Brown, 1997. 3-13.

"John Cheever and Indirection." *Conjunctions* 29 (1997): 216-30. Available at <http://www.conjunctions.com/conj29.htm>.

"Surveyors of the Enlightenment." Rev. of *Mason & Dixon,* by Thomas Pynchon. *Atlantic* July 1997: 106-10. Available at <http://www.theatlantic.com/issues/97jul/pynchon.htm>.

Introduction. *The Magic Kingdom.* By Stanley Elkin. Normal, IL: Dalkey Archive Press, 2000. v-xiii.

"The Creature Lurches from the Lagoon." *Zoetrope* 5.3 (2001): 30-34. Available at <http://www.all-story.com/issues.cgi?tImage=back&action=show_story&story_id=121>. A look at the difference between film and narrative.

"Reading Stanley Elkin." *Context: A Forum for Literary Arts and Culture* 5 (January 2002): 1, 3. Available at <http://www.centerfor bookculture.org/context/no5/moody.html>.

"Writing in the Dark." *Salon Premium* 24 January 2002. Available at <http://www.salon.com/books/feature/2001/09/18/dark/>. About the 11 September 2001 terrorist attacks.

Introduction. *The Mayor of Casterbridge.* By Thomas Hardy. Oxford World's Classics Series. New York: Oxford UP, 2002. v-xxiv.

The Black Veil: A Memoir with Digressions. Boston: Little, Brown, 2002; Boston: Back Bay, 2003.

Poetry

Fair Use: Poems and an Afterword. 43–page limited edition. Boston: Lame Duck Books, 2001.

The author would like to acknowledge the help of Jeffrey Pruchnic, doctoral candidate in American literature at Penn State University, for his help in accessing websites in assembling this checklist.

Ann Quin

Brian Evenson and Joanna Howard

Raised under complicated conditions in Brighton, Sussex, Ann Quin nevertheless enjoyed a deep, but short-lived camaraderie with many of the most notable experimental British writers of the 1960s and 1970s. While her first book, *Berg* (1964), received much general attention from reviewers, by her second book, *Three* (1966), she was easily garnering the praise of such writers as B. S. Johnson, Robert Nye, and Alan Burns, all of whom offered appreciative reviews of her work. When Quin went on to publish *Passages* in 1969 and her last completed novel *Tripticks* in 1972, these two later works were regarded as difficult and alienating by many reviewers, an attitude seen retrospectively by her publisher as having less to do with the works themselves than with the changing climate of English readership. *Tripticks*'s release was soon followed by Quin's presumed and somewhat mysterious suicide by drowning in 1973. Not long after, Quin's impact on innovative fiction largely subsided, and her novels slipped out of print; although *Berg* served as the basis for the British movie *Killing Dad* in 1989 (directed by Michael Austin, starring Richard E. Grant), the movie hardly made a splash and little attention fell back on Quin's work. In America in particular, Quin's novels were unavailable for nearly thirty years and have only recently been reprinted (and in the case of *Passages* and *Tripticks* issued in America for the first time) by Dalkey Archive Press.

Little is known about Ann Quin's life. She was born in 1936 and raised by her mother, her father having abandoned them shortly after her birth. She was educated in a convent (though she was not Catholic), which she described as "A ritualistic culture that gave me a conscience. A death wish and a sense of sin. Also a great lust to find out, experience, what evil really was" (qtd. in Mackrell 608). In her teens she grew interested in drama, leaving school to join a theater company for a short-lived stint as an assistant stage manager. She applied to the Royal Academy of Dramatic Art, but experienced intense stage fright when faced with the prospect of auditioning and soon surrendered any hopes for the stage, though dramatic performance and gestures inform her novels in terms of both form and content.

After leaving school, Quin began to write, poetry at first, later fiction. While employed as a secretary, she wrote two manuscripts, both of which were rejected by publishers. Trying to juggle her writing with the need to work for a living, she experienced her first nervous breakdown. Unable to get out of bed, she found herself subject to severe hallucinations, but after visits to a psychiatrist, she managed to pull herself together, for the "loneliness of going over the edge was worse than the absurdity of coping with day-to-day living" (qtd. in Mackrell 608). Soon after this decision, *Berg* was accepted for publication by John Calder and published to critical acclaim. *Berg*'s success opened up new possibilities for Quin, allowing her to travel in the United States and Europe, where she would experiment with both sexes and drugs—travels that would serve as the basis for her last two novels. Quin would struggle with mental illness throughout her life and was hospitalized several times. In 1972 while traveling in Switzerland, Quin suffered a breakdown so severe that she was unable to speak for quite some time and ended up hospitalized in London for a month. She recovered sufficiently to begin work on a new novel and, because of insecurity about not being educated, took college entrance exams. She had been, at the age of thirty-seven, admitted to the University of East Anglia, but before she could begin, she died by drowning, presumably a suicide.

The peculiar appeal of Ann Quin's work is to be found in her style, which, according to Wilmott is "unconventional and goes against accustomed reading habits" (3). Formally, Quinn's work remains, even for the most knowledgeable readers, quite challenging. Much of her work is relatively unpunctuated, and her exterior and interior dialogue (from speech to many different manifestations of thought) are often elided into the exposition instead of being set off; narrators, whether first person or third, remain intimately behind the shoulder of the characters, offering the world through a lens made wavery by subjectivity, while refusing explanation or interpretation of the characters' interior states. Rather, the narration functions like an invasive camera, with actions and events unfolding cinematically, simultaneously with the dialogue and the narration. In this sense, Quin's strongest work seems unique in its almost claustrophobic equalization of the narration: one moves from one narrative level to another abruptly and often without warning. The dilemma, however, remains that precisely those things that set her work apart from the mainstream of contemporary writers and caused her to be accepted by the experimental community ultimately formed a barrier for many readers of her work.

Ann Quin's content, on the other hand, shows her work to have an interest beyond formal innovation. In *Berg* a man goes to a seaside resort to kill his father, only to become immediately sucked into a triangular relationship with his father and his father's mistress, which culminates in the brutal mock-assassination of a ventriloquist's dummy. With *Three,* Quin returns to the tumultuous seaside setting, offering a suffocating triangle between a stilted, childless couple and a missing (and presumed dead) unstable young girl they have taken under their wing. With both *Berg* and *Three,* several narrative elements recur. There is always a triangle, a peculiar power dynamic, heavily laden with subtle eroticism as well as overt sexual interaction. Likewise, there is the recurrence of the sea, whose constant undulation parallels the subterranean movement of consciousness between narration and dialogue and which represents the yawning possibility of finality through sinking or drowning. In addition to this, there is the horror of the carnival, in *Berg* as linked to the dance hall and in *Three* in the masked miming which the characters regularly enact in an empty swimming pool. And, above all, both narratives revolve around violent death, murder/suicide or attempted murder, each coupled with acts of ambiguous, unpredictable, and permeating violence.

Passages and *Tripticks* pick up on many of the aspects of *Berg* and *Three.* For instance, as in *Three,* the interrelationship in *Passages* is triangular, with an absent third. More important, *Three* arranges itself around alternative types of narration, providing both third-person narration and first-person diary narrative, a technique picked up on in *Passages* as well and used to more disorienting effect. In *Tripticks* too, a chapter of letters interrupts the novel's other narration. And generally speaking, the narration of *Tripticks* picks up on aspects of *Berg.* Nondifferentiation of the narrative in *Berg* becomes in *Tripticks* amplified to the level of collage and pastiche: in *Berg* (and to some degree in *Three* as well) it is often difficult to tell where narration stops and interior thought starts, all of it fading together; in *Tripticks* any given paragraph can contain all sorts of narration, some of it appropriated from magazines or television and nestling uncomfortably against the narrator's own words.

Criticism regarding Quin's work is scarce. Those few essays in existence place their emphasis on *Berg* and *Three.* Philip Stevick in his article "Voices in the Head: Style and Consciousness in the Fiction of Ann Quin" examines Quin's use of style as a way of classifying her as an experimental woman writer. In this essay he comments on the "theatrical" nature of narration and dialogue, especially in *Berg*: "Berg's talk scarcely seems 'inner' at all, seems rather actual speech, acted out in the theater of the mind, and one imagines Berg talking aloud to himself . . ." (232). Stevick sees this style of theatrical consciousness as organic to the mental meanderings of the characters. He adds, "far from seeming a gratuitous experimentalism,

Quin's fictional technique comes to seem a perfectly natural way of rendering a mode of mind that is, in its way, at least as central to the general experience of the last two decades as . . . Joyce's Bloom" (233). While Stevick's reading of Quin's experimentalism is complimentary, his approach to Quin's style doesn't go very far beyond the assertion that she is in fact outside of the canon of traditional literature because she avoids classical notions of meaning and understanding and because she subverts the Aristotelian notions of beginning, middle, and end.

Both Stevick and critic Andrew Hassam compare Quin to Nathalie Sarraute, who in her book *The Age of Suspicion* sets out several tenets for the new novel which Quin seems to pick up readily: the emphasis on undercurrents of consciousness (what Sarraute terms subterranean movement), formal rendering of dialogue to appear without quotes and as elided into exposition, and the refusal to explicate character psychology through narration. However, Stevick points out that, at least prior to *Berg,* Quin had not read the new novelists, nor had she much interest in the French new wave novel as a constituted movement. Stevick further notes that it is "not a movement that interests her but the odd and inscrutable recesses of the mind [which] tends to organize itself as a reflection of sensory experience, rendering the visual, the tactile, and the auditory, creating a movement among them . . ." (237). Her publisher, Marion Boyars, reinforces this when, while acknowledging that Quin has been compared to the French nouveau roman, he suggests that Quin had "a very individual style and if any influences are to be found in her later work, it seems more appropriate to name people like Robert Creeley and John Cage" (qtd. in Gordon, *Beyond* 251).

The so-called "inscrutable recesses of the mind" which arise in Stevick's article are more deftly explored in Andrew Hassam's book *Writing and Reality,* in which Hassam examines the role of the diary in Ann Quin's novel *Three.* He sees the use of overlapping diaries in *Three* as an attempt to locate a "deeper reality and a lasting, if not totally unqualified freedom. In particular this search for a deeper, freer reality involves in the writing of a diary an entry into fantasy . . ." (129). In this way Hassam is able to move some of the formal elements of the novel, primarily the diary entries of the three characters, into close relationship with the content of the text, thereby strongly justifying some of the experimental elements that could seem otherwise gratuitous. Hassam goes on to render a close reading of *Three* which emphasizes the use of the diary, but which, more important, identifies the mental barriers provided by the married couple who are the subject of the third-person narration, juxtaposing them to the mental meanderings of the dead girl S's first-person narrative. For Hassam, much of the complexity of the text comes from the overlapping of mental interiors, and the elision of the interiors as the voices of the two living characters begin to overlap with the tape-recorded journals of S.

While Stevick makes several useful points about Quin's work, he maintains a tendency to read the text as more determinant than Quin's language would often suggest. For instance, in a meticulous explication of an early paragraph of *Berg*, Stevick separates the utterances out and firmly attributes them: "A little later, an encounter with a dance hall girl in which Berg was embarrassed by his impotence is recalled, as talk . . . or later, in no particular context, Berg recalls his school boy humiliation as speech . . ." (233). In both instances the speech in question is deliberately unattributed, as is all the dialogue in these first two novels, and this type of reading does much to destroy the ambiguity that Quin's elision and lack of explication work so hard to create. On another problematic issue, the fact that Stevick's essay is written specifically for a collection of essays on women experimental writers does much to complicate in advance the way in which he views Quin's work; such a narrow objective naturally leans toward a rather one-sided reading. Hassam's argument, on the whole, is much more careful and measured. His explication of the narrative events in *Three*, while closely examinative, avoids overly determinant readings, instead emphasizing the way the ambiguity of the three narratives replicates the confusion felt by the characters. Hassam's understanding of the style relies heavily on reading it as an organic rendering of the diary, and therefore the fact that many of the stylistic traits of *Three* existed previously in *Berg* (which does not make use of diary forms) goes untreated.

Other than two articles written in German on *Three* and published in the 1970s, the only other academic article with a connection to Quin that we know of is Kathleen Wheeler's "Reading Kathy Acker," which makes reference to Quin's "marvelous *Tripticks*," and begins with a quotation from the end of that book. Though the article is primarily on Acker, Wheeler argues for Quin as a precursor of Acker in her willingness to dispense with

> almost all familiar conventions of the novel. They both sought to reveal the fact that familiar order and logic are much less native to our experience than we realize, whether we mean inner mental experience or the apparent order of nature and the "external" world. Sanity is, arguably, merely the most familiar form of irrationality. Both authors challenge conventional assumptions about individual identity. They also examine its construction, perpetuation, and its breakdown. . . . (6)

Wheeler goes on to declare that Quin, like Acker, plays with gender stereotypes and categories. Certainly Quin seems as comfortable with crossing gender and writing from the perspective of a male character, and in *Passages* there is a sense that the male and female main characters might actually be one and the same.

Wheeler's reading of Quin is accurate and perceptive (though more relevant to some of the novels than to others, perhaps), though the usefulness of her argument is limited by the fact that, other than the quotation that opens the article, there is no actual quotation or close reading of an individual work by Quin, and thus no differentiation. It remains provocative but, nevertheless, general.

Berg (1964)

It is not surprising that, having grown up in Brighton, Ann Quin chooses a seaside resort for the setting of her first novel, *Berg.* Critics also connect the plot of *Berg,* which consists of a man seeking retribution against the father who abandoned him, to Quin's own biography: Quin's father, an opera singer, abandoned her and her mother in her childhood. However, after this is noted, biographical links become more tenuous. Judith Mackrell in her literary biography would suggest that "*Berg* is highly autobiographical in its underlying emotional impulse if not in particular detail" (608).

The first words of *Berg* stand apart from the text on an introductory page, in the form of a single, incomplete sentence: "A man called Berg, who changed his name to Greb, came to a seaside town intending to kill his father. . . ."[1] Says Dulan Barber, "There in one dangling sentence, incredibly well designed to lead the reader in and on, is the plot and essence of *Berg*. What follows is embroidery" (169). Alistair Berg establishes himself in a boardinghouse in a room that adjoins the room rented by his father and his father's mistress, Judith, separated from them by only a partition. He slowly manipulates his way into a relationship with his father and Judith, transforming their bond into a triangle which crumbles as Nathaniel, Berg's father, begins to look for opportunities to get out of his relationship with Judith and get into a traveling vaudeville act with a ventriloquist's dummy. On Guy Fawkes day, when Nathaniel's dummy is mistaken for an effigy and nearly burned, Berg and his father end up disoriented in Berg's room in the aftermath. Berg, convinced that he has been drugged by Judith, has difficulty interpreting the situation and convinces himself that he has killed his father and wrapped the body in a rug, only later to find that all he has is the dummy. Still he persists in an attempt to dispose of the dummy, clinging to the possibility that it somehow is the dead body of his father. When Nathaniel returns drunk and dazed to the apartment, Berg quickly dresses as Judith but then has to thwart an onslaught of sexual advances. It is not until a later day, perhaps the following day, that Nathaniel returns for Berg, realizing there has been a murder attempt. He and several other men chase Berg ultimately into the sea, where he clings to the ventriloquist's dummy, fading in and out of consciousness while asserting the hope that if his father would just drown, things would be easier. Berg awakens washed ashore with the dummy and returns to take Judith as his mistress. Shortly thereafter, a body washes up on the shore, a body which most likely is not that of his father, but which Berg chooses to identify as his father. The book ends as a new tenant moves into the room adjoining that of Berg and his mistress, Judith, the tenant suspiciously resembling Berg's father in disguise.

Running simultaneously with the narrative of Berg's pursuit of his father are the intermittent letters from Berg's mother that urge him to reconnect with his father and to view his father in a positive and loving light. Berg rejects his mother's advice and begins to replace her affection through his new relationship with Judith, returning his mother's letters with less and less frequency. By the end of the novel, Judith's voice seems entirely colored by the nagging voice of Berg's mother, as if Judith has come to occupy her role, and the implication exists that Berg intends to stay with Judith, assuming his father's position. With the arrival of the new tenant, there is every indication that the triangular relationship will begin anew, with Berg in his father's role this time.

Berg is remarkable because it operates in the space of innovative literary fiction while holding on to certain tropes associated with genre. *Berg* is unmistakably reminiscent of sixties British spy drama, in television and film as well as popular fiction. This can be seen in Berg's stakeout of his father and his mistress, in the hoodlum chase, in the tawdry affair between the pursuant and the mistress of his target, and in the barrier of the sea which keeps Berg from leaving for good the horrific resort town. Likewise, the question raised at the crisis moment in *Berg,* the moment in which he is finally given the opportunity to kill his father, the moment in which he is convinced he *has* killed his father, is straight out of the pulp crime genre: "My God what had she put in that drink—something lethal?" (71). However, by the end of the novel what has successfully played out, perhaps literally, but at the very least symbolically, is the Oedipal myth as refracted through the story of Hamlet.[2] And through this the novel regroups itself as being in the literary tradition. In the end it is a remarkable combination of high and low, of literary and nonliterary impulses. Says Giles Gordon of the book, "Here was a working-class voice from England quite unlike any other, which had absorbed the theatrical influences of John Osborne and employed the technical advances of the nouveau roman. *Berg,* to use shorthand, is a Graham Greene thriller as if reworked by a somewhat romantic Burroughs" (Introduction ix).

Stylistically, however, *Berg* remains challenging and innovative. The opening of the book sets up a stylistic pattern which is manipulated throughout the text:

> Window blurred by out of season spray. Above the sea, overlooking the town, a body rolls upon a creaking bed: fish without fins, flat-headed, white-scaled, bound by a corridor room—dimensions rarely touched by the sun—Alistair Berg, hair-restorer, curled webbed toes, strung between heart and clock, nibbles in the half light, and laughter from the dance hall opposite. Shall I go there again, select another one? A dozen would hardly satisfy; consolation in masturbation, pornographic pictures hanging from branches of the brain. (1)

The passage begins with an image rather than a point of narration, and here the image is truncated so that it is strictly visual. The narration continues in this fashion, so that the view moves in through the window, now marked as "Above the sea," a phrase that rhetorically defines the setting; however, the phrase remains vague and ambiguous. Berg is first described as a body rolling on a bed, and through this he is stripped of any particular humanity or agency. From this the metaphor extends and the rolling body, now linked to the sea, becomes a fish or fishlike creature described as finless, but with scales and curled webbed toes. At this point the third-person narrator enters to give Berg a name (that name being Berg, obviously), to give him what at first seems to be a professional title (hair-restorer), and to attach him to an action, nibbling. What follows is a first-person utterance, "Shall I go there again, select another one?," presumably Berg commenting on the girls of the dance hall, but here the stylistic confusion of inside and outside is acute. Is this utterance an exterior monologue by the character? Is this interior thought process? In either case the object of the utterance must be interpreted. Often, as in the case of this statement, the context must provide some understanding of both the subject and object of the statement, and here it seems likely that this must be interpreted as coming from the mouth or mind of Berg himself. However, in many other cases, the possibility of alternative interpretation is present. What follows this utterance, "A dozen would hardly satisfy," is thinly linked back to the previous statement, but could be read variously as a judgment by the third-person narrator (whose speech, even in this first paragraph, is already defined as quite textured and quite judgmental) or as third-person narration taking on the characteristics of Berg's voice or as a further utterance, either internal or external, by the character. Here the concern is one of the level of narration, which throughout *Berg* remains shifting, ambiguous, and indeterminate.

However, in any reading of the style, the narrative discourse remains always quite close to the central character's consciousness. Whether it is third-person objective, over-the-shoulder, or camera eye and whether it is interrupted by internal or external dialogue, voices from the past, present, or presumed future or whether it is purely fantasized, always the narration and internal utterances remain closer to Berg himself than to any other character, and often it seems to be Berg's own questionable sense of reality that colors the narrative lens. Despite the disorienting nature of the style, Quin is careful to filter through Berg's consciousness all the details necessary for us eventually to sort through the convoluted plot. And while some aspects remain ambiguous—for instance the fact that Berg's father may or may not be the new tenant who has moved into the room next door at the end of the novel, Quin is still careful to use the dialogue of the other characters—Judith, Nathaniel, and the landlady—to offer an occasional grounding reality for the reader to compare against Berg's often skewed perceptions. At heart, despite its experimentation, *Berg* still shares many aspects of the traditional novel.

Three (1966)

Closely following the successful response to *Berg*, *Three* has been even more closely linked to Quin's own biography, to her sexual and emotional involvement with the couple to whom she dedicates her book. This is perhaps due as well to Quin's own willingness, in talking to John Hall, to trace lines between her work and her life, to speak about triangular relationships in both her life and art. In *Three*, S, the young girl who infiltrates the lives of an otherwise mundane couple, commits suicide by drowning (possibly), a suicide which seems also to prefigure Quin's own death. Again, Quin returns to a seaside town for the setting of this novel; however, while the sea in *Berg* proves a temporary refuge for Berg as he escapes pursuers, in *Three* the sea serves as a horrific barrier for the two insular characters trapped between it and the city on whose edge they live. Yet, for both *Berg* and *Three,* the sea also promises the escape of death, and while for Berg the possibility that his father may have finally drowned seems reassuring, S's presumed suicide is treated with much uncertainty, guilt and mixed emotion by the two other characters of the triangle.

Three opens with a married couple, Ruth and Leon, as their attention is drawn toward a scrap of news, italicized and set off before the beginning of the text proper, outlining a man's death from a fall. From this, it becomes clear that the couple has become interested in any news related to death or suicide, and they link it back to the recent apparent suicide of S, the girl who came to live with the childless couple shortly after having an abortion. All that is firmly known about S's death is that her boat capsized and her coat was found with a suicide note in the pocket. Ruth and Leon assume she has drowned and discuss her in this way, "But Leon hers wasn't like that—I mean we can't really be sure could so easily have been an accident the note just a melodramatic touch" (1). What follows is the slow unfolding of the story of their relationship, with great ambiguity, through more third-person narration and through the written and recorded voice of S, so that by the end of the book it seems possible that what has happened to S is not that she has drowned but that she has deliberately turned herself over to a group of men with knives, knowing them to be dangerous and violent. This is reiterated when Leon notes the news clipping of a body of a girl washed up on shore, her death caused by an angler's knife and a hammer. This detail comes for Leon after he has brutally raped Ruth in an attempt to force her to empathize with his sexual longing. Because Leon has had some involvement with these men with knives (they badly beat him in his own backyard) and because the degree of Leon's involvement with S is never completely clear, the possibility of Leon having some vague part in S's violent death remains a lingering possibility.

What S has left behind is a series of diary entries, both written diaries and tape-recorded diaries, which begin to intersperse themselves throughout the narrative of Ruth and Leon's attempt to cope with S's absence and with their ongoing and stifling life together. It is through S's diary that we learn that she intends to set out in search of these violent men and that she reads her role in the narrative as that of victim. Her reason for doing this seems to connect strongly back to her need to break Ruth and Leon out of their cycle of noncommunication. Her final pages are also preceded by a detailed, recurrent fantasy of sexual encounters with an anonymous male in a hotel room, seeming to solidify her position as a kept woman and giving perhaps some background on her need for an abortion. Whether or not this fantasy figure is Leon is unclear, but the intimacy between Leon and S is made clear from S's attempts to understand his involvement with the violent gang who assaults him in his garden, and though no sexual relationship between S and Leon is ever made explicit, enough hints are present to suggest the possibility of such a relationship. S's final words as she prepares for her death are also the final words of the book, "The boat is ready, as planned. And all that's necessary now is a note. I know nothing will change" (143). Likely, what will not change is Ruth and Leon's claustrophobic insularity or their ultimately violent schism created by Ruth's revulsion at Leon's sexual advances and Leonard's latent contempt for Ruth. Though another possible reading may be that what will not change is Leon's inability to respond to, or accept responsibility for, the women in his life.

Stylistically, as with *Berg,* the language and syntax of *Three* serves to disorient rather than root the reader. While in *Berg* the reader held onto punctuation for use in separating utterances of the main character from those of the other characters, as well as from the commentary of the narrator, in *Three* punctuation falls away significantly. While commas are maintained for separations in the action, dialogue becomes completely elided, periods used only to indicate (and not always then) a shift from one speaker to the next: "Thought it something I'd get over conquer in time with you Leon—with the three of us here together. It's very calm today clear enough to see the rocks the river too might see salmon in the waterfall. You go yes go on why don't you you're dying to get out. It's not that. . . . Not what?" (3). Here the quotation presumably begins with Ruth's voice, identified only by her direct address of Leon, and here she refers to her fear of the sea. In the next sentence Leon begins to speak, describing the weather as calm. Ruth's response, which again we must interpret, allows her to recognize his comment as a desire to go on an outing, and her response, though contained in a single sentence in terms of punctuation, is actually comprised of several independent clauses, syntactically run together. The effect of this collision of dialogue is severalfold: first, it forces a reader to slow down the natural pace of reading so that careful interpretation can begin. Second, it allows the reader to feel the uncomfortable closeness of their speech, his and her responses being so closely linked that each response seems a skewed interpretation of what has come before, though each character holds on to the notion that he or she has properly interpreted the other. These sections of Ruth and Leon together are carefully rendered by a cinematic, third-person eye, so that even when Ruth and Leon are in separate places, their narratives run parallel through alternating paragraphs. Stylistically they are separated only by their own journals. Ruth's is a written journal which seems to be a new project of hers, an attempt to express her own feelings related to what she sees as

Leon's possible infidelity and his unwanted sexual advances toward her. Leon has a written journal, a formal ledger of events recorded in objective distance, and these appear in the novel in a form that mimics the ledger itself:

March 31st	S moved in
April 3rd	R ill
April 4th	Lunch at the Club
April 5th	Petrinelli translation started (2)

In Leon's written journal all events are given equal weight, so that the entrance of S into their lives (significantly enough on April Fool's Eve) receives equal mention to lunch at the club or the beginning of a new translation. However, Leon's written journal is juxtaposed to his tape-recorded one, which Ruth listens to in the last section of the book. Here, the response is much more subjective and muddled, coming quite close to S's own style in her written journal: "That I've been in a trance no doubt. Confronted by an existence I can no longer believe in. But who can say there's any definition in what has been? . . . How to come to terms?" (120).

The most stylistically notable passages, their experimental nature overt, come in Quin's transcriptions of the tape-recorded journal of S. S's journal is rendered with line breaks and poetic spacing, which further enhance the nonlinearity of S's thought patterns and her response to the objects and people of her environment. These passages are dominated by the sensory and form an interesting pairing with Leon's ledger, which is likewise formally quite vertical on the page and which seems to give equal weight to people, objects, and lunches. S's journals, though incredibly personal and subjective, ultimately have the same effect of leveling the subject matter: "Shirts / clothes. On the line above. Theirs. Three toothbrushes. / Blowing bubbles. Glide over tiles / split / against windows / glass. The sea / sea" (17). She goes on later in the passage to talk about a "Woman naked / crushed / by grapes" in the same flow of description. All elements are dealt with in this flattened tone, allowing resonance only in the enjambment; however, because we are left with no explication of the diary passages, only the implication that they are being read or heard simultaneously by the characters, there is not much to suggest whether the line breaks are meant to operate poetically or as pauses in the tape between utterances. Either reading leaves interpretive possibilities for the reader.

As in *Berg,* the narrative of *Three* remains always close to the characters. But here the narrative attention is divided equally among the three characters of the triangle rather than remaining close to a main character. The coherency of *Berg,* the sense *Berg* had of being a narrative with a definite plot and clear characters, is beginning to disperse—plot now more implied than actual—and will continue to do so in Quin's next two books. The journal entries of S comprise roughly one half of the book, while the combined third-person narrative of Ruth and Leon form the other half. What is remarkably different about *Three* in relationship to *Berg* is that the necessity Quin felt in *Berg* to clarify plot points through the speech of outside characters and through exposition has here corroded. The story remains heavily gapped, with the events of the past behind the story like ghosts, unable to be fully determined. This narrative style of consuming ambiguity and openness points toward the path Quin will follow in her last two books.

Passages (1969)

Quin's first two books have similarities to the French nouveau roman and Nathalie Sarraute, even if these similarities were not conscious on Quin's part. While these connections can still be felt in *Passages,* the novel seems to be moving toward the cut-ups of William Burroughs and the textual pastiche of Kathy Acker. In *Passages* narrative progression is attenuated, other voices taking the place of a developing narrative in a way that encourages confusion in character and in identity, a swapping of voice and personality. Indeed, *Passages* offers a more aggressive exploration of the technical possibilities of prose, at the expense of coherent plot and development.

Like Paul Auster's *The Country of Last Things, Passages* is ostensibly about a woman's search for her vanished brother, a brother who might not be alive. "Not that I've dismissed the possibility my brother is dead" (5), are the first words of the book. Yet, unlike in Auster's novel, the search for the brother seems more of a pretense than the focus of the book, a good deal of which moves in other directions. The main characters are a woman and a man, both unnamed. Together they travel through an unnamed country in search of the woman's brother who has disappeared. "They say there's every chance. No chance at all. Over a thousand displaced persons in these parts, perhaps more. So we move on. Towards. Away" (5). The man is in fact the woman's lover, though at other points he is described as if he is another manifestation of the woman herself. In addition, there are moments when the woman herself seems to speak of herself in the third person—though at times it appears there may actually be a third person or at the very least anonymous strangers, both male and female, who become briefly involved with the man or woman. Indeed, at times there seem to be three people traveling, at others only one, and at no point can the number of characters be resolved once and for all. At times as well it seems that the lover is on quite a different search, a search of self-discovery. Both the man and the woman seem to be, at the very least, mentally imbalanced, though more likely verging on schizophrenia. With the narrative focalized through the woman's disconnected but intense perceptions in one case and through the man's annotated diary in another case, the result is a narrative that lies so close to the misperceptions of its main characters that it is hard to sort out the solid ground that might have been the basis for these misperceptions to begin with.

The narrative is divided into four sections which alternate between two separate styles of narration. The first and third consist of the perceptions of the woman, the second and fourth of the man's annotated diary. The woman's narration consists of paragraphs with spaces between them that sometimes seem complete paragraphs, sometimes break off or start up in the middle of a sentence. At times one can feel a connection between one paragraph and the next, see where the second paragraph picks up the ideas or even the incomplete ending sentence of the paragraph that preceded it. But at least as often the spaces between paragraphs, whether the paragraph ends with a period or in the middle of a sentence, serve as gaps, and the reader experiences a lesser or greater confusion. A paragraph tends to group itself more around a vivid description or a memorable moment than around a plot point: on page 19, for instance, Quin offers bits and pieces of impressions in a church, though what relevance this might have to the search for the brother, beyond creating a certain mood, is unclear. Consider as well this short paragraph: "The harbour deserted, shutters down. We couldn't find a cab. We went into a cafe. A woman with gold teeth behind the bar. She watched us, every move, gesture. He watched her, the way she swayed from the waist, hips, as she moved from bar to table. I went out" (22). The reader gathers a particular memorable moment in the same way that one might notice something new. One gathers as well a certain vague sense of menace and of tension between the characters, but in the end it is just a relatively anonymous moment in a bar that breaks off near the end (the next paragraph begins "along the deserted street," completing the sentence). But it is through such anonymous moments that Quin builds up the effect of her story.

This strategy of breaking off a paragraph before the end of a statement is used much more often in the first section than in the third, appearing only eight times (out of sixty-four paragraphs) in the third section as opposed to twenty-four (out of fifty-eight paragraphs) in the first. Indeed, the third section seems to be a more conscious attempt at least to imply a narrative arc and to overtly pursue the search for the brother, perhaps more surefootedness on the part of the narrator.

An unsigned review of *Passages* in the *Times Literary Supplement* titled "Lovers," provides a good description of the rigors of this portion of the book: "the language seems bent on effacing itself in favour of some musical or visual medium, so that though the time sequence, the order of events, is blurred, particular observations and moments are expressed with lucidity and directness" (341). Indeed, the reviewer suggests as well that the formal elements of these sections are very much welded to the situation itself, for they "suggest exactly the reactions of a traveller whose senses acquire a new responsiveness to detail, to particular sounds, faces, physical impressions" (341).

The second and fourth sections pursue a different strategy, offering the diary of the man, with annotations in the margins which the back of the British paperback edition indicates consist of "those thoughts that provoked the entries," i.e., starting points for the entries themselves. While the woman's sections worked with the relationship between and juxtaposition of formally similar paragraphs, these sections work with the relationship between and juxtaposition of two formally dissimilar things: the diary entries and the annotations. Annotations may include Talmudic-style sayings or descriptions of Greek pottery, but they may also include more personal statements, such as "Am I truer to her than to myself perhaps?" (35). The diary proper contains equally diverse material: descriptions of dreams, sexual fantasies, simple reflections, words on the political situation, and so on. In addition to lack of connection from entry to entry (a natural thing in a diary) and lack of connection from annotation to annotation, there may or may not be a direct connection between the annotation and the entry it has sparked. Sometimes the connection is obvious:

1 a.m.

gull: sense of fool, may come from the bird swallowing anything that's tossed to it. Bird name is common Teut. Hence also gullible.

I am vulnerable only as far as another's gullibility allows, can contradict this, certainly an aspect of vulnerability.

33)

Implied is that the seeing of the bird leads to reflections on the nature of its name which in turn leads to the man's reflections on his own internal state as defined in relation to the gullibility of others.

The movement is from perception to definition to ontological statement, the progression easily traced. Other connections, however, are more oblique:

Friday

From a grave jar: The lid has been removed; out of it have escaped fluttering upward, two Keres, a third one is about to emerge, a fourth dives headlong back into the jar.

Two weeks in the city and we seem to be going neither forward or back. The papers carry the same goddamn news. Rumors make for excitement, despair for natives and exiles. There seems very little difference now between them, except the exiles seem able to get the money and clear out of the country more quickly. Threats, suspicion. Talk of detention camps. A university town with security problems. Growth of police power. Court martials. The regime, apparently has admitted in writing to the International Committee of Jurists that telephones are being cut off; the reason offered is that it prevents left-wing elements from plotting over the telephone. Relatives of political opponents are victimised. Very few people now allow themselves to get drunk. (90)

Here one moves between art and life; if the jar has any relation to the passage on politics, it is a symbolic one, the figures escaping and diving representing the political shenanigans of the country itself. In addition, many of the journal passages do not have annotations beside them, which leaves one to wonder if the annotations apply to several passages in a row or if some simply aren't annotated, and sometimes the annotations locate themselves oddly spatially, beginning in the middle of a passage or even touching two passages at once.

In this diary Quin's work with cut-ups and rearrangements is done in a contained space (this will change with *Tripticks*) and largely restricted to quotations from various sources used as journal annotations. At a few moments, however, she expands her range. On page 102 she allows the man to offer first his dream and then to give a rendering of it, called "Cut-up dream," that begins to reprocess it and reverse the relations. Part of the ending as well suggests that what is about to occur is a rearrangement or cut-up of what has come before: "So let us begin another journey. Change the setting. Everything is changing, the country, the climate. There is no compromise now. No country we can return to. She still has her obsession to follow through and her fantasies to live out" (112). We would argue that this statement not only has relevance to the book itself—

to the fact that, having found nothing, a new journey may be taken, perhaps equally as futile—but that it is a metafictional statement pointing to Quin's next book. Having begun *Tripticks* well before she had finished *Passages,* Quin knew her next book would be set in the United States, in a different country, and that she would be entering, literarily, uncharted territory. But more than that, *Tripticks* is, in a sense, a cut-up of *Passages,* a reversed and mangled *Passages.*

As it operates by juxtaposition and image, providing brief narrative moments that fail to accrue into a larger narrative whole, *Passages* offers exceptional challenges to the reader. At slightly over a hundred pages, *Passages* pushes a certain range of possibility just about as far as it can go, asking readers to suspend a great deal of what they have traditionally read fiction for in exchange for fleeting narrative moments, arresting images, an unresolvable flux between the real and the imagined, and unusual juxtapositions. Without the alternation between the narrative lines, the reader would be likely to flounder, but as it is, Quin pulls off a tiny masterpiece, ultimately unlike any other book.

Tripticks (1972)

Tripticks was spawned from a short story by the same name that was published in *Ambit* in 1968, a story which later Quin would rework as the first chapter of the novel, so it seems that *Tripticks* was conceived, even if only as a story, while Quin was still working on *Passages.* In addition, "Tripticks" won first place in a creative writing and drugs contest that *Ambit* sponsored, and, in a letter to the editor published in the same issue, Quin discusses the effect that drugs had on her writing of the story. In this she can be seen to have an affinity to such writers as William Burroughs and Alexander Trocchi, as well as the Beats in general.

Tripticks is both the most ambitious (though perhaps not the most successful) and the most diffuse of Quin's novels. In 1965, speaking about her composition process, Quin stated, "Form interests me, and the merging of content and form. . . . I write straight onto my typewriter, one thousand words an hour but half will in the end be cut out. When I write the first creating parts of my book I can go on for three hours without a stop" (qtd. in Gordon, Introduction xii). In *Tripticks* the vertiginousness and rapidity of the process can be felt by the reader in a way it cannot be felt in Quin's earlier work, because here Quin has managed to use her writing style to best effect to blend form and content into a kind of assault. The novel offers a barrage of styles and images, the novel operating according to principles of collage which attenuate the importance of narrative progression and plot. Yet it has a central character in a way that *Passages* did not, and a single narrator as well—which gives readers something (or rather someone) to cling to as they move through the barrage. In addition, the novel's use of Carol Annand's images breaks up the text enough to give the reader relief; thus ultimately the novel can be apprehended as easily as, perhaps even more easily than, *Passages.*

At the very front of the original British edition, on an unnumbered page before the title page of the novel, is a summary; it is not clear if the summary is by Quin herself, is to be considered part of the book, or was an expedient on the part of her publishers:

> Pursued across America by his no. 1 X-wife, the narrator conjures up a super-satirical vision of that much maligned "American Dream." In a society where "if one escapes being hijacked in an aeroplane, mugged in the street, or sniped at by a man gone berserk, one apparently still runs the risk of getting accidentally zonked by the hors d'oeuvres at a friendly neighbourhood cocktail party," the narrator treats us to some totally amazing revelations about the strange network of convoluted interpersonal relationships he seems to be evading—his ultra-modern, supersonic tycoon wizard of a father-in-law, a mother-in-law who aspires simultaneously to membership of the Daughters of the American Revolution and WITCH, whose life centres on an over-pampered, under-nourished all demanding poodle, plus an assortment of three pepped-up, freaked-out culturally-confused X-wives, the weird, zonked Nightripper and a retinue of bizarre aunts, mothers, retainers etc.

This gives a fairly accurate description of the novel, suggesting as well that it is a novel that is very much part of the counterculture of the late sixties and early seventies. The novel's title can perhaps be read as a mangled version of the word *triptychs,* referring to a work of art that consists of three separate panels, but if that is the case, it's hard to imagine what the equivalent of those panels actually is in regard to the book. It is perhaps more productive to read it as: "Trip ticks" with "trip" both referring to a literal journey and a drug trip, "ticks" being the irregularities or idiosyncrasies of both literal and drug-induced journeying.

The novel proper begins not with language, but with one of Carol Annand's illustrations, typical of the types of images to be found throughout the text. At the top is a row of six regularly arranged boxes, each of them showing a part of a human face, some male, some female, and two giving slightly more of a body. Directly below are three irregular boxes, two of which contain distorted human faces and the third of which contains the portrait of a woman who looks like she might be the femme fatale of the hard-boiled genre. Beside these boxes is a vague map, overlaid by a grid, numbers floating to the left of it. All of this together constitutes the top third of the image. The bottom two-thirds of the picture is split into two halves, the portrait of a mysterious man in a hat and trench coat being reproduced on both sides, the right side drawn to seem like the photographic negative of the left. He looks like a graphic novel's interpretation of a spy or like a pulp detective.

If we go into this in such detail, it is because it is emblematic of the strategies pursued in the images of the book as a whole. Each image contains multiple parts and multiple frames, and never can an illustration be said to represent *one* thing or even most of the time one level of thing—within each image there are several separate boxes, separate frames. Similarly, Quin's text always has several different sorts of things going on at once. In addition, these images often seem to refer elsewhere, to the stock images of genre—film noir and private-eye fiction in particular, but also to pornography, the Western, and science fiction. It is hard to sort the images into a coherent whole or into a coherent progression; equally, the images' relation to the text is skewed; they are "illustrations" only in a vaguest sense, less something that is subsidiary to the text than something which complicates, and is complicated by, the text. In that sense *Tripticks* is similar to Alan Burns's novel *Dreamerika!* which combines visual collage with narrative. However, Burns's novel centers on the Kennedy family: as soon as the reader realizes this, he discovers a stable historical footing that the innovation of the text refers to. He gains some solid ground. With *Tripticks,* however, any ground behind the text is personal and much more evasive, making it ultimately a more demanding book than Burns's novel.

From the novel's first words (not to mention the first illustration), the intense collaging of the text is manifest:

> I have many names. Many faces. At the moment my No. 1 X-wife and her schoolboy gigolo are following a particularity of flesh attired in a grey suit and button-down Brooks Brothers shirt. Time checked 14.04 hours Central Standard Time. 73 degrees outside. Area 158,693 square miles, of which 1,890 square miles are water. Natural endowments are included in 20 million acres of public reservations. All outdoor sports are possible. Deep sea sleeping, and angling for small game are favourite pastimes. The man who doesn't reckon his pleasures on a silver platter is a fish that walks by night. Batman's the name, reform's the game. Farm out the elite, the Ruff-puffs, stinking thinking, temper tantrums, strong winds, captivating experiences, Burn Down Peyton Place, and inhale deeply stretched time with red eyes. (7-8)

The first two sentences seem like something out of a film noir; they create a sense of mood and of character and are an indication as well that at the heart of the text is multiplicity. In the third sentence we are located in time and in situation and given a plot point: we come to know that the narrator is being followed by his first ex-wife and her boyfriend. These plot points are few and far between. In addition, the way the narrator describes himself as "a particularity of flesh" is quite odd and very deliberately anonymous: it is similar to the "body rolling on a bed" at the opening of *Berg,* but more extreme. We end up learning a great deal more about what he's wearing than about what he looks like, as if, being a man of "Many faces" (7), what he's wearing is, in a sense, who he is. This is followed by a series of statistics that seem increasingly absurd, a twisted and nonsensical proverb, the melding of Batman's voice with a common formula and a set of three generalized commands.

If one chooses to read *Tripticks* for plot, then one isn't likely to get very far. There is something of a plot, very tenuous, but plot is one of the least important things about the novel: plot is little more than an excuse to allow the book to move about; to read *Tripticks* is like being barraged with spliced-together advertisements and other information, with a plot vaguely wending through, vanishing and reappearing. It is as much a commentary on/immersion in capitalist American society as it is a story about a given character.

In addition to the rambling, loose paragraphs like the one reproduced above, *Tripticks* offers a series of lists that range from personality traits to the types of businesses in a town, from sex toys to types of fish; descriptions of/advertisements for hobbies; some headlines; a drive-in movie plot that gets worked in; twisted advertisements and jingles; an interview with a man who claims, when dressed in a wig and the right clothes, to look exactly like Shirley Temple; a series of letters, each (often ironically) titled. Each individual paragraph as well consists of a pastiche of information culled from magazines, statistic manuals, encyclopedias, television and pulp fiction—a wealth of significant and insignificant detail.

On the level of plot, the pursuit continues, rife with detail from the landscape and with reflections on the narrator's part about his past three wives, their foibles and their relatives, intermixed with glimpses of a sinister Nightripper. Indeed, one of the series of letters is from Nightripper himself, asserting kinship and urging the narrator, "let us remember who the enemies are and not waste our energy fighting each other" (103). Though he never meets Nightripper face to face, the narrator often suspects that he is only one or two steps away, and he sees Nightripper's handiwork everywhere. The narrator speaks about the sexual desires and fantasies of his ex-wives, reflecting as well on his divorces, one of which, he tells us, was on the grounds of extreme cruelty. Perhaps he is more like the Nightripper than he'd like to let on. Sexist and highly paranoid, the man seems to be undergoing a breakdown, his selfhood dissolving in the flow of images. The pursuit of the narrator by the ex-wife becomes, at one point, reversed, and he finds himself the pursuer rather than the pursued, spying on her. But soon even that seems to have lost meaning: "And this ridiculous drama now? Pursuing my first X-wife, or rather being pursued. Who was chasing who I had forgotten. Perhaps I should put a call through and ask them?" (136).

In the last quarter of the novel, the narrator finds himself beset by his "inquisitor," a man full of whispery advice and performative gestures who seems involved in a mock-religious, mock-sexual ritual circling around one of his ex-wives' karma and the attempt to locate her spirit. The inquisitor guides him through a series of rooms, where he discovers that the inquisitor "tape-recorded everything, aiming his microphone at conversations, monologues, freak-outs, and stream of consciousness raps. Certain moments stood out with clarity and boldness" (167). In a sense what Quin is describing here is her own style, which is largely quotation, threaded through with bits and pieces of narration. After a journey through many rooms with his inquisitor and after encounters with psychiatrists, attendants, and madmen of every stripe, the narrator is back on the road again, stopping to pick up a lone and somewhat mysterious figure who may be an Indian or may be "Some hippy having me on. All part of the conspiracy" (183). Paranoid, he continues to drive, coming at last to an adobe village. Confused, he wanders about, but then begins to feel that this is not an Indian village at all, but instead a village filled with members of WITCH: "Women's International Terror Conspiracy from Hell" (188). In a scene that is a hybrid of Western and film noir, he is jumping from roof to roof, trying to escape. As the novel ends, he is hiding in a church, in a state of high panic, about to begin screaming from a "Fear for safety and sanity, helplessness, frustration, and a desperate need to break out into a stream of verbal images" (191-92). But when he tries to express himself, nothing happens: "I opened my mouth, but no words. Only the words of others I saw, like ads, texts, psalms, from those who had attempted to persuade me into their systems. A power I did not want to possess. The Inquisition" (192).

If he has only the words of others then there is nothing innately his to express. Yet, without the words of others he remains mute. Indeed, Quin recognizes that no word comes into the world without a context, everything a response to something that comes before.

Theorist Mikhail Bakhtin sees this belief as a joyful thing, the collision and flux of language allowing for intersubjectivity, constant
dialogue, and constant struggle; for him, this very flux of language
makes it possible for no word ever to be finalized, for no monolithic
power ever to completely dominate.

For Quin, however, Bakhtin's notion of dialogism is complicated
by sheer volume: the issue lies more with frequency, the barrage of
information, the repetition of information, the rewiring of the brain,
as the words of others overwhelm the ability of the individual to express. Is this a bad thing? Yes and no. On the one hand it challenges
selfhood, but if that selfhood is an illusion to begin with, what is the
difference? On the other hand, there's something exhilarating
about Quin's use and manipulation of the barrage—she does manage to make it do something, to comment ironically back on the
capitalist world, and she herself invites the reader to step into the
flux himself, to get lost in it. Stylistically, too, Quin isn't interested
in rendering a modernist order out of the ruins. For that reason,
Quin is on the cusp of postmodernist celebration, less looking backward to modernism than looking forward to Kathy Acker's hearty
acceptance of irretrievable flux.

Again, Quin allows Carol Annand's drawings to have the last
word. While the opening drawing offered a multitude of faces, the
six panels that make up the final illustration have none: we see
only pieces of a building, mostly balustrades and high walls, one of
the drawings with a vague series of lines in the air suggesting that
someone might have jumped. We are left with the world as orga-
nized by humans, with the signs of human work, but deprived of
actual human presence. Earlier in the book, the narrator suggests
that "a truly perfect duologue would be two TV sets tuned in and
facing each other" (53)—again, a sign of human creation with humanity itself, after creating, having become obsolete. Perhaps this
indicates better than anything the impasse that *Tripticks* has
reached.

Uncollected Writings

At the time of her death by drowning, Quin was working on a new
novel, tentatively entitled *The Unmapped Country*. The first chapter was published by Giles Gordon in his groundbreaking anthology
Beyond the Words: Eleven Writers in Search of a New Fiction (1975),
an anthology which contained the work of many luminaries of British innovative fiction of the 1970s, including Alan Burns, Eva Figes,
B. S. Johnson, Gabriel Josipovici, and Gordon himself. It is not clear
how much of the novel Quin had finished; not enough, in any case,

for her publisher Marion Boyars to feel that they could publish it as a book.

The first chapter of *The Unmapped Country* suggests that Quin was pursuing a strategy much different from that of her previous novels. Perhaps with *Tripticks* she felt she had reached the limits of possibility for collagist fiction, or perhaps she turned away from overt formal experiment for other reasons. In any case, the published portion of *The Unmapped Country* is the most straightforward writing Quin had ever done. At the heart of the narrative is Sandra, a woman who is confined to a psychiatric hospital. The novel concerns her interactions with staff and patients and with her former lover Clive who visits her. Quin attempts to paint, relatively realistically, life among mental patients. While Quin's earlier work recalls the nouveau roman and the writings of the Beats, this piece is closer to the semi-autobiographical writings of Janet Frame.

Though the excerpt from *The Unmapped Country* does contain diverse sorts of writing, it contexts such writing in a much different way from Quin's earlier work. In addition to third-person narration, Quin offers sections of Sandra's journal, a journal which is much more narrative in impulse than the journals of *Three* or *Passages,* containing Sandra's thoughts and also records of dialogues with analysts. Instead of juxtaposing journal sections to the third-person narration as she might have done in the past, Quin always gives a context: we see Sandra open the journal, then we read what she either writes or sees, and then she closes the journal. At no moment does the reader feel the vertigo that accompanies Quin's other work. Despite this, however, the writing is often strong, the intensity of the piece building as it goes, and one remains curious about whether the entire novel, had it been completed, would have remained in a similar stylistic realm or if Quin would have varied the style as the novel progressed.

This novel excerpt, taken in conjunction with Quin's published stories, would be enough to make a short volume of unpublished writings—or perhaps a thicker one, depending on how much more of *The Unmapped Country* Quin managed to finish—but whether any publisher will choose to pursue such a project is doubtful unless the republication of Quin's work by Dalkey Archive Press encourages a major reconsideration of her place in British letters. Her remaining literary writing, as far as we have been able to determine, consists of six short stories, one of which was written in collaboration with Robert Sward and another of which served as the basis for her novel *Tripticks.* Her first published story, "Every Cripple Has His Own Way of Walking," is about a child living with her aunt and grandmother who becomes invisible when her father pays them a visit. "Never Trust a Man Who Bathes with His Fingernails," published in a periodical in Mexico City, concerns a willingly triangular relationship between a man, his wife, and a woman described as "the other," with a fourth person, a half-Cherokee laborer, changing the dynamic temporarily when they go to a hot springs. It reads like thinly veiled autobiography. Though classified as a story in R. D. Willmott's *A Bibliography of Works by and about Ann Quin,* the piece is broken into long lines and functions as a fairly traditional and fairly flat narrative poem. "Tripticks" served as the basis for the novel of the same name. "Motherlogue," published in the *Transatlantic Review* and later anthologized in Philip Stevick's *Anti-Story* anthology, provides the mother's half of a telephone conversation between her and her daughter and might be productively compared to Lily Tuck's *Interviewing Matisse, or the Woman Who Died Standing Up* or to Joyce Carol Oates's story ". . . & Answers." The mother's side of the conversation consists largely of trivialities with a few brief moments that dig deeper. "Eyes that Watch behind the Wind" is set in Mexico and is described by Willmott as being "probably her best short story. It contains a powerful image of man and woman as being eternally back to back" (7). It was published posthumously. In "Living in the Present" Quin collaborated with Robert Sward to create a very short collage piece that includes a pastiche of the Bible as well as excerpts from journalism.

Would republication of these stories add to Quin's reputation? Probably not. Publication of the remainder of *The Unmapped Country* might, however, add a chapter to critics' sense of Quin's artistic development, particularly if there is more to the novel than the single published chapter. However, Quin's reputation for the time being must rest largely on her four completed novels, novels that show her as an important figure in British innovative writing, one whose work still remains intriguing today.

Notes

[1] The first American edition of the novel begins with the same sentence but divides it into four lines, like a poem: "A man called Berg,/who changed his name to Greb,/came to a seaside town/intending to kill his father. . . ." The effect is slightly different, more lyrical yet at the same time less provocative.

[2] Dulan Barber explores the relation of Berg to *Hamlet* and "the Oedipal bones" (170) of the book in more detail in his afterword to *Berg.*

Works Cited

Barber, Dulan. Afterword. *Berg.* By Ann Quin. London: Quartet, 1977. 169-77.

Evenson, Brian. Introduction. *Three.* By Ann Quin. Normal, IL: Dalkey Archive Press, 2001. vii-xiii.

Gordon, Giles, ed. *Beyond the Words: Eleven Writers in Search of a New Fiction.* London: Hutchinson, 1975.

—. Introduction. *Berg.* By Ann Quin. Normal, IL: Dalkey Archive Press, 2001. vii-xiv.

Hassam, Andrew. *Writing and Reality: A Study of Modern British Diary Fiction.* Westport, CT: Greenwood Press, 1993.

"Lovers." Rev. of *Passages,* by Ann Quin. *Times Literary Supplement* 3 April 1969: 341.

Mackrell, Judith. "Ann Quin." *Dictionary of Literary Biography, Vol. 14: British Novelists Since 1960.* Ed. Jay Halio. Detroit: Gale Research, 1983. 608-13.

Quin, Ann. *Berg.* 1964. Normal, IL: Dalkey Archive Press, 2001.

—. *Passages.* 1969. Normal, IL: Dalkey Archive Press, 2003.

—. *Three.* 1966. Normal, IL: Dalkey Archive Press, 2001.

—. *Tripticks.* 1972. Normal, IL: Dalkey Archive Press, 2002.

Stevick, Philip. "Voices in the Head: Style and Consciousness in the Fiction of Ann Quin." *Breaking the Sequence: Women's Experimental Fiction.* Ed. Ellen G. Friedman and Miriam Fuchs. Princeton: Princton UP, 1989. 231-39.

Wheeler, Kathleen. "Reading Kathy Acker." *Context* 9 (2001): 5-6.

Wilmott, R. D. *A Bibliography of Works by and about Ann Quin.* London: Ealing College, 1981.

An Ann Quin Checklist

Novels

Berg. London: John Calder, 1964; New York: Scribner's, 1964; Normal, IL: Dalkey Archive Press, 2001.

Three. London: Calder & Boyars, 1966; New York: Scribner's, 1966; Normal, IL: Dalkey Archive Press, 2001.

Passages. London: Calder & Boyars, 1969; Normal, IL: Dalkey Archive Press, 2002.

Tripticks. London: Calder & Boyars, 1972; Normal, IL: Dalkey Archive Press, 2002.

Uncollected Fiction

"Every Cripple Has His Own Way of Walking." *Nova* Dec. 1966: 127-35.

"Living in the Present." Co-written with Robert Sward. *Ambit* 34 (1968): 20-21.

"Never Trust a Man Who Bathes with his Fingernails." *El Corno Emplumado* 27 (July 1968): 8-16.

"Tripticks." *Ambit* 35 (1968): 9-16.

"Motherlogue." *Transatlantic Review* 32 (1969): 101-05.

"Eyes that Watch behind the Wind." *Signature 20–A Signature Anthology.* London: Calder & Boyars, 1975. 131-49.

"From *The Unmapped Country:* An Unfinished Novel." *Beyond the Words: Eleven Writers in Search of a New Fiction.* Ed. Giles Gordon. London: Hutchinson, 1975. 255-74.

Casebook Study of
Silas Flannery

Contents

Introducing Silas Flannery

Anna Rubenstein

He was born 18 April 1913 in a residential part of Dublin, the last child in a middle-class family of six.

The Ha'penny Bridge, crossing the river Liffy. Joyce, O'Brien, Beckett crossed this bridge. As a youth he wrote poetry on the northern bank.

The family spent its summers at this cottage on Achill Island.

He dreamed of joining the navy and sailing to Puerto Rico.

The father's mother: she fell in love only once.

The father, a journalist and fervent nationalist, killed in service of the Irish Citizen Army during the Easter Uprising of 1916.

His mother, a seamstress. She raised Silas and his three siblings
with the help of her brother.

The mother's brother, a widowed manufacturer.

The younger generation. His siblings were, on the whole, emancipated in social matters, politics, and religion. Breaking away from the orthodoxy of their parents left them eager to adopt all sorts of substitutes.

His mother again. She aged well.

University College Dublin. In the fall of 1930 he began his studies here, revealing a writer of limited potential. He graduated in 1934, and obtained a position as research librarian at the university the following year.

A little gentleman.

In 1937 he married Windy Pearson. She died in a house fire six months later while carrying the couple's first child. He would never remarry.

The University College Dublin library, where Flannery attended meetings of the *UCD Journal of Literature.* In 1946 he submitted for publication a critical survey of nineteenth-century Gaelic fiction and a short story, "The Cask of Amontillado." Both submissions were rejected.

The Palace Bar, cultural center of Dublin. Early evenings he could be found drinking whiskey in the lounge at the back. He may have had too frequent a recourse to so palatable a medicine, in the hope of banishing for a time the recollection of his sorrows. If such a fault is to be regarded as venial, it may be excused in one who was more than a widowed husband and a childless father.

He followed his passions freely; this allowed him to write the history of literature as the history of Silas Flannery. It was merely unfortunate that the very intensity with which he insisted with an almost religious conviction upon the nobility and the universal significance of these passions and of creative expression, tricked him into saying too much.

Writing was for him a piece of deductive work, a magnificent cross-word puzzle, which he played in any forum that would present him with an interesting problem. It was the opposite of what it was for faculty at his nationalist university: it was transnational and based on experience. Writing eventually became his substitute for a belief or culture in which to be at home.

He found literature often and intensely boring. This evidently began very early, and it continued his entire life. He was always seen reading the newspaper.

At his flat in Dublin. He died here of a heart failure on 21 June 1975.

Another Besting of Both Englishmen

Silas Flannery

The evidence shows that this is how the murder was committed: Furriskey, the murderer, took up his post about nine o'clock one night in clear moonlight by the corner where Lamont, his victim, had to turn from the street where his office was into the street he lived in.

The night air was shivering cold. Yet Furriskey was wearing only a thin blue suit; the jacket was unbuttoned, too. He felt no cold; besides, he was moving all the time. His weapon, half a bayonet and half a kitchen knife, he kept firmly in his grasp, quite naked. He looked at the knife against the light of the moon; it glimmered, perhaps; at least enough for Furriskey. He bent forward, standing on one leg, and listened for any sound out of the fateful side street.

Why did Lamont, the industrious night worker who was watching it all from a window nearby in the second story, permit it to happen? Unriddle the mysteries of human nature! A sudden whim. The night sky invited him, with its dark blue and its gold. Knowing, he gazed up at it, knowing he lifted his hat and stroked his hair; everything up there drew together in a pattern to interpret the immediate future for him; everything stayed in its sensible, scrutable place.

Five houses further along, on the opposite side of the street, Ms. Lamont, with a fox-fur coat over her nightgown, peered out to look at her husband.

At last there rang out the sound of the doorbell before Lamont's office, too loud for a doorbell, right over the town and up to heaven. Trellis, a private citizen who was lingering unusually late that night, issued from the building, still invisible in that street, only heralded by the sound of the bell; at once the pavement registered his quiet footsteps.

Lamont bent far forward; he dared not miss anything. Ms. Lamont, reassured by the bell, shut her window with a clatter. But Furriskey knelt down; since he had no other parts of his body bare, he pressed only his face and his hands against the pavement; where everything else was freezing, Furriskey was glowing hot.

At the very corner dividing the two streets Trellis paused, only his walking stick came around into the other street to support him. With his collar turned up, his dressing gown girt around his portly body, he stood looking down, shaking his head. In itself it was a highly reasonable action that Trellis should walk on, but he walked onto Furriskey's knife.

"Lamont!" shrieked Furriskey, standing on tiptoe, his arm outstretched, the knife sharply lowered, "Lamont! You will never see Sheila again!" And right into the throat and left into the throat and a third time deep into the belly stabbed Furriskey's knife. Water rats, slit open, give out such a sound as came from Trellis.

"Done," said Furriskey, and pitched the knife, now superfluous blood-stained ballast, against the nearest house front. "The bliss of murder! The relief, the soaring ecstasy from the shedding of another's blood! Lamont, old nightbird, friend, alehouse crony, you are oozing away into the dark earth below the street."

Lamont, choking on the poison in his body, stood at the double-leafed door up above as it flew open. "Furriskey! Furriskey! I saw it all, I missed nothing!"

Lamont and Furriskey scrutinized each other. The result of the scrutiny satisfied Lamont; Furriskey, with a crowd of people on either side, came to no conclusion, his face grown quite old with the shock. He collapsed on top of Trellis; the gowned body belonged to Furriskey, the blue suit spreading over the couple like the smooth turf of a grave belonged to the crowd.

Furriskey, fighting down with difficulty the last of his nausea, pressed his mouth against the shoulder of the policeman who, stepping lightly, led him away.

An Examination of the Work of Silas Flannery

George Bliser

About 1941, in a city outside Belfast, I was one of many men conspiring for Irish independence. Of my comrades, some survived to engage in peaceful pursuits; others, paradoxically, fought in the desert and at sea under English colors. Silas Flannery, the man of greatest worth, died of heart failure in his Dublin apartment, at dawn, before a firing squad of soldiers could make him drowsy with sleep.

That all those who knew Flannery should write something about him seems to me a very felicitous idea; my testimony may perhaps be the briefest and without doubt the poorest, and it will not be the least impartial. The deplorable fact of my being an Irishman will hinder me from falling into a dithyramb — an obligatory form in Dublin, when the theme is a Dubliner.

Before undertaking an examination of Flannery's works, it is necessary to repeat that Silas Flannery, a member of the Irish Catholic faith, was deeply religious. In some salon in Paris, or even in Belfast, a literary person might well rediscover Flannery's method; but his method, presented in such a setting, would seem like a frivolous and idle exercise in irreverence or blasphemy. Apart from a few friendships and many habits, the problematic practice of literature constituted Flannery's life. Like every writer, he measured the virtues of other writers by their performance, but asked that they measure him by what he conjectured or planned. All of the books he published merely moved him to a complex repentance.

In Flannery's labyrinth there are three lines too many. Along the line so many critics have lost themselves that an experienced detective might well do so too. When in *Another Besting of Both Englishmen* Furriskey hunts Lamont, he feigns to commit (or does commit) a crime at A, then a second crime at B, eight kilometers from A, then a third crime at C, four kilometers from A and B, halfway enroute between the two. He waits for Lamont later at D, two kilometers from A and C, halfway once again, between both. He kills Trellis at D, as Lamont kills Ms. Lamont in the succeeding volume.

It is not illogical, I say, to think that Flannery's works are infinite. Those who judge them to be limited postulate that in remote places the reproductions and reformulations and repetitions could inconceivably cease — a manifest absurdity. *Another Besting of Both*

Englishmen is a picture, incomplete yet not false, of the universe such as Flannery conceived it to be. Differing from Unamuno and Jouandeau, Flannery did not think of his works as absolute and uniform. He believed in an infinite series of works, in a dizzily growing, ever spreading network of diverging, converging and parallel works. This web of literature—the strands of which approach one another, bifurcate, intersect, or ignore each other through reading—embraces every possibility.

Flannery understood that modeling the incoherent and vertiginous matter of which novels are composed is the most difficult task that a person can undertake, even though one should penetrate all the enigmas of a superior and inferior order; much more difficult than weaving a rope out of sand or coining the faceless wind. He affirmed that of the various pleasures offered by literature, the greatest is invention. Since Flannery was not capable of this pleasure, he had to content himself with shams.

Among Flannery's doctrines, none has occasioned greater scandal than the doctrine of *expropriation*. Flannery formulated it with less clarity than zeal, as one might put forward a paradox. To clarify the general understanding of this unlikely thesis, Conto Avalili offers the parable of book collecting, which enjoys in Dublin the same noisy reputation as did the Eleatic paradoxes of Zeno in their day:

> In the twilight hours, all the bibliophiles of Ireland gather on their respective porches to admire the night sky, dreaming of expensive books and cheaper women. Palmart's first printing of *Edicts and Ordinances for Valencia,* Granger's *Biographical History of England,* letters from the Earl of Chesterfield to his son are in the stars. As it grows dark, the Vincentes and Paxtons of the world dawn their nightcaps and retire, each bringing his personal stake in the fate of the cosmos safely to bed.
>
> But the sleeping bibliophile never dreams—at least not of books. Behind the curtains, beneath a stack of periodicals, in the folds of the bed sheets, Flannery lies in wait, anxious to sniff out the dozing bibliophile's Deepest Secrets and Darkest Desires. Tomorrow's auction tips, the name of a locksmith who designed the mistress's boudoir, the address of a summer chateau that hasn't been used in years are in the stars.
>
> In the evening and night hours, Flannery rouses a national literature from its slumber, stealing the twinkle from each participant's eye. One by one.

Flannery, the most discerning literary mimeotician in the world, invented a method for correcting chance. It is well known that the operations of this method are in general trustworthy; although, naturally, they are not divulged without a measure of deceit. In any case, there is nothing so contaminated with fiction as the methodology of Flannery. He (perhaps without wishing to) has enriched, by means of a new technique, the hesitant and rudimentary art of writing. This technique, with its infinite applications, urges us to run through his works as if they were written before *Ulysses,* and to read *Another Besting of Both Englishmen* by Silas Flannery as if it were by Silas Flannery: "Firmly clutching his knife, which he perhaps would not know how to wield, Furriskey went out into the plain."

There is a moment in *Another Besting of Both Englishmen* when the author is on the verge of saying something. He never says it, or perhaps he says it infinitely, or perhaps we do not understand him, or we understand him and he is as untranslatable as music. Lacking a common memory, lacking that other social memory which is language, scattered across the face of the earth, differing in color and features, only one thing—the method—unites Flannery's works, and will unite them until the end of time. In all Flannery's work, the passages copied from other sources are the *least* dramatic; I suspect that the author interpolated them so that one person, in the future, might realize the truth. I understand that I, too, form part of Flannery's plan. At the end of some tenacious caviling, I resolve to keep silent my discovery. I publish an essay dedicated to the glory of the author; this, too, no doubt was foreseen.

The Man at Night's Window

Silas Flannery

The evidence shows that this is how the murder was committed: Lamont, the murderer, took up his post about nine o'clock one night in clear moonlight by the corner where Ms. Lamont, his victim, had to turn from the street where her husband's office was into the street they lived in.

The night air was shivering cold. Yet Lamont was wearing only a thin blue suit; the jacket was unbuttoned, too. He felt no cold; besides, he was moving all the time. His weapon, half a bayonet and half a kitchen knife, he kept firmly in his grasp, quite naked. He looked at the knife against the light of the moon; the blade glittered; not enough for Lamont; he drew it like a violin bow across his boot sole while he bent forward, standing on one leg, and listened both to the whetting of the knife on his boot and for any sound out of the fateful side street.

Why did Trellis, the industrious night worker who was watching it all from his window nearby in the second story, permit it to happen? Unriddle the mysteries of human nature! With his collar turned up, his dressing gown girt around his portly body, Trellis peered out to look for Ms. Lamont, who was lingering unusually late tonight.

At last there rang out the sound of the doorbell before Lamont's office, too loud for a doorbell, right over the town and up to heaven. Ms. Lamont, with a fox-fur coat over her nightgown, issued from the building, still invisible in that street, only heralded by the sound of the bell; at once the pavement registered her quiet footsteps. Trellis bent far forward; he dared not miss anything. Lamont knelt down; since he had no other parts of his body bare, he pressed only his face and his hands against the pavement; where everything else was freezing, Lamont was glowing hot.

At the very corner dividing the two streets Ms. Lamont paused, only her walking stick came around into the other street to support her. A sudden whim. The night sky invited her, with its dark blue and its gold. Unknowing, she gazed up at it, unknowing she lifted her head and stroked her fur; nothing up there drew together in a pattern to interpret the immediate future for her; everything stayed in its senseless, inscrutable place. In itself it was a highly reasonable action that Ms. Lamont should walk on.

But she walked onto Lamont, standing on tiptoe, his arm out-stretched, the knife sharply lowered. And right into the throat and left into the throat and a third time deep into the belly stabbed Lamont's knife. Water rats, slit open, give out such a sound as came from Ms. Lamont.

"Done," said Lamont, and pitched the knife, now superfluous blood-stained ballast, against the nearest house front. "The bliss of murder! The relief, the soaring ecstasy from the shedding of her blood! Sheila, you are oozing away into the dark earth below the street."

Furriskey, choking on the poison in his body, stood at the double-leafed door of his house as it flew open. "Lamont! Lamont! I saw it all, I missed nothing!" Furriskey and Lamont scrutinized each other. The result of the scrutiny satisfied Furriskey, Lamont came to no conclusion. With a crowd of people on either side, Lamont stood before his wife shaking his head, looking at her face grown quite old with the shock.

"Furriskey!" shrieked Lamont, fighting down with difficulty the last of his nausea, "Furriskey! You will never see Sheila again!" Lamont collapsed on top of his wife, he pressed his mouth against her shoulder. The nightgowned body belonged to Lamont, the fur coat spreading over the couple like the smooth turf of a grave be-longed to the crowd.

A Certain Weariness in Moonlight

Silas Flannery

The evidence shows that this is how the murder was committed: Trellis, the murderer, exited the double-leafed door of his house about nine o'clock one night in clear moonlight by the corner where Furriskey, his victim, had taken up his post.

The night air was shivering cold. Yet Furriskey was wearing only a thin blue suit; the jacket was unbuttoned, too. He felt no cold; besides, he was moving all the time. His weapon, half a bayonet and half a kitchen knife, he kept firmly in his grasp, quite naked. He looked at the knife against the light of the moon; the blade glittered; not enough for Furriskey; he struck it against the bricks of the pavement till the sparks flew; regretted that, perhaps; and to repair the damage drew it like a violin bow across his boot sole while he bent forward, standing on one leg, and listened both to the whetting of the knife on his boot and for any sound out of the fateful side street.

Why did Trellis not permit it to happen? Unriddle the mysteries of human nature! With his collar turned up, his dressing gown girt around his portly body, standing on tiptoe, he approached Furriskey. And right into the throat and left into the throat and a third time deep into the belly stabbed Trellis with his knife. "Done," said Trellis, and pitched the knife, now superfluous blood-stained ballast, against the nearest house front.

Five houses further along, on the opposite side of the street, Ms. Lamont, with a fox-fur coat over her nightgown, peered out to look for her husband, who was lingering unusually late tonight. She came rushing down, shaking her head, her face grown quite old with the shock. She collapsed on top of Furriskey, her fur coat spreading over the couple like the smooth turf of a grave.

At last there rang out the sound of the doorbell before Lamont's office, too loud for a doorbell, right over the town and up to heaven, and Lamont, the industrious night worker, issued from the building, still invisible in that street, only heralded by the sound of the bell; at once the pavement registered his quiet footsteps.

Trellis bent far forward; he dared not miss anything. Ms. Lamont knelt down; since she had no other parts of her body bare, she pressed only her face and her hands against the pavement; where everything else was freezing, Ms. Lamont was glowing hot.

At the very corner dividing the two streets Lamont paused, only his walking stick came around into the other street to support him. A sudden whim. The night sky invited him, with its dark blue and its gold. Unknowing, he gazed up at it, unknowing he lifted his hat and stroked his hair; nothing up there drew together in a pattern to interpret the immediate future for him; everything stayed in its senseless, inscrutable place. In itself it was a highly reasonable action that Lamont should walk on, but he walked onto Furriskey's dead body.

"Lamont!" shrieked Trellis, "Lamont! Furriskey and your wife are oozing away into the dark earth below the street!" Lamont and his wife scrutinized each other. The result of the scrutiny satisfied Lamont, his wife came to no conclusion.

"Lamont! Lamont! I saw it all, I missed nothing! Lamont, old nightbird, friend, alehouse crony, you will never see Sheila again!"

Water rats, slit open, give out such a sound as came from Ms. Lamont. Lamont, choking on the poison in his body and fighting down with difficulty the last of his nausea, pressed his mouth against the shoulder of Trellis who, stepping lightly, led him away.

Imitation(/)Reproduction: Flannery's "Style"

Joseph Gonsieur

> The Jews have discussed for a million years the coming of the Messiah; they discuss his message and what it will be. Perhaps the message of the Messiah is *wait*.
>
> —Hélène Cixous

Why do I dedicate this essay to Hélène Cixous? First of all because it deals with a text by Silas Flannery. I am thus recalling a beginning. The first seminar that I gave at the Sorbonne, at the invitation of Hélène Cixous who introduced me there, was on Silas Flannery. *Fakes* was the title of this ongoing seminar; it continued for nine months, touching upon a number of related subjects: mimesis and amniocentesis, the signature, the antisignature, lovelessness, and death. In addition, I wish to dedicate this reading to Hélène Cixous because of the resemblance Flannery's corpus, bespeaking a unique intersection of fecundity and fruitlessness, bears to Cixous's messiah. Both are fabulous inventions, by which we mean inventions of language as the intention of language as the same and the other, of oneself as of the other.

Nothing can be invented *on the subject* of Flannery. Everything we can say about *A Fratricide Trilogy,* for example, has already been anticipated there, including, as we have seen, the scene about academic competence and the ingenuousness of metadiscourse. We are caught in this net. All the gestures by which we might attempt to take the initiative are already announced in an overpotentialized text that will remind you, at a given moment, that you are captive in a network of language, writing, knowledge, and *even narration.* All this has its narrative paradigm and is *already* recounted in *A Fratricide Trilogy.* Everything that happens to me, including the narrative that I will attempt to make of it, already has been predicted and pre-narrated in its dated singularity, prescribed in a sequence of knowledge and narration, within it, by a hypermnesic machine capable of storing in an immense epic work, along with the memory of the West and virtually all the languages in the world *up to and including traces of the future.* Yes, everything has already happened to us with *A Fratricide Trilogy* and has been signed in advance by Flannery.

A Fratricide Trilogy is erected on the base of the history of writing as an adventure of relationships between imitation and reproduction. Here, by a precaution whose scheme we must constantly repeat, let us specify that Flannery's writing is not explained by what we believe we know of imitation and reproduction, of plagiary, of the repeated word, and of apocrypha. We must, on the contrary, disturb this familiar knowledge, and awaken a meaning of imitation and reproduction in terms of Flannery. Now, if we consider the chain in which Flannery's writing lends itself to a certain number of nonsynonymous substitutions, according to the necessity of the context, we have recourse to the "reserve," to "archi-writing," to the "archi-trace," to "spacing," that is, to the "supplement," or to *mimesis,* and soon to the hymen, to the margin-mark-march, etc.

Flannery's writing does not recount something, the content of an event which Freud would call the fort:da. This remains unrepresentable, but produces, there producing itself, the scene of writing. In *A Fratricide Trilogy* there is a double narrative, the narrative of the vision enclosed in the general narrative carried on by the same narrator. The line that separates the enclosed narrative from the other marks the upper edge of a space that will never be closed. In *Another Besting of Both Englishmen:*

> Lamont and Furriskey scrutinized each other. The result of the scrutiny satisfied Lamont; Furriskey, with a crowd of people on either side, came to no conclusion, his face grown quite old with the shock. He collapsed on top of Trellis; the gowned body belonged to Furriskey, the blue suit spreading over the couple like the smooth turf of a grave belonged to the crowd.

Or in *The Man at Night's Window:*

> Furriskey and Lamont scrutinized each other. The result of the scrutiny satisfied Furriskey, Lamont came to no conclusion. With a crowd of people on either side, Lamont stood before his wife shaking his head, looking at her face grown quite old with the shock.

Or again in *A Certain Weariness in Moonlight:*

> Lamont and his wife scrutinized each other. The result of the scrutiny satisfied Lamont, his wife came to no conclusion. "Lamont! Lamont! I saw it all, I missed nothing! Lamont, old nightbird, friend, alehouse crony, you will never see Sheila again!" Water rats, slit open, give out such a sound as came from Ms. Lamont.

What is the *topos* of the murderer who remembers himself in a narrative (in a dream, a vision, a hallucination) within a narrative, including , in addition to all his ghosts, his *hallucination of ghosts,* still other visions within visions? What is his *topos* when he remembers, in the present, a past murder formulated in another sort of present and which he narrates as something that presented itself in a vision, and so on? If Flannery has always intended, from his point of view, to maintain his relation with the nonflannerian, that is the antiflannerian, with the practices and knowledge, empirical or not, that constitute his other, if he had constituted himself according to this purposive *entente* with his outside, if he has always intended to hear himself speak, in the same language, of himself and of someone else, can one, strictly speaking, determine a nonflannerian place, a place of exteriority or alterity from which one might still treat *of Flannery?* The truth of Flannery's writing, that is, as we shall see, (the) nontruth, cannot be discovered in ourselves by ourselves. And it is not the object of a science, only of a history that is recited, a fable that is repeated.

The absence of the signified. Flannery analyzes this too. He considers it always possible, even if, according to the axiology and teleology that govern his analysis, he deems this possibility inferior, dangerous, or "critical": it opens the phenomenon of the *crisis* of meaning. It is here that the value of *mimesis* is most difficult to master. A certain movement effectively takes place in *A Fratricide Trilogy,* a movement one should not be too quick to call contradictory. On the one hand, as we have just verified, it is hard to separate imitation from reproduction. But on the other hand, while Flannery often discredits mimesis and almost always disqualifies the mimetic arts, he never separates the unveiling of truth from the movement of *reproduction* (which is, as we have seen, to be distinguished from *plagiary*). Once one has distinguished, as does the entire philosophical tradition, between imitation and reproduction, it immediately follows that imitation declares itself in a structure of reproduction. Flannery insists a great deal on the opposition imitation–reproduction, which he advances as a paradox. This opposition, which is as orthodox as can be, facilitates the passage of the truth through fiction: common sense always will have made the division between reality and fiction.

We should return to Flannery himself. And I don't know yet where to start from. I don't know if he must be talked or written about. Producing a discourse, making a speech on the subject of Flannery, on the subject of anything at all about him, is perhaps the first thing to avoid. Of *mimesis,* one can readily remark, yes, Flannery speaks as little as possible, perhaps he has never spoken of it. Perhaps he has never said anything, by that name or the names under which we recognize it.

I would say the same about *method*. Flannery's way of writing is not a method and cannot be transformed into one. Especially if the technical and procedural significations of the words are stressed. It is not enough to say that *A Fratricide Trilogy* cannot be reduced to some methodological instrumentality or to a set of rules and transposable procedures. Nor will it do to claim that each of the three works remains singular or, in any case, as close as possible to something like an idiom or signature. It must also be made clear that Flannery's way of writing is not even an *act* or an *operation*. What Flannery is not? everything of course! What is Flannery? nothing, of course!

Flannery's way of writing is not some determinate thing, or a formal structure the undifferentiated generality of which applies itself to every moment. Flannery's way of writing is history, the becoming of its own proper presentation, of its own proper differentiating determination, and it is subject to the law, to the same law as what it is the law of: it first gives itself as immediate, then mediatizes itself by denying itself, and so on. That it is subject to the law of what it is the law of, this is what gives to the structure of the Flannerian system a very twisted form so difficult to grasp.

If you wish to talk of Flannery's operation when he sets himself into his work, when he writes "at this moment," and if you ask, "What is he doing?" and "How does he do it?" then not only must you dislocate the "he" who is no longer the subject of an operation, agent, producer, or worker, but you must right away clarify that the Work, as his work gives and gives again to be thought, is no longer of the technical or productive order of the operation. The heterogeneity of *A Fratricide Trilogy* makes it very plain: Flannery does not delude himself into thinking he knows what is going on with the effects called mimesis or the *ontological* effects of presence or absence. Rather, he analyzes this very delusion. He is very careful to avoid the sort of precipitous denegation that would consist in erecting a simple discourse against fiction and its system. Without a discreet parody, without a writing strategy, without a difference or divergence of pens, in a word, without style—the grand style—such a reversal comes down to the same thing in a noisy declaration of the antithesis.

When Flannery imposes and opposes *A Fratricide Trilogy,* he ruptures the rational transparency and interrupts also the violence of linguistic origins. He destines his works to reproduction, he subjects them to the laws of reproduction both necessary and impossible; in a stroke with his reproducible-irreproducible works he delivers a universal text (it will no longer be subject to the rules of a particular copy), but he simultaneously limits its very universality: forbidden transparency, impossible univocity. Such is the Flannerian performance.

The Cask of Amontillado

Silas Flannery

It was about dusk, one evening during the supreme madness of the carnival season, that I encountered my friend. He accosted me with excessive warmth, for he had been drinking much. The man had on a tight-fitting parti-striped dress, and his head was surmounted by the conical cap and bells. I was so pleased to see him again that I thought I should never have done wringing his hand.

I said to him: "My dear Fortunato, you are luckily met. How remarkably well you are looking today. But I have received another pipe of what passes for Amontillado, and I have my doubts."

"How?" said he. "Amontillado, a pipe? Impossible! And in the middle of the carnival! Come, let us—that is—Amontillado!"

"I have my doubts," I replied, "and I was silly enough to pay the full price without consulting you in the matter. You were not to be found."

"Amontillado!"

"I have my doubts, and I must satisfy them. I am on my way to Luchresi. He will tell me."

"Luchresi! Come, let us go to your vaults. I have no engagement; come. Luchresi! You have been imposed upon. Luchresi cannot distinguish Amontillado from Sherry."

Thus speaking, Fortunato possessed himself of my arm; and putting on a mask of black silk and drawing a roquelaire closely about my person, I suffered him to hurry me to my palazzo.

I had told my attendants that I should not return until the morning, and had given them explicit orders not to stir from the house. These orders were sufficient, I well knew, to insure their immediate disappearance.

I took from their sconces two flambeaux, and giving one to Fortunato, bowed him through several suites of rooms to the archway that led into the vaults. I passed down a long and winding staircase, requesting him to be cautious as he followed. We came at length to the foot of the descent, and stood together upon the damp ground of the catacombs of the Montresors. The gait of my friend was unsteady, and the bells upon his cap jingled as he strode.

"The pipe," he said.

"It is farther on," said I; "but observe the white web-work which gleams from these cavern walls."

"Nitre?" he asked, at length.

"Nitre," I replied. "A draught of this Medoc will defend us from the damps."

Here I knocked off the neck of a bottle which I drew from a long row of its fellows that lay upon the mould.

"Drink," I said, presenting him the wine.

He raised it to his lips with a leer. He paused and nodded to me familiarly.

"I drink," he said, "to your long life."

"And I to the buried that repose around us."

He again took my arm, and we proceeded.

"These vaults," he said, "are extensive." The wine sparkled in his eyes and the bells jingled. We had passed through long walls of piled skeletons, with casks and puncheons intermingling, into the inmost recesses of the catacombs.

"The nitre!" I said; "see, it increases. It hangs like moss upon the vaults. We are below the river's bed. The drops of moisture trickle among the bones. Shall we go back before it is too late. The cold—"

"It is nothing," he said; "let us go on. But first, another draught of the Medoc."

I broke and reached him a flagon of De Grave. He emptied it at a breath. His eyes flashed with a fierce light. He laughed and threw the bottle upwards with a gesticulation I understood well. I looked at him in surprise. He repeated the movement—a grotesque one.

"But let us proceed to the Amontillado."

"Be it so," I said, offering him my arm. He leaned upon it heavily. We continued our route in search of the Amontillado. We passed through a range of low arches, descended, passed on, and descending again, arrived at a deep crypt, in which the foulness of the air caused our flambeaux rather to glow than flame.

At the most remote end of the crypt we arrived at another less spacious. Its walls had been lined with human remains, piled to the vault overhead, in the fashion of the great catacombs of Paris. Three sides of this interior crypt were still ornamented in this manner. From the fourth side the bones had been thrown down, and lay promiscuously upon the earth, forming at one point a mound of some size. Within the wall thus exposed by the displacing of the bones, we perceived a still interior crypt or recess, in depth about four feet, in width three, in height six or seven.

It was in vain that Fortunato, uplifting his dull torch, endeavored to pry into the depth of the recess. Its termination the feeble light did not enable us to see.

"Proceed," I said; "herein is the Amontillado. As for Luchresi—"

"Yes, yes, Luchresi," interrupted my friend, as he stepped unsteadily forward. In an instant we had reached the extremity of the niche; a moment more and he had fettered me to the granite. In its surface were two iron staples, distant from each other about two feet, horizontally. From one of these depended a short chain, from the other a padlock. Throwing the links about my waist and wresting the key from my left pocket, it was but the work of a few seconds for him to secure it. Withdrawing the key he stepped back from the recess.

"The Amontillado!" I ejaculated.

"True," he replied; "the Amontillado."

As he said these words, he busied himself among the pile of bones of which I have before spoken. Throwing them aside, he soon uncovered a quantity of building stone and mortar. With these materials and with the aid of a trowel, he began vigorously to wall up the entrance of the niche.

Fortunato had scarcely laid the first tier of the masonry when I let escape a low moaning cry from the depth of the recess. There was then a long and obstinate silence. He laid the second tier, and the third, and the fourth. I attempted the furious vibrations of the chain. The noise lasted for several minutes, during which, that he might hearken to it with the more satisfaction, Fortunato ceased his labors and sat down upon the bones. When at last my clanking subsided, he resumed the trowel, and finished without interruption the fifth, the sixth, and the seventh tier. The wall was now nearly upon a level with my breast. He again paused, and holding the flambeaux over the mason-work, threw a few feeble rays upon my figure.

A succession of loud and shrill screams, bursting suddenly from the throat of my chained form, thrust him violently back. For a brief moment he hesitated, he trembled. Unsheathing his rapier, he began to grope with it about the recess. He placed his hand upon the solid fabric of the catacombs, and felt satisfied. Fortunato reapproached the wall; he replied to my yells. He re-echoed, he aided, he surpassed them in volume and in strength. He did this, and my clamoring grew still.

It was now midnight, and Fortunato's task was drawing to a close. He had completed the eighth, the ninth and the tenth tier. He had finished a portion of the last and the eleventh; there remained but a single stone to be fitted and plastered in. He struggled with its weight; he placed it partially in its destined position. But now there came from out the niche a low laugh that must have erected the hairs upon his head. It was succeeded by a sad voice, which he undoubtedly had difficulty in recognizing as that of myself. I said—

"Ha! ha! ha!—he! he! he!—a very good joke, indeed—an excellent jest. We will have many a rich laugh about it at the palazzo—he! he! he!—over our wine—he! he! he!"

"The Amontillado!" he said.

"He! he! he!—he! he! he!—yes, the Amontillado. But is it not getting late? Will not they be awaiting us at the palazzo, the Lady Fortunato and the rest? Let us be gone."

"Yes," he said, "let us be gone."

"For the love of God, Fortunato?"

But to these words I hearkened in vain for a reply. I grew impatient. I called aloud:

"Fortunato?"

No answer. I called again:

"Fortunato?"

No answer still. Fortunato forced the last stone into its position; he plastered it up. Against the new masonry I heard him re-erect the old rampart of bones. My heart grew sick; it was the dampness of the catacombs that made it so.

In total darkness I released myself from the granite. The iron staples securing my arms slid out easily from the surface of the wall. With my free hands I felt for my key to the padlock; it was but the work of a few seconds for me to throw off the links about my waist.

To my right and rear stood the granite wall; to my left was the narrow passageway through which we had entered the interior crypt, in width about two feet, in height about six or seven. I put my ear to the stone wall before me, hearkening to hear Fortunato's actions within the innermost crypt. There came forth in return only a jingling of the bells.

The Second Degree

Rachel Perkins

No doubt the moment we turn a source into a subject (for an article, for a conversation) there is nothing left but to give it predicates; in the case of Flannery, however, such predication unfailingly takes the most facile and trivial form, that of the epithet. The work of Flannery seems to me bound up with this literary problem, not as the straightforward expression of a particular moment (the transition from imitator to plagiarist) but as the powerful germ of a disturbance of civilization, Flannery at once bringing together its element and sketching out its solution; an ambiguity which is that of Flannery's two literary roles: the villainous role which he was made to play during the last five decades and the modern role which our own decade is beginning to accord him.

Some people talk avidly, demandingly of Flannery's technique in "The Cask of Amontillado"; what they want in his work is method, which can never be too rigorous or too formal for their taste. Flannery's method becomes a Law, but since that Law is devoid of any effect outside itself it is infinitely disappointed. Posing as a pure metalanguage, Flannery's method partakes of the vanity of all metalanguage.

The text can be described technically through a simple nomenclature of its elements and their functions; imitation is adulterated as long as the text remains functional, produced with a view to an actual use; but if the text is only the spectacle of itself, as it were, and passes itself off as a signaletic copy of a genre (for example, in a parody or a pastiche), there is imitation and the beginnings of a "poetics" of reproduction. Thus is born an ensemble of texts and sources no longer linked to one another by a logic of uses and signs, but by constraints of an entirely different order, i.e., those of narrative: imitation shifts the semantic units from pure combinative discontinuity to *tableau vivant,* or, one might say, from structure to event.

Although "The Cask of Amontillado" is full of narrative, there nonetheless remains in Flannery's work, insofar as the literal message is sufficient, a kind of natural *being-there* of sources: nature seems spontaneously to produce the sources represented. A pseudotruth is surreptitiously substituted for the simple validity of openly semantic systems; the absence of attribution disintellectualizes the message because it seems to find in nature the signs of originality. This is without doubt an important literary paradox: the more Flannery develops the imitation of texts (and notably of words), the more he provides the means of masking the constructed meaning under the appearance of the original meaning.

It is impossible however that Flannery's words "duplicate" their sources; in the movement from one narrative to the other, second signifieds are inevitably developed. What is the relationship of these signifieds of connotation to the source? To all appearances, it is one of making explicit, of providing a stress; Flannery's text most often simply amplifying a set of connotations already given in the source. Furthermore, because Flannery is entirely absorbed in an imitation, his "Cask of Amontillado" cannot derive from Poe, however "well-turned" it may be: it can parade Poe (by copying its tone), but precisely because Poe is what it signifies, it cannot achieve Poe. There is an erotic, an aesthetic of the *second degree.* "The Cask of Amontillado" becomes a maniac of the second degree: rejects denotation, spontaneity, platitude, innocent repetition, tolerates only languages which testify, however frivolously, to a power of dislocation: parody, amphibology, surreptitious quotation. As soon as it *thinks itself,* Flannery's language becomes corrosive. But on one condition: that it does not cease doing so *to infinity.*

In order for Flannery's work to be really bereft of origin and exceed its geometrical nature without ceasing to be imitation, the price that must be paid is enormous—no less than death. In "The Cask of Amontillado" the narrative moves from double-crossing to quadruple-crossing reshaping what its characters do: such is the extreme limit at which imitation is outplayed; the reader can no longer take up any position, for he cannot identify the murderer and his victim; the narrative has no point of departure, no support, it gapes open. Paradoxically moreover (for redundancy habitually serves to homogenize, to clarify and assure a message), when read after Poe's "Cask of Amontillado" (Poe being the principal origin of the narrative) the redundancy of Flannery's text creates an abrasion, a grating of readability.

Thus is revealed the total existence of Flannery's writing; his texts are made of multiple writings, drawn from many literatures and entering into mutual relations of dialogue, courtship, contestation, but there is one place where this multiplicity is focused and that place is the reader, not, as was hitherto believed, the sources. The reader is the space on which all the quotations that make up a Flannery text are inscribed without any of them being lost; his work's unity lies not in its origin but in its destination:

We continued our route in search of the Amontillado. We passed through a range of low arches, descended, passed on, and descending again, arrived at a deep crypt, in which the foulness of the air caused our flambeaux rather to glow than flame.

A detail overwhelms the entirety of our reading; it is an intense mutation of our interest, a fulguration. By the mark of *something,* Flannery's text is no longer "anything whatever." This *something* has triggered us, has provoked a tiny shock, a *satori,* the passage of a void (it is of no importance that its referent is insignificant). It is clear that "The Cask of Amontillado" is the epitome of a counter-narrative; disseminated, reversible, set to its own temporality, it inevitably determines (if one follows it) a quite different analytical segmentation to that in shots, sequences and syntagms (technical or narrative)—an extraordinary segmentation: counter-logical and yes "true." Flannery's text is only the imaginary contemporary of Poe: contemporary of its languages, its utopias, its systems (i.e., of its fictions), in short, of its mythology or of its philosophy but not of its history, of which it inhabits only the shimmering reflection: the *phantasmagoria.*

So the method: Flannery's "The Cask of Amontillado" can be Poe only in its difference (which does not mean its individuality), its reading is semelfactive (this rendering illusory any inductive-deductive science of his work—no "grammar" of the text) and nevertheless woven entirely with citation, references, echoes, cultural languages (what language is not?), antecedent or contemporary, which cut across it through and through in a vast stereophony. The intertextual in which Flannery's text is held, it itself being the text-between of another text, is not to be confused with some origin of the text: to try to find the "sources," the "influences" of his work, is to fall in with the myth of filiation; the citations which go to make up his texts are anonymous, untraceable, and yet *already read:* they are quotations without inverted commas.

"The Cask of Amontillado" does not reproduce, does not plagiarize Poe; the passion which may excite us in reading it is not that of a "vision" (in actual fact, we do not "see" anything). Rather it is that of meaning, that of a higher order of relation which also has its emotions, its hopes, its dangers, its triumphs. "What takes place" in "The Cask of Amontillado" is from the referential (reality) point of view literally *nothing*; "what happens" is language alone, the adventure of language, the unceasing celebration of its coming. It is no longer the sources which need to be unmasked (the academics now take care of that), it is the text itself which must be shaken; the problem is not to reveal the (latent) origin of an utterance, of a trait, of a narrative, but to fissure the very irreproducibility of meaning, is not to change or purify the sources but to challenge the source-concept itself.

It is thus futile to ask oneself as do certain critics (contributors to this volume among them) whether or not the reader can forget the presence of Edgar Allen Poe. Flannery practices neither the dissimulation nor the emphatic disclosure of his various sources, hence ridding the animation of the text of any suggestion of its origin and abolishing the metaphysical bond that critics cannot stop from setting up between cause and effect: If the source is not hidden, then why and how turn it into an origin? In Flannery, the text is held by no thread; without a thread, there is no longer any metaphor, any Fate; text no longer aping source, "The Cask of Amontillado" is no longer a puppet in the hands of Poe, the *source* no longer controls the *text*.

"The Cask of Amontillado" possesses reasons which seem to reconnect it to a more manageable, more distant time, and which are the politeness or—the regret—of the murder it commits of its own past, as if it vaguely heard that possessive voice of the slain source saying to it: *Yesterday I was what you are, tomorrow you will be what I am.*

Eveline

Silas Flannery

Every morning before his classes begin Frank does an hour of jogging; he feels the need to move, and also to relieve his nerves. During the day, if he does not go to the campus or into the library, he does not know where to go; therefore he runs this way or that on the hill, as many students do and also many of his colleagues. He crosses on the rustling paths of leaves. Sometimes he says hello to the others, sometimes nothing, because he has to save his breath.

The hill is entirely built up. As Frank runs he passes two-story wooden houses with yards, all different and all similar. Every so often he hears a telephone ring. This makes him nervous; he slows down; he pricks up his ears to hear whether somebody is answering and he becomes impatient when the ringing continues. Continuing his run, he passes another house in which a telephone is ringing. He thinks: "There is a telephone chasing me. There is somebody looking up all the numbers on Aston Quay in the directory, and he is calling one house after the other to see if he can overtake me."

As he runs, he feels a vague sensation of alarm. Even before he can pick up the sound with his ear, his mind records the possibility of the ring; at that moment from a house comes, first muffled then gradually more distinct, the trill of the bell; it puts Frank in an absurd frenzy. He is the prisoner of a circle in whose center is the telephone ringing inside that house; he runs without moving away; he hovers without shortening his stride.

"If nobody has answered by now, it means nobody is home. But why do they keep calling, then? What are they hoping? Does a deaf man perhaps live there, and do they hope that by insisting they will make themselves heard?" He thinks he should try to make himself useful, help the deaf man. At the same time he thinks that in doing so, he could insure that the call is not by chance for himself.

Still running, he pushes open the gate, enters the yard, circles the house, and explores the ground behind it. Everything seems deserted. Through an open window in the rear a room can be seen, in disorder, the telephone on the table continuing to ring. The shutter slams; the window frame is caught in the tattered curtain.

Frank has circled the house three times. He continues to perform the movement of jogging, breathing with the rhythm of his run so that it is clear his intrusion is not that of a thief. A dog barks; this is enough to open a passage in the circle that is holding him prisoner. He resumes running among the trees along the street, leaving behind him the increasingly muffled ringing.

He runs until there are no more houses. In a field he stops to catch his breath. He looks at the time; he is late, he must go back if he does not want to keep his students waiting. He flings himself onto the return road, paying no attention to anything. He will not even recognize that house; he will pass it without noticing. The house is exactly like the others in every respect. The only way it could stand out would be if the telephone were to ring again, which is impossible.

The more Frank turns these thoughts over in his head, the more he seems to hear that ring again; it grows more clear and more distinct; he is again in sight of the house and the telephone is still ringing. He enters the garden, goes around behind the house, and runs to the window. He has only to reach out to pick up the receiver. Breathless, he says, "He's not here . . ." and from the receiver a voice says: "Now, you listen to me. Eveline is here, she'll be waking in a little while, but she's tied up and can't get away. Write down this address carefully: one-fifteen Middle Abbey Drive. Come get her. Otherwise, in half an hour this house will go up in flames."

"But I'm not—" Frank begins to answer.

They have already hung up.

Frank starts running again; he circles the house once more; he resumes his way. He is sorry for this Eveline, but if he stepped forward to save her, nobody would believe that he does not know her; there would be a great scandal. Frank slows down. He could enter any one of these houses, ask them if they will let him call the police, and say first of all quite clearly that he does not know this Eveline; he does not know any Eveline.

To be truthful, at the university there is a student named Eveline. Frank noticed her immediately among the girls attending his classes; she appealed to him a lot. However, the time he invited her to his house to lend her some books an embarrassing situation may have been created. It was a mistake to invite her. This was during his first days of teaching; they did not yet know the sort he is; she could misunderstand his intentions. That misunderstanding took place, an unpleasant misunderstanding, even now very hard to clarify because she has that ironic way of looking at him; the other girls also look at him with an ironic smile.

Frank would not want this uneasiness now reawakened in him by the name Eveline to keep him from intervening to help another Eveline, whose life is in danger. Unless it is the same Eveline; unless that telephone call was aimed personally at him: "A very powerful band of gangsters is keeping an eye on me; they know that every morning I go jogging along that road; when I approach that deserted house they call on the telephone; it is me they are calling, because they know the unfortunate impression I made on Eveline that day and they are blackmailing me."

Almost without realizing it, Frank finds himself at the entrance to the campus, still running; he did not stop by his house to change and pick up his books. He continues running across the campus; he meets some girls drifting over the lawn in little groups; they are his students already on their way to his class. He stops Lorna O'Brien and asks her, "Is Eveline here?" The girl blinks. "Eveline? She hasn't shown up for two days. Why?"

Frank has already run off. He leaves the campus. He takes Dame Street, then Galway Avenue, then Maple Road. He is completely out of breath; he is running only because he cannot feel the ground beneath his feet, or his lungs in his chest. He reaches Middle Abbey Drive. Eleven, fifteen, twenty-seven, fifty-one; the numbers go fast, skipping from one decade to the next. He reaches 115. The door is open. He climbs the stairs and enters a room in semidarkness. There is Eveline, tied on a sofa, gagged. He releases her. She vomits. She looks at him with contempt.

"You're a bastard," she says to him.

Frank hears the telephone ringing, a bell clanging upon his heart. He seizes her hand:

"Come!"

All the seas of the world tumble about Eveline's head. Frank draws her into them; he would drown her. She grips with both her hands to the sofa.

"Come!"

No! No! No! It was impossible. Her hands clutch the sofa in frenzy. Amid the trill of the bell she sends a cry of anguish.

"Eveline! Evvy!"

He rushes outside the house and calls to her to follow. She shouts at him to go on, but still he calls to her. She sets her white face to him, passive, with that ironic smile he cannot bear. Her eyes give him no sign of love or farewell or recognition.

A General Statement about Fiction: Unpacking the Work of Silas Flannery

Leon Schneider

Adventavis asinus, pulcher et fortissimus: these words may have been intended as a general statement about fiction. So books like *Finnegan's Wake,* Balzac's *Peau de chagrin,* and Musil's *Man without Qualities* have their fates. Silas Flannery, however, interprets this Latin saying differently. For him, not only books but also copies of books have their fates. And in this sense, the most important fate of a copy is its encounter with him, with his own reproduction.

I am not exaggerating when I say that to Flannery the reproduction of an old book is its rebirth. And yet Flannery does not dare attach to this rebirth the promises which tradition has attached to the renaissance of art. His novels are sextons who have lost their house of prayer, his shorter works are pupils who have lost their Holy Writ. Now there is nothing to support them on their "jog." Flannery has found the law of this resurrection—at least on one occasion he succeeded in bringing its breath-taking speed in line with the slow narrative pace that he presumably sought all his life. He expressed this in "Eveline," a little prose piece which is his most perfect reproduction not only because it is an interpretation:

> As he runs, he feels a vague sensation of alarm. Even before he can pick up the sound with his ear, his mind records the possibility of the ring; at that moment from a house comes, first muffled then gradually more distinct, the trill of the bell; it puts Frank in an absurd frenzy. He is the prisoner of a circle in whose center is the telephone ringing inside that house; he runs without moving away; he hovers without shortening his stride.

From this story it may be seen what the nature of the reproduction is. The value of Joyce's original does not survive the moment in which it was new. It lives only at that moment; it has to surrender to it completely and explain itself to it without losing any time. Flannery's work is different. It does not expend itself. It preserves and concentrates its strength and is capable of releasing it even after a long time.

Reproducibility is an essential quality of Flannery's "Eveline," which is not to say that it is essential that it be reproduced; it means rather that a specific significance inherent in Joyce manifests itself in his reproducibility. It is plausible that no reproduction, however good it may be, can have any significance as regards the original. Yet, by virtue of its reproducibility Joyce's "Eveline" is closely connected with Flannery's reproduction; in fact, this connection is all the closer since it is no longer of importance to the original. One might generalize by saying: Flannery's technique of reproduction detaches the reproduced work from the domain of tradition. By making many reproductions he substitutes a plurality of copies for a unique existence. And in permitting the reproduction to meet the reader in his own particular situation, it reactivates the object reproduced.

The crisis of artistic reproduction which manifests itself in Flannery's "Eveline" can be seen as an integral part of a crisis in perception itself. What prevents our delight in the reproduction from ever being satisfied is the image of the original, which Flannery regards as veiled by the tears of nostalgia. "She sets her white face to him, passive, with that ironic smile he cannot bear. Her eyes give him no sign of love or farewell or recognition." — This declaration of estrangement is the tribute which the reproduction as such is entitled to claim. Insofar as Flannery's "Eveline" aims at the original and, on however modest a scale, "reproduces" it, it conjures it up (as Menard does Cervantes) out of the womb of time.

Flannery's "Eveline" is in league with this course of fiction in an entirely different way from that of Joyce. Because suspense belongs less to the outcome than to the individual events, a reproduction can cover the greatest spans of time. We know that in this short work Flannery does not reproduce Joyce's original as it actually is, but the work as it is remembered by the one who reproduces it. And yet even this statement is imprecise and far too crude. For the important thing for the remembering author is not what he experienced, but the earnestness of his reproduction, the Penelope work of a professional. To do justice to "Eveline" in its purity and its peculiar beauty one must never lose sight of one thing: it is the purity and beauty of a simulacrum. The circumstances of this *simulacrum* are manifold. One is tempted to say: once Flannery was certain of eventual reproduction, everything worked out for him *en route* as in a dream. There is nothing more memorable than the fervor with which "Eveline" emphasizes its sincerity.

Flannery cannot do without the notion of an original that is not a reproduction, but in which fiction stands still and has come to a stop. For this notion defines the situation in which Flannery himself is reproducing fictions. His "Eveline" gives the eternal image of the original; it supplies a unique experience with the fiction. Flannery leaves it to Joyce to be drained by the whore called "Once upon a time" in fiction's bordello. He remains in control of his work, man enough to blast open the artifice of fiction. Thus for Flannery the representation of literature by "Eveline" is incomparably more significant than that of Joyce, since it offers, precisely because of the thoroughgoing permeation of literature with mechanical reproduction, an aspect of literature which is free of all reproduction. And that is what one is entitled to ask from a work of fiction.

Selected Bibliography

Zachary Hammerman

Flannery's Works

Another Besting of Both Englishmen (1950); out of print.
"The Cask of Amontillado" (1946). *Trinity College Journal of Literature* Volume X, Issue 2; 1946.
A Certain Weariness in Moonlight (1957); out of print.
Collected Poems, 1929-1934. Tokyo: Unagi Press: 1980.
"Eveline" (1968); *Trinity College Journal of Literature* Volume XXXII, Issue 3; 1968.
The Man at Night's Window (1953); out of print.
"A Survey of Modern Gaelic Fiction" (1946); *UCD Journal of Literature* Volume XLIV, Issue 2; 1978.

Articles
(excluding articles in this issue of the *Review of Contemporary Fiction*)

Bliser, George. "Silas Flannery's Homage to Joyce (and Tradition)." *Yearbook of Irish Studies* (U.K.) 15 (1985): 179-200.
Easlum, Adam. "Flannery's 'Eveline.'" *Cripsi* (Melbourne, Australia) 5.2 (1989): 131-51.
Eiler, Sven. "Silas Flannery on the Grid." *Irish Review* 57.6 (1984): 820-32.
Gonsieur, Joseph. "Literary Quotations in Flannery's *Another Besting of Both Englishmen.*" *Gaelic Studies* (U.K.) 42.2 (1978): 181-94.
—. "Silas Flannery's Puzzling Style." *Cripsi* (Melbourne, Australia) 5.1 (1988): 63-77; reprinted with variants in *NP Review* (Manchester, U.K.) 15.6 (1989): 12-17.
—. "Silas Flannery and the Art of Deception." *Dublin Memoirs* 128 (1990): 107-18.
—. "The Language of Silas Flannery's 'Eveline.'" *Journal of the Institute of Comedy Studies* (Dublin) 1 (1992): 325-33.
Hisanaga, Yuka. "An Optical Disillusion." *Subculture* 29 (1981).
Kuo, Una. "On Translating 'The Cask of Amontillado.'" *Timu Literary Supplement,* 2 September 1988: 958.
—. "Flannery Translations." *NP Review* (U.K.) 15.6 (1989): 18-19.
Murphy, Fergus. "Silas Flannery." *Grand Avenue* (London) 3.1 (1983): 136-45.

Nadia, Abigail. "Note on *The Man at Night's Window.*" *Quinzieme* 6 (1983): 102-105.

—. "A Certain Weariness in Silas Flannery." *Orbis Terrarum* 39 (1984): 148-59.

O'Neill, Harley J. "Allegory in Silas Flannery's *A Certain Weariness in Moonlight.*" *Modern Irish Notes* 102.6 (1987): 866-76.

Perkins, Rachel. "Doing Flannery." *Colon* (U.K.) 12 (1989): 56-64.

Schneider, Leon. "Silas Flannery: Portrait of the Artist as Iconoclast." *Perspectives on Contemporary Fiction* 12 (1987): 11-17.

Scheinkman, Marlene. "Silas Flannery: The Puzzles of Fiction." *Yale Gaelic Studies.* The Irish Novel Today (Special Issue) (1989): 185-88.

Twain, Alberta. "Narration and Story in Silas Flannery's A *Fratricide Trilogy.*" *Western Symposium* 43.4 (1989-1990): 248-59.

Selected Reviews

(in chronological order)

Gumbrecht, Hans Ulrich. "Dubliner." *New York Times Book Review* 16 June 1950: 32.

Dolens, Irena. "Words but Not People." (London) *Independent* 24 September 1950.

O'Lehr, Seth. "The Bartleby Follies." *New York Times Book Review* 15 October 1953: 7.

Newman, Hildegard. "Celebrations in a Mirror of Fiction." *Times Literary Supplement* 30 October 1953: 1191-92.

Austein, Paul. "Perpetual Xerox Machine." *Voice Literary Supplement* 5 November 1957: 11.

Moeller, Sal. "That Ephemeral Thing." *New London Review of Books* 6 June 1994: 34-37.

Rebholz, Cordelia. "Brilliant Book by Flannery." *Literary Review* (London) October 1994: 20-21.

Sonino, Terri. "Flannery's Rules of the Game." *Cripsi* (Melbourne, Australia) 5.1 (1995): 79-87.

Jorisenn, Harbinger. "An Elusive Search." *Encounter* (London) July 1995.

Bliser, George. "In Search of Silas Flannery." *Dublin Morning Herald* 15 January 1996.

Zamler-Carhart, Sasha. "Unfair Kind of Fame." *London Review of Books* 10 January 1996: 18.

Casebook Contributors

GEORGE BLISER was a founding member of the Literary Studies Department at University College Dublin. He is the author of *Joyce: Impetus and Impediments* (1982) and *Illusions of Grandeur: A Primer of Contemporary Literary Theory* (1991), of many essays on Joyce and of the study "Towards a Politics of Irish Literature."

JOSEPH GONSIEUR is Professor of Literature at the Ecole des Hautes Etudes en Sciences Sociales in Lyon. He has held posts at the University of Minnesota, Glasgow, and Awolowo University, Nigeria. Among his many works translated into English are *Fictions of Desire* and *The Mimetic Impulse*.

ZACHARY HAMMERMAN is a graduate of the program in Comparative Literature at Stanford University and holds a J.D. from Stanford Law School. He practices intellectual property law in Palo Alto, California. His work includes *Futurist Machine, Oulipo mode d'emploi* and numerous essays on Calvino, Perec and Flannery.

RACHEL PERKINS taught literature at the University of Missouri from 1963 to 1978 and has been a professor of literature at the College de France since 1980. She is a member of the Centre National de Recherche Pataphysique and an honorary Professor of English at Trinity College, Dublin. Her works include *Signals in Discourse, Saussure / Saint-Beuve,* and *Empirical Lexicons.*

ANNA RUBENSTEIN regularly exhibits at the Peggy Radin Gallery in London. Her artworks hang in public collections, including the Guggenheim. Her illustrated fiction has been published as *Beneath the Sheets* (1995); she also has co-edited with Michael Rubenstein *In Name Only: A Compendium of Literary Insignia.*

LEON SCHNEIDER has written extensively on Lispector, Stendhal, and Queneau. He has published eleven volumes of criticism and autobiographical works, including *Philological Analytics* and *Miserable Iconoclasts.* He is now giving his greatest attention to the O'Brien Academy and to his responsibilities as editor of the *O'Brien Journal of Literature.*

Book Reviews

Don DeLillo. *Cosmopolis*. Scribner, 2003. 209 pp. $25.00.

Cosmopolis is set in April 2000, a postmillennial, pre-9/11 time significant for being a month removed from the NASDAQ's record-setting closing number, 5048.62. This, then, is the beginning of the end of the nineties boom, and DeLillo's protagonist, billionaire currency- and stock-speculator Eric Packer, is poised on the surface of a bubble that's about to burst. On one level, the narrative is quite simple: Eric leaves his multistoried, multi-million-dollar apartment on Manhattan's east side and takes a trip across town on 47th Street in his custom-made limo to get a haircut, a journey delayed by midtown traffic, a presidential motorcade, a broken water main, a rap star's funeral procession, an anti-global-capital riot, and Eric's whims. It is also a journey from riches to rags (as Eric's hubristic speculations bring his empire crashing down), from morning to night, from life to death—all reinforcing the inevitability of time's arrow. Yet at the same time it is a journey from the present to the past: Eric's destination is his father's childhood neighborhood and the barbershop where Eric had his first haircut—this man whose success is based in his ability not just to predict the future but to bring that future into being needs the familiarity, the repetition, the sameness of his distant past. The novel's structure reflects this tension between the forward and backward movement of time: the bulk of the narrative follows Eric's trip from river to river chronologically, but two interpolated excerpts from the journals of Benno Levin (a.k.a. Richard Sheets), ex-currency analyst and current homeless person who will, apparently, kill Eric, are presented chronologically backward and out of sync with Eric's narrative.

These structural and thematic explorations of time provide the context for Eric's search for patterns—the predictable and controllable—in numbers, nature, and life, versus life's tendency to offer us uncontrollable random phenomena—surprise. Within the rigid order of the day, Eric is offered many surprises: several unexpected encounters with his mysterious wife; the unaccountable and (for him) disastrous rise of the yen against the dollar; a cream pie in the face courtesy of an international pastry terrorist; and his chance encounter with Benno, who has staked his own identity on Eric's death. As surprise overwhelms him, Eric tries more and more rashly to assert control, swinging from the homicidal to the suicidal.

Once again, DeLillo has captured the essence of a particular American moment: the solipsism of power, the paranoia of control, the inequities and immateriality of wealth, the shock of recognition as a system begins to collapse. *Cosmopolis* is a beautiful and brilliant book. [Robert L. McLaughlin]

Aleksandar Hemon. *Nowhere Man.* Nan A. Talese/Doubleday, 2002. 242 pp. $23.95.

Josef Pronek appears in Hemon's novel as the narrator, who, calling himself "Victor Plevchuk," tours an English-language school for immigrants like himself while seeking work in Chicago. In one class sits Pronek, a one-time writer displaced stateside from the nineties Bosnian horror, whom "Plevchuk" vaguely recognizes and whose bleakly comic exploits and affecting nature thereafter take center stage. In a series of carefully disjointed episodes ushering Pronek back and forth in time, through childhood and youth in Sarajevo, Yugoslav army service, university, a brief junket at a Ukrainian heritage center in Kiev (he and the narrator room together), to life as an exile in Chicago, Hemon delves into Pronek's representative nature to mock the masquerades we buy and sell to live. Hemon's readers have met Pronek before, but here he is given more scope while revealing the same winsome candor, hounded by the wonder of his experience, searching for but never finding harmony in relationships, society, and language. Pronek grew up disaffected from his family, whom he could never please. Moved by adolescent angst to form a rock band to sing his own songs and get girls in the years before certain murderous Serbs descended like wolves on the sheepfold, Pronek assumes the mantle of Nowhere Man, intelligent if feckless booby whose hopes continually go awry. Later, inadvertent if penetrating witness to American pop culture, he plays hapless participant in the absurdist bubble of his life as it takes on the character of a black sitcom. Wistful outrider from a time warp whose charm and broken English prove finally, maddeningly appalling, Hemon's antihero stumbles down the path his mercilessly humorous creator takes in dissecting, item by item, the postmodern nightmare. The concluding parable on a clever Russian spy lays out his cards for all to see. [Michael Pinker]

Kathy Acker. *Essential Acker: The Selected Writings of Kathy Acker.* Ed. Amy Scholder and Dennis Cooper. Intro. Jeanette Winterson. Grove, 2002. 335 pp. Paper: $15.00; *"Rip-Off Red, Girl Detective" and "The Burning Bombing of America: The Destruction of the U.S."* Grove, 2002. 201 pp. Paper: $14.00.

"I just read passages at random," a character in Stewart Home's *69 Things to Do with a Dead Princess* says. "It makes no sense to read Kathy Acker from beginning to end." This is the sense of Acker we have to understand if we are to read her. Her project is to reject the master voice of literature because it does not permit her to say what she needs to say. As a woman she is dispossessed, marginalized, and as an American, estranged from her homeland. (One cannot separate language from politics.) Thus she must educate—uneducate—us to read differently, including reading a text from beginning to end. ("Why . . . make a work that cannot be read through?" Stanley Cavell writes in his review of Walter Benjamin's *Passagenwerk*. "Perhaps to remind the reader his or her work must perpetually find its own end. Why make a work that cannot be written to an end? Perhaps to remind the writer of a reason to suffer awakening without end.") Acker often adapts marginalized genres, such as the detective novel (its charge to find out who did what and why is crucial to her own writing) or pornography ("I won't go against the truth of my life which is my sexuality," she writes). She also rewrites texts, layering them against history (not so much plagiarism as an act of rereading). Her method here is analogous to how we use quotations, which we give new meaning by removing them from their original context. "Myself or any occurrence is a city through which I can wander," Acker writes to describe her method. We do not read such texts from beginning to end, but do so as if walking through a city we do not know, stopping at what interests, puzzles, or confuses us. Such a reading can never be planned or directed, except as aimlessness itself directs attention (or inattention). This does not mean that her work does not coalesce. She returns again and again to what we might consider a primal scene: the patriarchal, repressive father she loves and the mother, a victim like her daughter. (In her last work, unpublished before her death, her last words are for her mother: "For it was you I loved.") All her history, politics, language, and psychology come from the moment desire was subverted. (R. D. Laing was an early influence.)

Rip-Off Red, Girl Detective and *The Burning Bombing of America* are two early works written in the early 1970s and not published before. The first is an example of her use of the detective novel, and the second emphasizes the political nature of her writing. *Essential Acker* is selections from all of her texts (except essay collections). The title is too academic and, for Acker, misleading. There can be no essential Acker. Only that where each of us finds a foothold. [Robert Buckeye]

Joseph McElroy. *Actress in the House.* Overlook, 2003. 432 pp. $26.95.

Joseph McElroy's dazzling, multidimensional novel brilliantly unfolds a seismic map that charts the tumultuous, uncertain relationship between Becca Lang and Bill Daley. The novel opens as Daley witnesses an actress at a warehouse theater violently struck in the face during a performance; as she is hit, Becca, the actress, catches Daley's attention. From this initial connection McElroy explores the "joint venture" between actress and audience, storyteller and listener, that spirals backward and forward from several events in Daley's past, including his wife's death, his mugging, and a botched helicopter mission in Vietnam. Through the intersection of these two lives, this "plunge into another person," McElroy navigates Becca and Daley's emerging romance and negotiates their individual (perhaps linked) pasts, crafting a prismatic narrative that mimics the complex evolution of memory, as the diverse cast of characters recycles experience into multiple narratives. *Actress in the House* engages themes of love and abuse, memory and action in Daley's passionately imagined New York, with "people and enterprises all linked like street noises or evidence." Amid "the subtly dislodging, dissolving layers and vibrations" of McElroy's deep vision, Daley operates as a hinge between people. "People take from what you give them something or other and you don't know what it might be," he observes. Throughout the novel Daley encounters many forms of physical and psychological abuse—the "misuse of actual people"—which spread in concentric waves across the narrative as Daley tries to maintain control of his past and discover the truth of Becca's previous life. *Actress* serves as a masterful evocation of McElroy's earlier work, displaying the same subtle perception and uncompromising intelligence as *A Smuggler's Bible, Lookout Cartridge, Plus,* and *Women and Men.* Yet *Actress* is a remarkable, insightful novel in its own right, and readers should seek out McElroy's distinctive voice, immense range of knowledge (geology, jazz, law, engineering), and unparalleled genius. [Trey Strecker]

Rikki Ducornet. *Gazelle.* Knopf, 2003. 208 pp. $21.00.

Rikki Ducornet scares me. I don't know where all this stuff comes from: the capitalist Tubbs arriving in Egypt and wanting instantly to turn it into a pudding with raisins, Secundo ejaculating into the flames of a public execution. And yet . . . when I teach, I tell my students: write about what frightens and disturbs you. "All my novels do a sort of dance over the coals," Ducornet has said. Repeatedly, she speaks of writing as waking hallucination, of fiction as a species of magic, of a fiction informed not just by the quotidian and pressures of physical experience but by dreams, reverie, philosophy, and intuition: all the noumena that form the shimmer of our minds at their meeting place with the world. She wants not just to create whole new worlds—which she brilliantly does in *Phosphor in Dreamland,* the stories of *The Word Desire,* the tetralogy consisting of *The Stain, Entering Fire, The Fountains of Neptune,* and *The Jade Cabinet*—but to take in the whole of this one as well, to mark its imprint on her soul, to possess it. In *Gazelle* the story is of a young girl coming to age and sexuality in Egypt. Her beautiful blond mother has departed; her father, olive-skinned and dark of hair like herself, has sunk into an obsession with chess and war games; and she has been taken under wing by a family friend, the perfumer Ramses Ragab. As always, Ducornet writes of the eternal struggle, within and without, between forces of repression and those of liberation, trying to retrieve for self and characters a space in which creation and transformation remain possible. "I believe," she has said, "in the sexual soul." [James Sallis]

Robert Ostaszewski. *Troję pomścimy* (Get Even for Troy). Ikon, Kraków, 2002. 193 pp. No price given.

Robert Ostaszewski's second novel is an ironic guide through the parallel worlds of contemporary Poland. At first the division of the book into three parts—the Gierek Era, the Jaruzel Era, and the Brown Era—seems neatly chronological, beginning with slightly nostalgic memories of a childhood spent in the 1970s. Such a reading soon proves false, however. Whereas the first two eras are named after historical figures (Party leaders Edward Gierek and Wojciech Jaruzelski) symbolic of Polish politics in the 1970s and eighties, the third, with its allusion to Brownian movements or heroin ("brown sugar"), refers to someone or something representing a totally different order. While such an acerbic designation of the nineties as a decade heralding the end of history seems apt, the novel is clearly at odds with any linear sequence. The plot weaves through time, either tracing circles within circles or running in parallel lines. All in all, flashbacks included, the story spans some sixty years and is set all over the country. The narrative points of view also change: the child telling the story gives way to a teenager, a student, and finally an adult, though the perspective is always that of a slightly alienated bystander. The narrator seems to have had a fairly typical biography yet for some reason does not succumb to the collective mania that infuses everyone else's life with meaning. A token of this bizarre normality is the absurd graffiti calling to "Get Even for Troy." Living in the past makes all the characters obsessively intent on getting even for old indignities. Their hostility is directed toward other Poles, Germans, Russians, and other neighboring nations, as well as Jews. The book paints a recognizable picture of Poland's collective fixations, currently being reflected in political commentary and often making the front pages. [Cezary Konrad Kéder]

Lynne Tillman. *This Is Not It*. Distributed Art Publishers, 2002. 283 pp. $27.50.

Lynne Tillman's *This Is Not It* offers a pastiche of stylistic responses to contemporary works by such artists as Jeff Koons, Kiki Smith, Barbara Kruger, and Peter Dreher. Through her own unconventional approach to the short story, Tillman blurs barriers between art and life, writer and reader, and fiction and truth. Tillman bookends the collection with two long, intricate stories—"Come and Go" and "Thrilled to Death"—which pull together characters whose tenuous bonds twist together briefly only to fan out again as their lives separate. Many of the collection's central stories perform more ethereally, closely reflecting the mood or effect of their paired artworks. "A Picture of Time" responds beautifully to Stephen Ellis's *Untitled,* a work of primary color in oil scraping across linen in vertical and horizontal bands, interrupted centrally by twisting thicknesses of light. Tillman's story picks up the texture of the paint, and its linen foundation, in an examination of time and imagination through the conceptual language of color. "Ode to Le Petomane" tightly reflects Roni Horn's *Between Visibility and Nonexistence* as a man tries to erase himself from his fiancée's life. These stories also hold a deep continuity in absence and negation, as most acutely demonstrated in the title story, whose narrator tells us, "In the wrong place at the wrong time, the wrong people and I are obviously in a drama, a tragedy or comedy." Tillman's characters either never quite connect or, in connecting, recognize that there is little to hold them together. Tillman's attention to double entendres and wordplay allows an eerie humor to break into the overwhelming loss and fear permeating the text, to offer slippage only in the possibility of lies and stories. Beautifully designed, with cover pages for each story, Tillman's *This Is Not It* offers a fresh exploration of the expectations and effects of art and imagination. [Joanna Howard]

Paul Auster. *The Book of Illusions*. Holt, 2002. 321 pp. $24.00.

In his best novel in over a decade, Paul Auster revisits several of his familiar themes: traumatic regrets, mysterious pasts, chains of miraculous and diabolic coincidences, and the quest for redemption through unusual and obsessive creative activity. *The Book of Illusions* is narrated by a comparative-literature professor named David Zimmer, who has lost his wife and two sons in a plane crash. He suffers from a severe case of survivor's guilt, which is exacerbated by meditations on the small coincidences that caused them to die without him: "Everything was part of it, every link in the chain of cause and effect was an essential piece of the horror." To save himself from emotional and alcoholic self-destruction, Zimmer takes up a book project on a forgotten silent film comic named Hector Mann. He eventually visits the dying Mann, escorted by a woman with close personal ties to Mann named Alma Grund. Zimmer's brief encounters with Alma and with Mann's life and works parallel his own private explorations of art's potential to redeem action. Although Auster is known for his formal experimentation, his most well-honed skill is still the judiciously paced, transparent narration characteristic of novels like *The Music of Chance* and *Leviathan*. His set pieces on Zimmer's and Mann's personal tragedies, for example, read so compellingly that one can easily forget the mediation of the printed page. More technically impressive, though, are Zimmer's transcriptions of Mann's silent films into the written word. To Zimmer, silent films are "like poems, like the renderings of dreams, like some intricate choreography of the spirit." Auster tough-mindedly denies both cinematic and narrative art the transcendent powers that could fully redeem Mann's, Grund's, and Zimmer's lives. But for all the bizarre tragedies that punctuate their stories, Auster does invest these art forms with the power to affirm a vague, yet nevertheless life-sustaining, sense of hope. [Thomas Hove]

Alain Robbe-Grillet. *Repetition*. Trans. Richard Howard. Grove, 2003. 191 pp. $23.00.

Marking Robbe-Grillet's return to fiction after a twenty-year absence, *Repetition* details the story of a secret agent, Henri Robin, as he makes his way through Europe in the late 1940s. His adventures include possibly witnessing or committing three or four murders (including a rather gruesome stabbing with a champagne flute), multiple changes of identity, apparent kidnapping and being kidnapped, encounters with Nazis and sons of Nazis, a little S&M with a woman who could be his half sister or even half daughter, a mother/sister named Joëlle Kast (Jocasta); all with accompanying druggings, dream states, vague recollections, and hallucinations. There's more: the narrator is himself being watched and narrated by another voice, possibly his twin brother, possibly someone else. (As an interesting aside, the physical book itself has been *repeated* with a difference: Grove Press mistakenly placed a large part of one of the chapters—"The Third Day"—in footnote form, causing Grove to *recall* the flawed edition. I now hold in my hands two books: the original, flawed *Repetition* and the corrected, repeated *Repetition*.) While the plot twists, character mutations, and multiple points of view would be hopelessly confusing in the hands of a less sure hand, R-G's crystalline and precise prose somehow manages to keep all the textual threads in place. There's a real joy here, an exuberance and humor one does not always associate with the sometimes dour and distant (although always emotive) writing of the nouveau roman. It is this delight, combined with the adult mastery of the writing, that makes this book a welcome and important addition to R-G's oeuvre. More than a journey through divided Europe, the protagonist's wandering is a tour of Western literature and film, a pastiche composed of elements of de Sade, Graham Greene, Breton, Sophocles, Hitchcock, Freud, Kierkegaard, and Robbe-Grillet's earlier novels, especially *The Erasers* and *Jealousy*. These cultural references are all remixed, as it were, and transformed into a work of remarkable complexity and, dare I say it, beauty. [Jeffrey DeShell]

Oleg Pavlov. *Povesti Poslednikh Dnei* (Tales of Recent Days). Tsentropoligraf, Russia, 2001. No price given.

Oleg Pavlov is one of the most gifted exemplars of what has been dubbed the "renaissance in Russian literature." Like all of the great Russian writers, he eschews overt social and political commentary, approaching his subject matter with the satirical, darkly comic panache of a contemporary Gogol. *Kazennaya Ckazka* (A Barracks Tale) is the first in a compilation of short novels entitled *Povesti Poslednikh Dnei*. *Kazennaya Ckazka* is set during the last years of the crumbling Soviet Union in a remote and neglected outpost of the Empire. Its subject is that of the fate of men faced with the deprivations, cruelties, and absurdities of army life—men striving to retain a sense of their own dignity and humanity in a system crushingly indifferent to even the most basic of human needs. Resistance to that indifference comes from the novel's unlikely hero, Captain Khabarov, a man determined to ensure that his soldiers don't go hungry. The enterprising Captain Khabarov has hit on the idea of cultivating a potato crop on army land, thus keeping the wolf from the camp door. This act of defiance attracts the attention of the novel's scheming antihero, who confiscates and dumps the entire crop, thus leaving Khabarov and his soldiers marooned with dwindling rations. The stalwart Captain embarks on a futile journey to retrieve the potatoes—a journey into the venal and selfless nature of humans.

Karagandinskii Devyatina (A Ninth-Day Wake at Karaganda) is perhaps the most surreal of Pavlov's novels, set in a landscape almost lunar in its desolation. The title refers to the Orthodox wake on the ninth day after a person's death, in this case that of a young soldier. The novel begins with the swirling approach of winter in the town of Karaganda. Private Alexei Mikhailovich Kholmogorov has just demobilized and has been asked by a mouse-phobic doctor to perform one last task before leaving Karaganda: he is to collect the body of the soldier on the ninth day after his death and expedite it home. As Alexei goes about this lugubrious business, events take an increasingly fantastical, comic, and harrowing turn, leading to Alexei's imprisonment and the dwindling hope of his ever leaving Karaganda. The characters are exposed both to an arbitrary and cruel military bureaucracy and to the pitiless indifference of the natural environment, embodied in the novel by an infestation of hungry mice.

Karagandinskii Devyatina and *Kazennaya Ckazka* are reminiscent of *Catch-22* in their evocation of the absurdity of army life. Pavlov's sense of the grotesque and his black humor serve to shore up the painful pathos that permeates all of his work. The author conveys the sense that the characters are buried alive in the hostile reaches of the steppes. The poignancy comes from the characters steeling themselves to survive, however nobly or ignobly, in this soul-destroying environment. [Susan Anne Brown]

Nicholson Baker. *A Box of Matches*. Random House, 2003. 178 pp. $19.95.

To say that no one writes like Nicholson Baker is at once a compliment and a simple fact. Whether he is writing about sex, libraries, or corporate bathrooms, Baker's works are characterized by humor, precision of language, and an acute perception of the ordinary world's little details. The narrator of *A Box of Matches,* a medical-textbook editor named Emmett, constructs his world for us in typical Bakeresque fashion by observing his surroundings and indulging in imaginative fantasies. Emmett is an admirable, gentle soul who wants to protect those around him, including his two children, his wife, and his pet duck. Because he allows himself a moment of contemplation at the start of each day, he has an unusual appreciation for small things of beauty, like an airplane's contrail lit by moonlight or the "brief vortex, like a rainbow after a storm" of a bathtub drain he plunges. The scope of this book is at once tiny and immense. The vehicle for the novel is the tradition of lighting a fire each morning while the world sleeps. Baker seems determined to restore a sense of wonder to ordinary things while he restores the diarylike aspect to fiction. The more we enter Emmett's private world, the more it has the ability to amuse us or disturb us or both at the same time, as when he describes the "suicide fantasies" he employs to help him fall asleep. These private thoughts are every bit as entertaining as his minute observations of the world around him, and as they accumulate, they form a clear, coherent picture of a character, if not a life. Traditional narrative elements like plot or dramatic action are not to be found here. What we do find is a narrator who is real, who describes the world with uncanny precision, and who amuses us. When Emmett finishes his box of matches, the reader is sorry to see him go. [D. Quentin Miller]

Alicia Borinsky. *All Night Movie*. Trans. Cola Franzen with the author. Northwestern Univ. Press, 2002. 204 pp. Paper: $15.95.

There is something tantalizingly audacious about a tango, the paradox of bold passion and playful immediacy despite the intricate choreography and demanding execution. Such is the feel reading Alicia Borinsky's intoxicatingly playful, highly irreverent mood-piece on the erotic chaos and chilling nightworld of contemporary Argentina. With guerrilla insouciance and giddy confidence, Borinsky challenges the picaresque genre, playing through a madcap array of narrative asides, capturing a culture in chaos, indeed a culture feeding upon its own chaos, a cartoon culture suspended uneasily between comic-opera irony and self-inflicted apocalypse. Here characters appear for a quirky narrative turn or two and then tumble back within the enfolding narrative's furious rush toward (appropriately enough) nonclosure (a promise, at the end, that more will follow). Prostitutes ply their trade in phone booths, renegade nuns search for an iconic adolescent (afflicted with leprosy, maybe) known only as the Scarred Girl, nefarious politicos scheme and posture, crusading journalists cling to the idea of truth somewhere in such murkiness, a cult of girls devoted (apparently) to the memory of Eva Peron wander the back streets—and at the center (if such a carnival fantasy can have such a steadying thing) is a murder trial that closes, appropriately, in a dismissal by reason of insanity. Structurally diced into fragmentary chapters that frustrate the need for conventional linearity, the novel justifies its own momentum without the hokey intrusiveness of sustained plot and character development. Like the seductive tango so richly involved with its own elaborate flourish and so intensely aware of its own energy, the narrative propels rather than engrosses, mesmerizes rather than involves. To capture such a defiant hybrid of comic and ghastly, the pitch-perfect translation sustains the game. It is an absorbing read, at once lyrical and harsh, erotic and barbaric—it is, like the tango itself, both intimate and cool. [Joseph Dewey]

Lyn Hejinian. *Happily*. Post-Apollo, 2000. 39 pp. Paper: $7.00; *Slowly*. Tuumba, 2002. 43 pp. Paper: $10.00; *The Beginner*. Tuumba, 2002. 42 pp. Paper: $10.00.

These short books by poet, essayist, and translator Lyn Hejinian are not quite a series, but read together, it's difficult not to take them as one. In all three Hejinian explores happiness, time, fate, logic, birth, and death (and music, photography, film, and writing) in run-on lines and paragraphs of a sentence or two that often seem only peripherally related to one another. But subjects and objects recur (within each book and from book to book), creating a network of motifs from the earliest, *Happily*, through *Slowly* and *The Beginner*. A key motif is an "outside" physical world in constant contact with an "internal" intellectual/emotional self. Hejinian writes from a specific domestic spot and with a keen awareness of the activeness of things, to the point where objects are often personified. In *Happily* there are "buckets taking dents" and "persevering saws swimming into boards"; in *Slowly* "film proceeds without inhibitions." And in *The Beginner*, "If someone referred to by a personal pronoun feels emotions too great to continue, the pronoun will come to refer instead to a rock, a natural thing." Everything is dynamic and exists in relation to everything else. Complex ideas in this world become as approachable as a bicycle or an egg, and references to Gertrude Stein, postmodern theories of photography, Gustave Flaubert, Rae Armantrout, or Plotinus maintain levity rather than becoming grave or portentous. Furthermore, the ongoing conversation with writers, thinkers, and theories places the reader consciously inside a continuum of literary thought, in the way that the development of ideas throughout the books creates a continuum. Upon finishing we are left with the sense that, taken together, the pieces don't have a specific beginning or end, but run much like a film on a loop, with banal and exquisite images flickering past, sinking and reemerging. In this way Hejinian creates an act of reading for the reader, a rhythmic temporal experience, like the duration of a day, film, or piece of music, all of which begin and end while maintaining the inherent possibility/assurance of beginning again. [Danielle Dutton]

John Banville. *Shroud*. Knopf, 2003. 257 pp. $25.00.

Banville gives us another thrilling exhibition. He returns (obsessively?) to his favorite themes of evidence, deception, and investigation, and his dazzling metaphorical power grips us. Vander, his central character, speaks to us at first, and on almost every page he explores his fear of disclosure, his (painful?) pleasure in his impersonation of his shrouded self. He boasts: "All my life I lied to escape, I lied to be loved, I lied for placement and power. It was a way of living; lies are life's almost-anagram." His reputation as scholar, oracle, and prophet has never been questioned. Once he gets a letter from a young woman who has discovered his clouded past and threatens to reveal his lost identity, his World War II status, he immediately travels back to the Old World, hoping to avoid her threats. But he discovers that his shadow, Cass Cleave, also has an unbalanced self. They are meant for each other; they are phantoms. Cass, we are told, is insane: "Her hallucinations were like real happenings, or memories of real happenings made immediate and vivid." Thus Vander and Cleave are perfect; their "marriage" is a kind of mad paradise. Of course, their "marriage" cannot last. They are unbalanced—a word that recurs throughout the novel—and although they explore their wounds, they are separated by each other's special needs and follies. Banville could have written a comedy of errors, but he knows that somehow reality exists, if only in the body's decay. After all the metaphors, the changes of narration, Vander (wander, wonder?) knows that the dead have their voice. And it is this voice that drowns out Vander's secret eloquence. It appears that even death doesn't stifle the longing for perfection: the novel eludes burial, closure—and it makes us wonder whether radiance can truly illuminate the shroud. [Irving Malin]

Juan Rulfo. *Pedro Paramo*. Trans. Margaret Sayers Peden. Photos Josephine Sacabo. Univ. of Texas Press, 2002. 161 pp. $35.00.

This handsome reissue of Juan Rulfo's classic *Pedro Paramo*, occasioned by the series of Josephine Sacabo photographs that appear here alongside the text that inspired them, should serve as an opportunity for readers to (re)discover a work that, while retaining every ampoule of its extraordinary power, seems to have fallen a little off the American radar screen. First published in Mexico in 1955, *Pedro Paramo* begins as the story of one Juan Preciado, who in hopes of meeting his father, the novel's eponym, travels to the village his mother fled years before, only to find a crumbling, wind-swept ghost-town. Welcomed by several of the village's ghostly former inhabitants, Preciado is gradually overwhelmed by the sad voices and bits of nightmarish story that gather around him. Soon he is left behind, and the narrative turns fully to Pedro Paramo—local tyrant, empowered psychopath—and his devastating obsessions. The principal of these is Susana San Juan, Paramo's childhood sweetheart, who despite his murderous machinations finds escape in madness. It is this side of the novel on which Josephine Sacabo's gorgeous, dream-inflected photographs focus, serving to fore-ground Susana's importance as the target of Paramo's withering attention and as a symbol of Comala's ruin. Rulfo's novel, in which phantoms and visions are constituent elements of the actual, has long been acknowledged as a signal precursor (with Borges) of magic realism. It is interesting to note, and Sacabo's photos generally help to underscore this, how unrelentingly understated Rulfo's haunting vision was compared to the hyperbole of the practitioners who made the movement famous. Whether in the company of Sacabo's photos, as we have it here, or in the standard Grove Press edition (which also features Margaret Sayers Peden's elegant translation), it would be hard to recommend a work more highly. [Laird Hunt]

Mehis Heinsaar. *Vanameeste näppaja* (Snatcher of Old Men). Tuum, Estonia, 2001. 155 pp. No price given.

Mehis Heinsaar attracted attention in Estonia with his earliest short stories, and his first book, *Vanameeste näppaja*, received the prestigious Betti Alver award. The book consists of sixteen short stories divided into three cycles. The author's unmistakable skill unites the exotic and local slum romanticism with traditions of world literature. It abounds in biological, spatial, and temporal mutations, mixed with Soviet kolkhoz life and weird characters. There is, for instance, a strange creature called Gerko living in a maize field, maize being a crop cultivated on Moscow's orders despite utterly unsuitable climatic conditions. Such true-life Soviet absurdities, like the campaign to make the Siberian rivers run in the opposite direction, greatly enrich Heinsaar's imagination and form the foundation of his work. The writer himself emphasizes the friction between the worlds of the everyday and that of myths: their convergences are surprising and novel, waking the reader from either real or magical sleep. The effect is all the more powerful, since readers cannot immediately understand into which of the two worlds they have been aroused.

Heinsaar notices details but does not heap them; his language is scant and his stories simple and "ordinary," at least at first sight. They become unusual by absurd twists and turns, which are rendered in a casual, everyday manner, as if fairy tales and witchcraft were natural parts of our lives. Heinsaar's stories could be described as magic realism: "How Death Came to Mirabel," for example, could easily be the title of a García Márquez short story. Although Heinsaar often operates in a clearly Estonian key, many of these stories could happen anywhere and have obviously been inspired by world literature. The cat dictating stories is probably related to E. T. A. Hoffmann's cat, Murri; some reviewers have cited influences in the Old Testament, Bulgakov, and especially surrealism. The last story, "Encounter in Time," is a depressing hallucinatory piece about a stinking tramp who rapes a girl on a park bench, mistaking her for the love of his youth. This, too, is a metamorphosis, mutation in time, and reference to *Lolita*. The story even has a moral side to it, although Heinsaar's work should be relished in the spirit in which it was written—with soaring imagination and inventiveness. [Janika Kronberg]

Joanna Scott. *Tourmaline*. Little, Brown, 2003. 279 pp. $23.95.

In *Tourmaline* Joanna Scott's lustrous Mediterranean landscapes echo the shadowy Italian romances of Nathaniel Hawthorne and John Hawkes. Inspired by her own extended tour of Italy, Scott weaves a simple tale with a mysterious and seductive allure. In the 1950s Murray Murdoch and his family flee his American past for the island of Elba, infamous as the land of Napoleon's exile, where he expects to lead a simpler life. A financial failure, Murray searches for a fortune in semiprecious tourmaline, which he expects will redeem his ruined reputation, but he becomes engulfed by the investigation into the disappearance of an entrancing local girl, Adriana Nardi, and the scandalous rumors that circulate about their illicit relationship. But Murray's misadventures are only part of Scott's story. More interested in "the murky private work of consciousness," Scott brilliantly orchestrates a multitiered narrative, relating many scenes through the contemporary perspective of Murray's wife, Claire, and his son, Oliver, as they struggle—often against each other—to compose a meaningful account of the family's life on the island from isolated fragments of memory and dreams. Throughout *Tourmaline*'s elegiac evocation of family and belonging, Scott writes crystalline prose that absorbs, reflects, and refracts the complex light of human desire and emotion. [Trey Strecker]

Kenzaburo Oe. *Somersault*. Trans. Philip Gabriel. Grove, 2003. 576 pp. $29.95.

In his first new novel since winning the Nobel Prize for Literature, Kenzaburo Oe offers an examination of the nature of faith when it is balanced against the potential for human self-annihilation in the twenty-first century. A complete departure from Oe's fiction concerning his retarded son, *Somersault* is a conventional narrative about a fictional religious cult, partly influenced by Aum Shinrikyo and their 1995 sarin attack on the Tokyo subway. Ten years before the novel begins, a religious group's two founding leaders, Patron and Guide, betray their own movement because a radical faction within the group threatens large-scale terrorism. The leaders contact the authorities and publicly ridicule the values and beliefs their group espouses, a complete disavowal labeled a somersault. After the somersault, Patron and Guide go into exile for ten years, but reemerge as a new group of followers converges to restart Patron's movement. If Oe's previous novels have often concentrated on a father trying to decide what role his retarded son can play in the world, here Patron and his followers conceive of how to live in a world they believe is doomed to an imminent and violent end. While Oe's writing on Hiroshima is not directly invoked in *Somersault,* the novel does focus on how to live in a world where unspeakable actions can destroy a people's faith and shatter them physically. Instead of addressing only the survivors of violence, Oe envisions a potentially violent cult that is both perpetrator and victim of its crimes, a microcosm of a twenty-first-century humanity that is hastening its own destruction. Akin to Oe's other novels, *Somersault* possesses a grotesque and dark view of the world that is nevertheless flavored by the author's immeasurable humanity and ability to find beauty in dark and disturbing characters and locales. Readers of Oe's prior work will find the length and approach of *Somersault* an entirely new venture for the Japanese author, one that yields disquieting and unexpected results while also broadening the scope and form that the author's future fiction might take. [Jason Picone]

Javier Marías. *The Man of Feeling.* Trans. Margaret Jull Costa. New Directions, 2003. 182 pp. $22.95.

Readers in the United States have been slower than those elsewhere to discover the sophisticated pleasures of Javier Marías, the fifty-two-year-old Spanish author who has been translated into more than two dozen languages. Following the successful reception of *Dark Back of Time* and *When I Was Mortal,* New Directions offers an English translation of an earlier, less ambitious Marías novel. First published in 1986 as *El hombre sentimental, The Man of Feeling* is a brief, intense portrait of an aberrant artist, an artist of aberrancy. Its narrator, Léon de Nápoles, is a promising opera star who declares, "I need to try to destroy myself or to destroy someone else," and accomplishes both objectives. During a sojourn in Madrid to perform Cassio in Verdi's *Otello,* Nápoles encounters Hieronimo Manur, a wealthy Belgian banker, and his restless wife, Natalia. With the connivance of the banker's factotum, Dato, Nápoles attempts to pry Natalia away from her husband. Hieronimo had in effect purchased Natalia, taking her as property in exchange for bailing her father and brother out of financial ruin. Believing that she will eventually learn to love him, Manur is the novel's eponymous *hombre sentimental,* and, recalling the events through a scrim of dreams four years later, Nápoles, a man of scant feeling but resentment, still marvels at the other man's patient faith in the eventual birth of love. Miscast as Cassio rather than Iago, Nápoles broods over the banker's devotion to a woman who remains indifferent to him. "Bear in mind that there is no stronger bond than that which binds one to something unreal or, worse, something that has never existed," observes Manur about his own uncommon marriage—and Marías about his own perverse and powerful fiction. [Steven G. Kellman]

Joseph Heller. *Catch as Catch Can: The Collected Stories and Other Writings.* Ed. Matthew J. Bruccoli and Park Bucker. Simon & Schuster, 2003. 333 pp. $25.00.

This volume collects all of the short fiction Joseph Heller published in his lifetime. It also includes five previously unpublished stories, a variety of pieces relating to *Catch-22* (1961) and its sequel *Closing Time* (1994), and some autobiographical reminiscences. Stories like "Castle of Snow," "World Full of Great Cities," and "MacAdam's Log" are certainly interesting documents from Heller's early career. But his journeyman stories don't have the manic and darkly humorous style that makes his novels such unique experiences. Bruccoli's introduction notes that this short fiction emulates the themes and realist techniques of Ernest Hemingway, William Saroyan, John O'Hara, and some of the proletarian writers of the 1940s. Most of these stories play out either during or soon after World War II, and they tend to focus on characters dealing with threats to their masculinity and autonomy. The rest of this collection, as the title suggests, revolves around *Catch-22*. Compared to Heller's early efforts, that novel truly does mark a significant turning point in his development—not just in its exuberant style, but in Yossarian's radically new take on traditional masculine anxieties. Several nonfiction pieces collected here are also of interest for their relation to *Catch-22*. Among these, the best is Heller's hilarious reminiscence of his sporadic encounters with Mike Nichols and the others who put *Catch-22* on film. As a whole, this collection will most likely appeal to Heller enthusiasts. Since enthusiasts would no doubt appreciate supplementary scholarly, historical, and biographical material, it's unfortunate that Bruccoli's introduction is so terse and that much of it merely reproduces large sections from Heller's 1998 memoir *Now and Then*. But for anyone who wants to round off their collection of Heller's works, this volume conveniently fills in some major gaps. [Thomas Hove]

Franck Pavloff. *Matin brun* (Brown Morning). Cheyne Editeur, France, 1998. 12 pp. €1.00.

A psychologist and children's rights expert who has spent years working for humanitarian causes in Africa and South America, Pavloff is a politically engaged French novelist and children's author. His antitotalitarian parable

Matin brun, originally published in 1998, became a phenomenon after the virulent National Front leader Jean-Marie Le Pen beat the official challenger, socialist prime minister Lionel Jospin, in the first round of the 2002 French presidential elections. The incumbent Jacques Chirac, a republican, won the decisive second round, but Le Pen's initial success at the polls shocked Europe, highlighting the presence of extremism and xenophobia.

What if the government suddenly announced that all cats, except brown ones, were to be outlawed for reasons of "overpopulation"? What if the authorities went on to say that all nonbrown dogs had to go as well? If all newspapers except the official "Brown News" were to be banned? And what if one day all those who had ever harbored nonbrown pets were hoarded up and taken away, together with their families and associates? *Matin brun* brings to life the incremental process by which an open society can succumb to totalitarianism. Apathy erodes freedom: a small concession today can pave the way for serious oppression tomorrow. The ultimate reference is to the specter of fascism, *"la peste brune,"* Europe's overrepresented trauma, which has become imaginatively unreal: It Could Never Happen Today.

What is most original about Pavloff's unusual, pamphlet-length bestseller is its vivid problematization of political quietism. How far do things have to go before minding your own business becomes a form of collaboration? Pavloff uses a children's story and absurdist narrative to pose a conundrum that only a mature, historically educated citizenry could ever hope to handle for real. A topical, devastatingly simple tale in the tradition of Camus, Orwell, and Saramago, *Matin brun* struck a chord with the French reading public, becoming a best-seller in the spring and summer of 2002. A classic instance of subversive literary experiment, it cuts to the quick of a political problem, offering protection against indifference in any society where entertainment rules, racism is an issue, and electorates are sluggish. A lucid starting-point for a debate on civic responsibility, diversity, and democracy, Pavloff's story deserves to become a classroom classic in Europe and beyond. [Philip Landon]

António Lobo Antunes. *The Inquisitors' Manual.* Trans. Richard Zenith. Grove, 2003. 435 pp. $25.00.

Bearing a certain resemblance to *The Sound and the Fury,* Antunes's most recent novel to be published in English recounts the fall of a Portuguese family in the time preceding and following the 1974 revolution. The plot revolves around Senhor Francisco, a minister during Salazar's reign, who abuses his power, rapes his milkmaid, is deserted by his wife, goes insane after the revolution, almost drinks himself to death, and ends up in a hospital with a nurse endlessly repeating, "wee-wee, it's time for wee-wee, who made a nice wee-wee, who was it?" His plight, and that of those who surround him, consists of five reports told to an unnamed—and generally unobtrusive—inquisitor researching Senhor Francisco's family for a book he's writing. Five characters directly impacted by the family's decline narrate these reports: Francisco's son João, their maid Titinia, Francisco's illegitimate daughter, his mistress, and Francisco himself. Each report is expanded upon—sometimes touchingly, sometimes sarcastically—with "commentaries" from a cast of minor characters. An indictment of Salazar's reign, this novel powerfully portrays the hopelessness of Portugal's lower classes, a situation that sadly doesn't seem to improve much after the revolution, when the already rich take advantage of the chaos and the poor find another decrepit apartment to live in. Like Antunes's other works, this isn't just a political novel, nor is it a tragedy of the human situation. In contrast to Faulkner, Antunes realizes that the misery of his characters can be quite funny. Antunes's grasp of the workings of his characters' minds is amazing, as in the situation of the veterinarian who organizes his life in order to see young girls arriving at school (the principal eventually files charges) and the way João's mother-in-law's comment—"Are you a moron, young man, or are you just pretending?"—infiltrates his being like a sadistic mantra. The overarching plot of this book is as flimsy as the premise that an inquisitor is gathering all of this material, but that really isn't the point. *The Inquisitors' Manual* will be remembered for the voices of its characters (which Richard Zenith captures so well) and the dark humor that emerges from the conflict between their desires and the hopelessness of their situations. [Chad W. Post]

Jay Cantor. *Great Neck.* Knopf, 2003. 703 pp. $27.95.

While not yet a large enough collection to call a subgenre, several books have appeared in the past few years with enough in common to hint at one. Their authors seem to have sublimated the lessons of postmodernism and used them to reinvent the novel of family life. Think of Franzen's *The Corrections* and perhaps also Eugenides's *Middlesex,* and now add *Great Neck* to the list. All of these are as ambitious as their ancestors in their willingness to sprawl, and they explode the details of domesticity across their many pages. Cantor's contribution concerns the residents of the eponymous Long Island suburb, particularly a group of privileged, mostly Jewish friends who pass from childhood into adulthood as the civil-rights movement of the sixties and seventies unfolds. Obviously, political and racial themes are prominent—one character states, "if the body on trial is a black one, then justice is always far from blind. Criminal *justice* is always only criminal *politics"*—but the real interest here is in the way the characters are built through a steady accretion of observation and incident. The book is densely written, with a knotty chronology that takes a step back every time it takes two steps forward, and in its surfeit of detail it captures the sense of living through an almost paralyzing era that featured far too much to think about and do. Reading *Great Neck* requires almost the same amount of effort as living a life; those who are willing to work will find that Cantor's created a rewarding plenitude. [James Crossley]

Vassilis Vassilikos. *The Few Things I Know about Glafkos Thrassakis.* Trans. Karen Emmerich. Seven Stories, 2002. 356 pp. $24.95.

Vassilikos creates an unnamed narrator who is writing a biography of the fictional writer Glafkos Thrassakis (pen name for Lazarus Lazaridis). An "afterword" devoted to Thrassakis's text "Conversations with Andreas Kalvos," identifying parallels between his own life and that of the *real* nineteenth-century Greek writer, adds yet one more layer to the patently palimpsestic quality of this work while at the same time blurring fact and fiction. Vassilikos probes the intriguing dynamics between biographer and subject: how the biographer is prone to identify with certain qualities of his subject and how his own life narrative is influenced by the subject as he retraces his subject's steps. Whose life is whose, we might ask in the end, and where does one life begin and another end? Woven into the fabric of the material (both the biographer's and Thrassakis's) are important historical references, particularly to the dark days of the junta in Greece, the nefarious actions of Henry Kissinger, the workings of American imperialism, and various leftist activities. The theme of exile and return is central as Thrassakis and others are either forced to leave their countries or choose to do so. The work performs the virtual impossibility of adequately and truthfully representing a whole life, accounting for all its multiple facets. There will be just "the few things I know" about the subject—a series of vignettes, or snapshots, or speculative reconstructions. The novel contains stories of the biographer's sleuthing as well as various documents, such as diary extracts and excerpts or synopses of his literary production. This results in a curious, unique structure. As the narrator/biographer reflects toward the end of the work, "I'm not a fan of 'statistical' biographies that start with the person's birth and end with his death." Rather, he says he has taken his material as it came, "following whatever path it might lead me down." [Allen Hibbard]

Nenad Veličković. *Sahib.* Stubovi Kulture, Serbia, 2002. 176 pp. € 5.00.

A young Englishman comes to postwar Bosnia, which lingers between "a preserve and a colony," to work on the implementation of Western principles and policies. Travel to another country and meeting with a new culture, as we have seen in E. M. Forster's *Passage to India* and *Room with a View,* rarely goes without at least a slight transformation of the newcomer. The young and nameless Englishman is no exception. The Englishman's e-mails to his male lover back in England unfold before our eyes, showing us the rigidity, stereotypes, and ideology in which we are all immersed when trying to understand the Other. At the end of the book, there is a translator's note telling us that the e-mail messages are a documentary thing, not invented stuff. What we were hoping was a deliberate exaggeration (the preposterous, arrogant, and ignorant nature of the Englishman) on the part of the writer turns out to be a translation of real e-mail messages, with only the names of the protagonists changed.

The meeting of the Orient with the Occident serves as a good source for all sorts of humorous situations, misunderstandings, and witticisms, with which Veličković's book abounds. Yet what Veličković seems to be concentrating on most is showing us how the encounter with the new culture is always a meeting with the Other, something inevitably inferior, lower than the subject itself. *Sahib,* at times, becomes a Swiftian satire, having as its main target the colonizing policies behind the rhetoric of liberating and democratizing nations. However, Veličković is far from idealizing the state of affairs in prewar Bosnia. His satire is also directed at the contradictions and shortcomings of the previous socialist and communist regimes. What foreign organizations in Bosnia seem to be mostly preoccupied with is finding techniques to dissuade young people from immigrating to Western countries, or, in other words, preventing the "weeds" from Bosnia from implementing themselves on Western soil. Foreign organizations are creating only the illusion that they are doing something worthwhile for the war-ravaged society, while in reality they are busy creating surreal and impossible projects for the "country's benefit." The only product, says the main protagonist of *Sahib* (in one of his half-serious, half-joking musings), over which the developed countries of the world still do not have a monopoly and which Bosnia can produce, is blood. If Bosnia exported blood, this would probably turn out to be beneficial for both Bosnians and other, more developed countries.

Veličković's book leaves us guessing what good comes out of today's mingling of the nations and what great migrations of populations bring when our efforts to perceive and experience foreign culture as anything besides simply the Other are hindered and thwarted in advance by the limits of our own subjectivity. In an age "when dollars can shut up every mouth," even bitter satire does not have the effect it once had. [Ana Lucic]

Robert Coover. *The Adventures of Lucky Pierre: Director's Cut.* Grove, 2002. 405 pp. $24.00.

In *Briar Rose* (1996) and *Ghost Town* (1998) Robert Coover took two identity- and culture-defining narrative genres—the fairy tale and the American Western—and turned them inside out. The more ambitious *Lucky Pierre* takes on another such genre, pornography, treating it through the idiom of another culture-constructing form, cinema. The eponymous hero's adventures consist of a series of erotic films, into and out of which he is perpetually falling, never sure when, if ever, he is in a real, noncinematic life. Taken together, these films trace the course of his life, from youth to old age; the history of film, from silents through classic Hollywood narratives to avant-garde; and a survey of film genres, as pornography is hybridized with South Seas adventure, slapstick comedy, Japanese monster movie, and dozens of others. The heart of all this is the exploration of identity amid these powerful cultural narratives. With no single narrative or even a single name (he has different names at different times in his career) to hold onto and with no sense of what around him is real and what illusion, Pierre is reduced to one defining trait: "He is he who ceaselessly desires." Yet the objects of his desire are always externally generated, making him the identity-less puppet of an unnervingly ambiguous authority. In a rare moment of self-awareness, Pierre thinks, "it has trapped him inside a box of artificial light even as it pulled him in all directions at once and has given him no life, no center of his own." This novel offers many outrageously funny, genuinely moving, and technically impressive sequences. Still, the overall effect of the repeated pornographic episodes is ultimately deadening; perhaps this is the point, but I suspect the novel could have been shorter without losing all that's wonderful in it. [Robert L. McLaughlin]

Ken Kalfus. *The Commissariat of Enlightenment*. Ecco, 2003. 295 pp. $24.95.

The years between the deaths of Tolstoy and Lenin were years in which the most artfully successful Russian revolutionaries recognized the emergent technology of the moving picture for its awesome ability to mediate reality. *Commissariat*'s Nikolai Gribshin (neither hero nor quite antihero) is among the first to grasp "how to assemble facts into something useful . . . facts that are not facts—that are, in fact, lies—until they're in the service of revolution," and he carefully uses this knowledge as he maneuvers through the creation of a new Soviet reality. Gribshin eventually comes to serve the postrevolutionary Commissariat of Enlightenment, through which he comes to understand that a canny government will "either starve the masses of meaning or expose them to so much that the sum of it would be unintelligible." The stark and grimly well-timed parallel between revolutionary Russia and today's capitalist West is clear, but it's not a point that Kalfus digs into our ribs: his storytelling is engaging, subtle, and written with a clarity that would border on cautious were it not for his palpable confidence. It's probably natural for a serious literary writer to comment on the fall of the written word to newer media, but circa 2003 the consequence is that the main and possibly only audience for that writer's book is comprised chiefly of the few people who noticed that the word had fallen in the first place. Thus Ken Kalfus writes a terrific, bleakly beautiful first novel (following 1998's *Thirst* and 1999's *Pu-239*, both collections, both great) that will effectively end up choir-preaching to the majority of its audience and go ignored by those most in need of its message. Whether it's naive to even point this out anymore, let alone fret about it, is another matter. [Tim Feeney]

Edward Carey. *Alva & Irva: The Twins Who Saved a City*. Harcourt, 2003. 207 pp. $24.00.

Edward Carey has carved himself a nifty little niche in the atmosphere of this world, by which I mean to say, he has, in only two books, successfully blown this world to slivers, and he seems poised to write each sliver back into existence one at a time. *Alva & Irva* is the story of twins with perfectly opposite dispositions. Alva, the historian with gasoline in her veins, fuel she hopes will propel her to an adventurous life. Irva, mousy and precise, preferring the sheltering quietude of kitchen cabinets to the idea of life outside their fictional city of Entralla, their "corner of existence . . . everything that we learnt and saw could be contained within it." Together, at the urging of an overbearing grandfather, they create a plasticine model of Entralla (shown throughout in black and white photographs; the model was actually built by Carey), which becomes the thing that may save Entralla following a massive natural disaster and immortalize the twins, together, forever. Like Carey's horribly overlooked first novel, *Observatory Mansions, A & I* skirts the line between clever convolution and just plain convolution, the latter at times making seemingly choice turns of phrase into toss-offs easily disregarded for their deliberate cuteness. But these instances are few. Carey's prose simultaneously pulls readers into the world of his creation and holds them at arm's length, dangling them in the air above this world, to demonstrate the wonder he has created. The reader becomes a kind of child or spectator at an amusement park: positioned safely to avoid danger, but with clear sight lines to all the best attractions. While this may potentially turn some readers off, there is no denying Carey's ingenuity. His is a voice both fresh and familiar: a writer who will continue to impress himself on *our* landscape. [Brian Budzynski]

———————

Christian Oster. *My Big Apartment*. Trans. and intro. Jordan Stump. Univ. of Nebraska Press, 2002. 155 pp. Paper: $20.00; *A Cleaning Woman*. Trans. Mark Polizzotti. Other Press, 2003. 197 pp. $22.00.

Since Preston Sturges, the American romantic comedy—with its anatomy of the sweet disorder of infatuation as it stumbles into love, its slight plots compelled nevertheless by the engine of heavy-handed complications, all set against the chaotic rule of coincidence—has been largely the province of film, disdained by contemporary serious fiction makers as too frivolous to reward extensive investigation, save as the subject of often withering parody. Too bad, really, as Christian Oster's marvelous entertainments testify—ultimately, sentimentality is merely the tension of aware minds burdened/salvaged by hearts that stubbornly refuse to accept the irony of their own evident vulnerability. Romantic comedy has always lingered dangerously close to existential despair: a slight turn of the plot, and the screen could darken into irretrievable sorrow. Oster understands that—his central characters are seekers: tender, intellectual men who linger against adulthood, who fear accepting the chilling reality that any life is a structureless drift made endurable only by the accidental collision of two imperfect, yearning hearts. Both hurt and hopeful, his narrators, who speak in unaffected directness rendered perfectly by these translations, move about a thin sort of everyday world, certain that love at first sight is viable, that the heart cannot err, that the rich and cutting disappointment of love is the sole reward for living. In *My Big Apartment* (1999) a man, bruised by a collapsing relationship with a live-in lover, chances upon a striking but very pregnant woman in a public pool. Impulsively, he agrees to accompany her to her brother's home in southern France, and there becomes involved with the idea of being involved with her even as he assists in the delivery and becomes hopelessly enthralled by the simple wonder of the newborn girl. By the close, they agree to stay together; perhaps, they reason, it is love enough. Jacques, the suffering romantic of *A Cleaning Woman* (2001), is also smitten by a stranger, specifically a young woman he hires to restore tidiness to his Paris digs in the aftermath of a careening relationship. Unlike the earlier novel, however, Oster here fleshes out this object of affection and creates a fragile, fascinating sort of love quadrangle as both Jacques and the cleaning woman have hearts haunted by lingering ghosts. Indeed, Oster examines the uneasy line separating passion and obsession. The attraction here is far more erotic, but that never becomes the saving impulse, Oster too aware that the frictions of sexuality are, compared to love, uncomplicated and inevitably dulled. The interest here is in the overwhelming hunger of attraction (Oster nicely manipulates the metaphor of the open sea and drowning) and the sweet risk of giving in to its dark suasion. Never collapsing into thin clichés, Oster stage-manages this romance through point of view, Jacques never entirely aware of all that he reveals: his needful heart, the poignant sadness of his aimless midlife, the intractable excess of his desire, and the insatiable jealousy that lurks, Oster argues, at the heart of every romantic. [Joseph Dewey]

Brian Evenson. *Dark Property*. Black Square/Hammer, 2002. 132 pp. Paper: $14.00.

Brian Evenson appreciates the discordant beauty of Old Testament verse and appropriates it in his novel *Dark Property*. In what might be called neobiblical language, Evenson alternates between the story of an unnamed woman carrying a dead infant and the story of a bounty hunter, Kline. Both characters journey through a postapocalyptic desert landscape teeming with menace. The novel tells of their encounters with the denizens of this blasted landscape and separate pilgrimages to a walled compound filled with grotesque resurrectionists. The interwoven narratives ask readers to compare the two travelers, each of whom carries human cargo over a shoulder—in his case, a woman bound for slave life in a brothel, and in hers, a dead infant. Readers of Evenson's other books, like *Contagion*, will find familiar subjects. What incites these characters to dark acts is left inscrutable for much of the novel—a hook pulling readers along to find out what lies behind their deeds. Evenson does not portray violence to shock or mortify (though a reader may be both shocked and mortified) but to illustrate the principle that murder is an adjunct to moral authority. Kline's conflict with the resurrectionists can be understood in abstract terms as a clash between religious practices—is the word or the deed stronger? Evenson dramatizes a struggle between truth communicated with language, as in saying something true, and truth communicated with deed, as in a death sentence. When the resurrectionists breach the divide between life and death, Evenson's Kline reflects that "Truth cannot be imparted. . . . It must be inflicted." Using sparse dialogue and almost no psychological reflection, the novel invites readers to reflect on the limits of language, which is a revealing—and sometimes unsettling—artistic endeavor. [Alex DeBonis]

Alison Bundy, Keith Waldrop, and Rosmarie Waldrop, eds. *One Score More: The Second Twenty Years of Burning Deck, 1982-2002.* Burning Deck, 2002. 240 pp. Paper: $15.00.

Burning Deck is one of those amazing independent publishers that seems to be in an eternal state of creation and recreation. What they publish consistently seems fresh, new, and noteworthy. Like Black Sparrow, Burning Deck has emphasized book crafts to the point that the physical aspect of the book reinforces the press's mission. This volume is an anthology of more than fifty authors whose works comprise a faithful sample of the artistic vision maintained by the press from 1982 to 2002. It provides insight into why Burning Deck has continued to be a solid influence in poetry and poetics, particularly in the application of the underpinning concepts and epistemological stances utilized by French poets writing in the late-twentieth century. For Burning Deck, philosophy is reflected in poetics, which in turn engages and informs philosophy. In the case of the works represented in the anthology, form and syntax undermine the narrative strategies of a sentimentalist realism. A fundamental questioning of subjectivity and a destabilization of the idea of essence allows the works to focus on how language creates meaning beyond the typical poetic stratagems of metaphor, simile, and structured prosody. The prose pieces in the collection are perhaps the most stunning, with Dallas Wiebe's ironic pseudoparodies of "hard-boiled" minimalism, Lissa McLaughlin's adrenaline-surging estrangement of the ordinary, Walter Abish's travelogues of the mind, and Elizabeth MacKiernan's faux genealogies, to name just a few. The poetry spans minimalist explorations of the edges of meaning and nonmeaning, including Burning Deck classics Gale Nelson, Jena Osman, Tina Darragh, and Keith Waldrop. Concrete and postconcrete poetry includes Susan Gevirtz, Ernst Jandl, and Peter Gizzi. Although it may seem sterile to emphasize metatexts dealing with self-reflexive investigations of poetic meaning, the results are exciting and important to late-twentieth-century poetry. *One Score More* provides an important overview. [Susan Smith Nash]

Jim Knipfel. *The Buzzing.* Vintage, 2003. 259 pp. $12.00.

Roscoe Baragon, the hero of this wonderfully zany and grim novel, is a reporter. He cannot take news seriously—he realizes that the usual catastrophes don't really interest him. All reporters repeat the same items about terrifying serial killings, child abuse, leaked Washington copy on health care, government projects for the public good. Baragon expresses himself in what he calls the Kook Beat—those events that are so bizarre, they must be true: "Now there was only a great, empty, echoed buzzing where the story used to be." And he begins to speculate that seemingly unrelated things are possibly linked: an unusual earthquake in Alaska; the disappearance of poor, wounded roomers from halfway hotels; the corporation of SVA, which owns these hotels. He lists the bizarre events that are occurring. Baragon thinks: "conspiracies, moreover, also help make the normal redundancies of life a little more bearable." At the same time, he believes that his referential mania is somehow more real than *other* paranoias. And as the novel moves to its end, we wonder—as does Baragon—whether there are secret patterns or only the lunatic ramblings of Kooks. *The Buzzing* then becomes an antiparody of conspiracy theories, or a very accurate rendering of a true conspiracy. Is Baragon mad? Is the world mad? The last page leaves us unsure. Baragon leaves the paper, trying to calm himself as he sings a "sweet Malaysian tune . . . He knew full well it wouldn't help. Still, he figured, it was worth a shot." What is *it*? Baragon puzzles over his account. Where will he go? Perhaps he will go to the library and read Pynchon, who, by the way, offers a blurb for this novel, citing Knipfel's "cheerfully undeluded American voice." *The Buzzing* is either undeluded or deluded or overdeluded. [Irving Malin]

Bruce Fleming. *A Structure Opera*. Six Gallery, 2002. 195 pp. Paper: $12.95.

Novelist Jim Chapman (*In Candyland It's Cool to Feed on Your Friends*) says that novels are food. If so, Bruce Fleming has served up with his latest offering, *A Structure Opera,* what could best be described as a "nouvealipo sandwich." Here's the recipe: take two thick slices of Robbe-Grillet's Nouveau Roman Meal bread and spread as many neo-Oulipo games in between as the bread will hold. The bread is rich in description, of course all objective, with no visible narrator. The invisible narrator is gender biased (e.g. "the creations of mere men," "so that to him who sees"—or is this the Robbe-Grilletian absent narrator referring to himself in the third person, à la *Jalousie*?), which gives us a clue to the narrator's personality. And then he leads us to games. The difference between Fleming's games and real Oulipian amusements is that Oulipo's exercises are to literary purpose— they are mechanisms employed to generate text. Fleming's experiments have different results: dances for watch hands, pocket calculators, semaphores, metronomes, fingers, photocopiers, playing cards, and chess boards seem less like literary devices than some absurd Peter Schickele/PDQ Bach composition. The final section, the other slice of bread, is served to us while we do some museum hopping (the flavor should remind you of the museum hopping in the first slice) along the Mall by the nation's capitol. The narrator reveals an almost *Harold and Maude*-like obsession for museums. And the fragments, to some extent, are pulled together in the novel's final thrust of film scenario and story narratives. As structure, this opera succeeds. Somewhere, Mies van der Rohe is applauding. The structure of the novel is architectural, and Fleming builds a postmodern sandwich that even Dagwood could admire. [Eckhard Gerdes]

Stewart Home. *69 Things to Do with a Dead Princess.* Canongate, 2003. 182 pp. Paper: $13.00.

Literary provocateur Stewart Home marries the pulp pornography of his previous skinhead novels with fundamentally more "highbrow" attributes—literary criticism, political theory, and other avenues of philosophical discourse—to produce the style he describes affectedly as "proletarian postmodernism." In this latest work Home has muted his characteristic prankster plagiarism, choosing instead to cue his inspiration more conventionally by way of literary influence. Ann Quin is the most evident influence guiding *69 Things,* as made apparent in an opening line that recalls Quin's opening to *Berg* and made blatant when narrator Anna Noon describes how her prosaic inspiration should avoid certain authors and "detour instead towards Ann Quin." When Anna, a twenty-year-old university student in Aberdeen, Scotland, meets Alan, a book-obsessed older man, the two quickly hit it off. It is from here that the main structural pattern of the book is established: scholarly discourse—from diatribes on Fromm's misconceptions about mechanization to acclamations of Trocchi's literary hoaxes—followed by a whole lot of fucking. Home is clearly having fun drawing parallels between the masturbatory self-importance of theoretical discourse and the masturbatory voyeurism of reading detailed accounts of sexual intercourse. One book that Alan is obsessed with is "69 Things to Do with a Dead Princess," in which author K. L. Callan claims to have taken the body of Princess Diana on a tour of sixty-nine of Aberdeenshire's ancient stone circles. Attempting to test the plausibility of Callan's claim, Alan straps a weighted-down ventriloquist's dummy (another nod to Quin) to his back and sets out with Anna to replicate the tour. While this stone-circle expedition provides some amusing psychogeographical "facts" and adds an interesting historical framework to the discourse/sex construct, the deliberate repetitiveness could have easily grown tedious. Fortunately, Home never lets that happen—as the repetition begins to exhaust itself, the narrative fractures, and the main characters' identities become as inverted as the numerals in the book's title. With *69 Things* Stewart Home has proven that he's a skilled author capable of much more than pulp appropriations. [Cory Weber]

Curt Leviant. *"Ladies and Gentlemen, the Original Music of the Hebrew Alphabet" and "Weekend in Mustara."* Univ. of Wisconsin Press, 2002. 156 pp. $21.95.

In these two novellas, two American Jewish scholars set out for foreign lands to find letters and artifacts from the dead that will advance their academic careers. The places they travel to, both foreign and mythical, lead them not to what they sought but to something of more value, "the undiscovered countries of the self," particularly their Jewish selves. Their quest, in the tradition of other recent novels about scholar-adventurers, leads to tastes of the scholarly fruit of the tree of knowledge, a fruit that turns to ashes. They are led to questions: "Collecting knowledge and manuscripts and pitchers and coins; whom did this all benefit? Had any of this saved one human being from sorrow?" What joins the stories is the theme of "possession." Though they overtly describe the waiting and struggle for possession of academic artifacts that will yield knowledge (and tenure!), the stories are not just about tepid academics in search of dead letters but about poets and mystics and the nature of desire. The energy and passion of this desire flashes in Leviant's scintillating language and imagery that emerges from his knowledge of Jewish culture and literature. To foreground the two kinds of knowledge that the scholars discover—the conventional and the hidden—Leviant also uses surrealist techniques, juxtaposing reality and dream, as well as using modernist wordplay and punning (also a part of the Hebrew tradition). Writing, like music, is about "the shaping of the invisible," and like any fine writer, Leviant provides us with things to see. His painterly effects and surrealistic scenes lift poetic, dreamlike, and mad moments out of the "cotton-wool" of ordinary life. And yet these stories have a strong sense of place, the gathering place for Leviant's strong emotions about the history of the Jews. *Ladies and Gentleman* takes place in Budapest, "a convention of the mad: war survivors, survivors of attics, cellars, forests, sewers, survivors of death camps . . . survivors of fascism, nazism, communism." In *Weekend* the island of Mustara, Italy, is presented as a place where Moorish, Christian, and Jewish cultures blend, a place that the Ashkenzai Jews fled to from central Europe to form a *kehillah* (community) that has survived Nazism and totalitarianism. What the protagonist, Leviant, finds in Mustara is his double, his name inscribed into the Book of the Dead in the Jewish Museum. In this book he also discovers the name of Ferdinand Friedman, the Holocaust survivor of the first story. It is then that he links to his past and "hears" the unbearable, silent melody of the Hebrew alphabet. [Patricia Laurence]

Gabriel Josipovici. *Goldberg: Variations.* Carcanet, 2002. 180 pp. Paper: £9.95.

Is a work of art supposed to calm you down or wake you up? Does literature function best when it solves problems or leaves readers with philosophical quandaries? These questions appear to be at the center of Josipovici's book, but as a backdrop to the experiments with narrative that take place and are illuminated only in the conclusion to a storytelling roller coaster. In the first chapter of the novel (and whether or not this is a novel is a relevant question too), writer Samuel Goldberg takes a job with aristocrat Tobias Westfield; his employment consists of writing during the day and reading that day's writing to Westfield through the night. Apparently, Westfield cannot sleep; his mind races, and he needs some type of (supposed) linear narrative to lull him. The reader expects, then, thirty-two (à la Bach) variations from Goldberg; however, on the first day, Goldberg finds that all he can write is a letter to his wife. The twenty-nine (!) chapters that follow are not (as might be predicted) further "variations" but disconnected stories about a variety of topics. Right about the middle of the book, a character named Gerald appears, plagued by writer's block affecting his novel about Westfield and Goldberg. Ah ha! But no: his story progresses past the block due to his examination of Paul Klee's painting *Wandering Artist*. When the "narrator" (who at that point is not Goldberg or Gerald) finds that the German meaning of "wandering artist" is that of a public and nomadic performer, like an actor or a con-man, the novel-long manipulation of "story" is understood. A little. This is a tough book, but immensely intriguing if you can appreciate the puzzle and relax about some of the frustratingly unrelated chapters. Along with pondering the questions that Josipovici poses about literature, the reader is forced to come to terms with the fact that he or she is, in fact, an individual reading a book, and examining what that responsibility might entail. [Amy Havel]

Ludwig Harig. *The Trip to Bordeaux*. Trans. Susan Bernofsky. Burning Deck, 2003. 103 pp. Paper: $10.00.

While German writer Ludwig Harig has earned a strong reputation in Europe over the last four decades, it's only now that his inventive work is being translated into English. The latest volume in Burning Deck's "Dichten =" German literature series, Harig's marvelous novel *The Trip to Bordeaux* plays host to all sorts of eccentric and intriguing characters as they embark on a two-week vacation in southern France. Harig deploys short, fast-paced chapters in a number of styles, ranging from Steinian descriptions of various household chairs; to Vladimir-and-Estragonesque Socratic dialogues on the taste of a fine wine or the profit of wealth; to depicting a family's easily defeated attempt to "rouse" themselves out of their house with Seussian absurdity; to surrealistic gunfights at a citadel, which result in the mummy of a general appearing only to get shot—again, the book provides a carnival of possibilities that would certainly make Raymond Queneau, Russell Edson, or Lewis Carroll smile. M. de Montaigne, possibly two characters, possibly not, offers reflective missives in the form of prose poems that ask questions like "What is there to say about childbirth and kidneys?" or cautions readers that "Everything published by contemporary writers, especially young ones, shall be ripped to shreds." Merely getting the characters to and from Bordeaux in a car is to witness a stylistic bridge from Samuel Beckett to David Foster Wallace. Harig even slips in a hilarious narrative poem about turtledoves and dung beetles. The formal acrobatics are as diverse as the characters themselves and make for a book that is as unabashed as a child in a sandbox yet as contemplative as, well, a German philosopher. The result is both generously intelligent and an absolute delight to read, and one can hope only that more of Harig's work appears in English. [Mark Tardi]

Pedro de Jesús. *Frigid Tales*. Trans. Dick Cluster. City Lights, 2002. 105 pp. Paper: $11.95.

Despite the title, there is nothing frigid about these tales—what appears to be coldness is all on the surface. True, the characters of these six interrelated stories are often uncomfortable with their sexuality and sometimes believe they would be happier if they weren't so horny all the time, and true, too, Pedro de Jesús makes use of the cerebral and distancing forms of postmodern fiction, although he cannot resist descending into a realism he has been taught to disparage—in short, the stories are the product of a young man who believes that his libido is getting in the way of his art but nevertheless cannot hide his old-fashioned passion for love stories. De Jesús seems to have taken Freud at his word that there are always at least four people having sex at any time. Usually in his stories there seem to be even more, since the characters keep changing their sex and their sexual orientation. In "Images, Questions Re: Beautiful Dead Woman" he gives the characters numbers, as if we couldn't tell them apart without a scorecard. In fact, even with the numbers I couldn't tell them apart. No matter. In one's twenties all heartbreaks are the same—painful, narcissistic, and self-destructive. Ironically, the volume rests on de Jesús's most traditional stories: "The Portrait" and the campily titled "How to Act in 1830," his homage to Stendhal. It is a story worthy of Stendhal in its passion, playfulness, and social and psychological subtlety. The story is so wonderfully perverse that it makes me wonder how de Jesús continues to work in Cuba and what might happen to him as an artist in the post-Castro world. [David Bergman]

George Singleton. *The Half-Mammals of Dixie*. Algonquin, 2002. 287 pages. $22.95.

In his second collection, George Singleton proves that southern humorists can definitely strike more than one note. Like his northern counterpart, George Saunders, Singleton manages both to write stories that make us laugh and to construct characters and situations that gesture toward the deeper and often disturbing undercurrents of existence. Singleton seems to realize that comedy can have an even greater resonance if there is the potential for misfortune, even tragedy. In the lead story, "Show-and-Tell," a young boy spins an amusing yarn even as we catch glimpses of his father's loneliness and longing through the narrator's third-grade consciousness. A similar strategy is employed in the collection's funniest piece, the wonderfully titled "This Itches, Y'all," a story about the decline of a young man's social standing after he plays the lead role in a head-lice documentary. But such humor takes place against the backdrop of social change, as the "entire nation transform[s] itself" at the end of the 1960s. Singleton's brilliance lies in the contrast of the specific and the general, and what seems to result is the kind of universality that Tolstoy famously argued for. At the same time, there is a Swiftian quality to the work, a kind of social satire working to correct the folly of our age. In the final story, "Richard Petty Accepts National Book Award," the NASCAR driver scrolls through the litany of objects that helped him accomplish his feat, among them LaserJet Laser Paper, Ball Roller Grip pens, the Intel Pentium III, and Jack Daniel's whiskey. Singleton's humor is biting, and yet we feel we are in the hands of a writer who forces us to laugh in the face of circumstances that, without the lens of a careful and precise art, would evoke only tears. [Aaron Gwyn]

Elisabeth Sheffield. *Gone*. FC2, 2003. 268 pp. Paper: $13.95.

Stella Vanderzee is lost and almost alone in upper New York State. She's looking for a painting, a Winslow Homer, an inheritance from her grandfather that will help her escape the series of dead-end jobs and relationships she is locked in. Interspersed with Stella's drink-and-drug-fueled monologues are letters from her Aunt Judith—usually to people Judith knew at best peripherally. The letters, which are given to Stella, who almost immediately loses them, are the best part of the book. Judith's voice is entirely convincing: educated, condescending, and cutting, and filled with putdowns, unverifiable claims, and lightly veiled insults. Judith, however, cannot stop herself from inserting her own story of how she and Stella's mother, an artist, now dead, grew up together and where, how, and why they separated. Sheffield explores this loss from both sides. Stella's faulty memory and hazy perceptions and Judith's unsent letters provide alternating and diverging viewpoints of Stella's mother and her life. There's more here than just a comparison of memories—this is no upstate *Rashomon*-lite. Sheffield's loser protagonist—searching for an inheritance that was gone before she arrived, losing her boyfriend, her job, her aunt's letters, even her hotel room—is the archetypal lost person searching for home. Even if it's only the idea of home, since the actuality is long gone. Stella has repudiated what remains of her family, but in need and desperation, she returns, only to find that her family is truly gone. Where is reliability? How can we go forward without looking back? And we haven't even explored the sexual peccadilloes yet. [Gavin Grant]

Ignacio Padilla. *Shadow without a Name*. Trans. Peter Bush and Anne McLean. Farrar, Straus & Giroux, 2003. 192 pp. $22.00.

Padilla's first novel to be translated into English starts off simply enough: pointsman Viktor Kretzschmar is being charged with causing a terrible train crash. His motives for this crime open the door into the mystery fueling the plot of this book, for as his son discovers, Kretzschmar was actually born as Thadeus Dreyer but won the name—and safety—in a chess game on a train that was to take him to the front, fighting for the German army in World War I. As it turns out, the stand-in Dreyer doesn't die in the war, instead becoming a major figure in Hitler's regime, responsible for creating a dangerous game of doubles involving the highest officers of the Party. In a twist straight out of a thriller, this Dreyer isn't the same person from the train, a fact that is somewhat irrelevant, as the name of Dreyer continues on through history, assuming a certain inevitable force along the way.

Putting aside the intrigues of the plot, the most interesting aspect of this novel is its structural form. A member of the Crack group, Padilla tells his story through four stand-alone yet interwoven sections, each narrated by a different character at a different time and place. These monologues are restricted by the character's point of view, presenting the reader with all the clues to the puzzle but no omniscient narrator to put it all together. So only the reader can figure out that Kretzschmar's son is trying to exact his revenge against a different Dreyer, and by paying attention to the seemingly extraneous dates and places where each section was written the reader can uncover the final clues to the novel's game. Aptly translated by Peter Bush and Anne McLean, this is an ambitious book executed with such style and ease to establish Padilla as a writer to watch for years to come. [Chad W. Post]

Ludmila Ulitskaya. *Medea and Her Children.* Trans. Arch Tait. Schocken, 2002. 320 pp. $24.00.

Ludmila Ulitskaya's Medea resembles the tragic villainess in name only. We meet this childless, introverted, fiercely independent, sweetly redoubtable Medea inhabiting an almost magical landscape in which time and memory jostle for attention in seasonal rhythms, stirred by bands of relatives and friends arriving in regular waves at her bucolic Crimean home each spring. Yet these often errant "children" bring affairs that cross her own tangled path in ways both heartfelt and disenchanting. Now past the median of life in what for centuries was a Greek enclave, then Tatar country, her husband dead, an extended family strewn over central Asia, Medea greets the season of awakening love, which serves as backdrop for events unfolding forward and backward in her life. Her husband, a Jewish dentist and one-time communist revolutionary, flits through her mind, as does her childhood friend Elena, now living far away in Tashkent. But after discovering an old letter unearthing a shocking secret, Medea abruptly undertakes the arduous journey to see this one person with whom she can share such confidences. Meanwhile, Medea's sister's youngest daughter, Masha, a poet, and another niece, Nike, are both seeing Valerii Butonov, who appears early on touted as a man of immense value but whose sexual attraction later supplants Masha's appetite for anything or anyone else. When she learns that Nike also sleeps with Butonov, Masha enters a hallucinatory realm of her own as her poetic faculty explodes in incandescent but pathetic beauty, charting an inner journey peculiarly complementing Medea's outward trek to Tashkent. Medea's old-fashioned romantic world gives way to Masha's more contemporary disorientation as the rhythms of life mount to fever pitch before a dying fall. Still, in Ulitskaya's beatific vision, while love and time take their toll, Medea's spirit knows and accepts all, much like Mother Nature herself. [Michael Pinker]

George Garrett. *Southern Excursions: Views on Southern Letters in My Time.* Ed. James Conrad McKinley. Louisiana State Univ. Press, 2003. 315 pp. $35.00.

Although the "excursions" in this surprising collection vary in length and form—essays, book reviews, tributes, introductions, dialogues—they are all gracefully written. They demonstrate that even in this solemn (absurd?) time of theory, there are critics whose written voice is always present. Garrett's words are *his*—they are not as cranky or moralistic or Jamesian as those of Winters, of Blackmur, of Leavis. Garrett recognizes that southern literature is one of the easy categories used to place writers who are, in some ways, remarkably different. He ranges widely, from Truman Capote to Madison Jones to David Madden to James Dickey to his own fiction. Who exactly is a "southern" writer? Garrett understands that many "southern" writers, especially after World War II, inevitably moved to other regions. Thus the notion of place is insufficient to categorize such works as *The Confessions of Nat Turner* or *Death of the Fox.* Garrett writes: "Sometimes imaginary history, and at its heart an imaginary sense of place, not only haunts our lives with ghostly voices and echoes but is, finally, stronger, even more accurate that the cut, shuffled, and dealt world of hard facts." I am pleased to see Garrett, a master of "southern" letters, a founder of the fellowship of "southern" writers, rebel against the very category in which he is usually placed. And he continually surprises me when he proclaims *In Cold Blood* a work of art, or condemns many of the omissions in the *Encyclopedia of Southern Culture,* or defends, in a conversation with George Core, the virtues of the *Hudson Review* (and other quarterlies). It is impossible to review this hefty collection of excursions; I can say that at times Garrett says enough in one sentence to make most other writers envious. Garrett defies convention, constructs real arguments, and remains a true ghostly presence in the "south." Therefore, I honor his excursions; he makes me watch my strides; he points out things I hadn't seen; and he makes me rethink my rash assumptions. [Irving Malin]

———————

Brian Littlefair. *Desert Burial.* Holt, 2002. 254 pp. $25.00.

Although a first novel, Brian Littlefair's *Desert Burial* reads like the work of a mature novelist—intriguing, carefully crafted, and intellectually engaging. Despite imagining a future of relative world peace, *Desert Burial* is a timely exploration of geopolitical maneuvering and old-style colonial manipulation. Set in the west African nation of Mali, the novel centers on Ty Campbell, an American geologist charting subterranean water tables. His placid routine is interrupted when an aid worker leads refugees into Campbell's region. Soon an enigmatic figure named Bud van Sickle, CEO of Timbuktu Earthware, appears, offering food and medicine to the homeless and a job for Campbell full of intrigue, power, and wealth. Campbell must become a corporate spy and inform on a series of competing plans to dump nuclear waste: Timbuktu Earthware's bid proposes burial in the Sahara. The novel offers a skillful interrogation of the politics of colonialism. Indeed, there is the process of exploitation as the colonizer purports to know what is best for the colonized, and van Sickle's methods amount to a primer on colonial disingenuousness. The processes of Othering and dispossessing the native population are clearly evident when what is presented as a boon to economic prosperity becomes an impediment to self-determination and fair government. Timbuktu Earthware is a multinational maze of holding companies that ultimately, as one character reveals, act as a proxy for United States interests. What van Sickle proudly announces as the New World Order amounts to the Old World Order, only in more technological dress. Despite a melodramatic love interest and a too-pat conclusion to what is an otherwise intricate plot, Littlefair writes with remarkable verbal facility and a keen eye for small, revealing details. It is surprising to learn that his background is in international finance, yet that background has inspired an audacious narrative. [David W. Madden]

Juan Tovar. *Creature of a Day*. Trans. Leland H. Chambers. McPherson, 2002. 160 pp. $20.00.

Creature of a Day is Mexican novelist Juan Tovar's first book to be translated into English. This edition also contains material that is not yet available in the original Spanish. Tovar's previous work consists of four novels, six collections of stories, and two dozen plays. It is not surprising, then, that this work combines elements of all the above. The result, a novel in the loosest sense, reexamines the genre and approaches it as a fluid interaction of several short-story strands. On the one hand, the novel has a modern frame-tale narrative that is peopled with characters borrowed loosely from Grimm. On the other, it is a pastoral drama scripted with a lyrical quality that owes much to Chaucer and the medieval poets. It subscribes to multiple theologies in its exploration of the rites of pagan and Christian ideologies. It is equally concerned with both universal mythologies and those found within the constructs of the world Tovar creates. The internal world of the novel is dominated by the labyrinthine strands of the multiple themes. In this way it has been compared to Borges but lacks his sense of structure, purpose, and intellectual energy. This, combined with the heavy rhetoric Tovar employs, allows the narrative to become sluggish in places. The novel's exploration of consciousness and belief in relation to the legends Tovar creates and manipulates contrasts with his explicit reminders that we are being told a tale. This metafictional quality has the alienating effect of a character aside to an audience, thus cleverly reinforcing the notion that what we are dealing with here is not, in fact, prose after all. Whether ballad or drama, Tovar successfully re-creates a pilgrimage in words. His band of pilgrims highlight the freedoms that lie in migration but also, conversely, the need for a foundation in belief. [Sarah McClellan]

Zoran Živković. *The Writer*. Trans. Alice Copple-Tosic. Polaris/Ministry of Whimsy, 2002. 81 pp. Paper: $8.00.

Živković is a Serbian writer whose stories often run in the tradition of Calvino/Borges-style fantasy—i.e., he'd be illustrated by the Brothers Quay, not Hildebrandt—but, like Calvino and Borges, he just as often presents nifty little metafictive exempla, as in 1998's *The Writer*. This compact novella offers a brisk examination of authorship and ontology, somehow managing to be really funny in the process. An unnamed narrator, suffering from writer's block, intends to write the final chapter of his book, which began as a novel but has morphed into a story collection. As if stalling, he instead discusses other matters, eventually mentioning a pretentious would-be novelist friend, one with a predilection for Freudian analysis. This novelist has written the narrator into his fiction with the stipulation that the narrator not recognize the character based on himself. When antagonism builds between the two, the narrator attacks the novelist's pretenses, whereupon the novelist attempts an analysis of the narrator; each is struggling to control—to write—the other. The narrator's dream sequence late in the story seems to offer an interpretation of the novel we've been reading, though naturally the sequence is itself open to the reader's interpretation; author and reader aren't so much braided as dreadlocked. Ultimately, we're not sure who the book's title refers to: we could be reading the novelist's work or the narrator's or someone else's entirely (and an ingenious textual feature serves to further complicate everything). While William Gass famously wrote that "one thing [the death of the author] cannot mean is that *no one did it*," Živković suggests that the complex relationship between writer and reader can indeed get knotty to the point that a novel might as well have literally *no one* as its author. [Tim Feeney]

Christian Gailly. *An Evening at the Club*. Trans. Susan Fairfield. Other Press, 2003. 133pp. $22.00.

An enigmatic painter-narrator tells the story of his friend, a middle-aged former jazz musician and alcoholic who, one night, starts drinking and playing again after ten years of abstinence from both. The plot is rather clichéd, but it is interesting to see how Gailly, taking up the age-old reflection on the sister arts, tries to create a verbal version of jazz. Gailly uses three methods to build the unique rhythm that, I believe, holds his book together. First, his prose is terse (short verbless sentences, interjections, etc.) and anaphoric, unfolding in elaborate parallels, generating subtle contrasts and, hence, rhythm: "His glasses weren't on his nose. Normal. He always takes them off to go to bed. His watch wasn't on his wrist. Not normal. He never takes it off to go to bed. What did I do with it?" The shift from the third to the first person points to the second direction in which Gailly works, juxtaposing direct, indirect, and free indirect speech. In this manner he creates another type of interval, smooth here, more strongly perceptible there, as in the following example: "She was telling me how once she got back home: Once I got back home, she said." The third aspect of rhythm in *A Night at the Club* is the contrastive use of tenses, as in the liminary break between the narrator's present-tense introduction to his fiction and its second beginning, in the past. Although Gailly's play with tenses is not always translatable (the English preterite corresponds to two different past tenses in French, which Gailly systematically contrasts), on the whole, the vivid presence and purely rhythmic suspense characteristic of Gailly's prose are well conveyed in the English translation. [Clarissa Behar]

Robert Phillips. *News about People You Know*. Texas Review Press, 2002. 175 pp. Paper: $18.95.

"News about people we know": to illuminate the already exposed. To shed light upon areas where there is no mystery is a far more imposing task than merely shedding light upon mystery. In Phillips's twice-told realism, no single word is innocent; there is the possibility with each one that it is freighted with meaning. Phillips's prose is utterly colloquial, contemporary, so you could step into it off the street, yet obeys the Keatsian injunction to load every rift with ore. An editor asked to cut even a few words from one of the stories in this book would be faced with a near-impossible task, as all but a few are essential. Referential in manner, but not so in shape, these stories veer between urban, rural, and European settings, using human relationships as glyphs. Some stories are set on the Delmarva Peninsula, a terrain Phillips wrestles, albeit only temporarily, away from John Barth. A man named Fallick (we are supposed to laugh not just at the pun itself but its conscious obviousness) is the *raisonneur* of several of the stories, chronicling couplings and betrayals, "visions and revisions" in the Eliotic sense. "Smokey Mary's," the High Anglican church of St. Mary the Virgin around Times Square, emerges as the strangely moving spiritual center of one of the stories—only to be followed up by Marilyn Monroe serving the same function in the next, in a kind of religious anticlimax. Phillips's narratives are antishort stories, yielding not epiphanies but discontinuous promptings. The imperative of Phillips's prose is to let narrative unfold, not seal it off—to let it *be* narrative: garrulous, indefatigable, unstinted by formal or doctrinal restraints. [Nicholas Birns]

Lewis Robinson. *Officer Friendly and Other Stories*. HarperCollins, 2003. 228 pp. $23.95.

Lewis Robinson's first collection is outstanding. These eleven stories reveal, by way of impeccable prose, the intricate world of rural Port Allison, Maine. In "The Diver" Peter, a restaurant owner from Portland, swims to shore after fouling his yacht's propeller. In a bar Peter finds a diver who agrees to help him only after mocking Peter for both fouling the prop and having to swim ashore. Yet the story's tension becomes fully realized only when Peter pauses to consider himself from the diver's perspective: "wearing a bright blue and yellow swimming suit, getting his propeller wound up in lines. A yachting jackass." In this story and throughout the collection Robinson achieves poignant depictions of the gravity and the grandeur of the human condition. In "Cuxabexis, Cuxabexis" Eleanor, a pregnant med-school student, travels with her boyfriend, Bill, to an island off Port Allison where he grew up. They stay with Bill's aunt, Fran, who hopes that Bill and Eleanor will get married and return to the island. Though Eleanor initially wants to keep her pregnancy secret, she abruptly tells Fran the morning after they arrive. For Eleanor, as an expectant mother, the island simply feels right, particularly as she explores her impending motherhood: "The baby is hers. She already loves it so much she could eat it—this is something else which Bill wouldn't understand. *I don't mean that literally*, she'd have to say." As a storyteller, one of Robinson's great strengths rests in his ability to realize the edginess inherent within situations, an edginess quite like what Mary Gaitskill achieves throughout *Bad Behavior*. *Officer Friendly* does not idealize Port Allison; life is simply lived in all of its uncertain complexity. Lewis Robinson is to be congratulated for his impressive and fully realized first collection. [Alan Tinkler]

Mark Dunn. *Ella Minnow Pea: A Novel in Letters*. Anchor, 2002. 208 pp. Paper: $12.00.

This odd, strangely moving novel, originally published in 2001 by Random House, teases us at first. The title, a girl's name, suggests a series of letters: *l, m, n, o, p*. The subtitle tells us that it is "a novel in letters." Aren't all novels written in letters? Or is this an epistolary novel like *Clarissa* or Barth's *LETTERS*? Next we are given some definitions: *epistolary, lipogram, Nollop,* and *pangram*. Nollop is said to be a nation "21 miles southeast of Charleston"; it "elevates language to a national art form." The Nollop nation honors "Nevin Nollop, the author of the popular pangram sentence: *'The quick brown fox jumped over the lazy dog.'* " The first letter written by Ella to her cousin Tassie introduces the fact that "one of the tiles from the top of the cenotaph at the town center came loose and fell to the ground." This descent is a significant event, interpreted by the governing council to mean that the letter, *z*, cannot be used in communication. Of course, Ella writes that *z* is usually insignificant; written communication doesn't exploit or employ it very much. But as the letters continue to fall, the very exchange of information becomes frightening: *What if each vowel falls?* The entire culture will fade; apocalypse will come. As the novel progresses, letter-writers continue to communicate, using evasive means. But the letters become less and less coherent. Danger lurks everywhere; paranoia reigns. We slowly conclude that without language, without culture—the two are inextricably bound—existence itself is at stake. And we forget that the novel is only playful. Soon we see that a void, a blankness, awaits us. I predict that Dunn will write more dazzling novels that remind of us of Perec and Mathews and Roussel and Abish. [Irving Malin]

Mark Swartz. *Instant Karma*. City Lights, 2002. 136 pp. Paper: $11.95.

Among the many ailments suffered by David Felsenstein, the narrator of Mark Swartz's *Instant Karma*, are paranoia, hallucinatory tinnitus, and a "directional deficiency" for which he wears a magnet taped to the top of his head. The novel is structured in short, tightly constructed journal entries in which we follow Felsenstein and his plans to blow up the Harold Washington branch of the Chicago Public Library. As a self-proclaimed anarchist, Felsenstein sees his plans to destroy the library as a kind of dadaist master-piece, making terrorism an artistic act once he frees it from the chains of politics and purpose. He starts small, burning American flags à la Jimi Hendrix torching the Star Spangled Banner at Woodstock before literally setting the flames to his own instrument at Monterey. And indeed, the li-brary is Felsenstein's instrument, his medium. He haunts the shelves, pin-ing after the librarian at the main desk and recording in his notebooks the gems he finds from his obsessive and eclectic reading. To these tidbits he adds his own thoughts on subjects from art and anarchy to bells and Bud-dhism, as well as ephemera such as notes on the movie *1941*, or as Felsenstein calls it, "Spielberg's other World War II farce." The secret to suc-cessfully rendered unreliable narrators is not that we are fooled by them but that we want to believe them. Such is the case with Swartz's Felsenstein. *Instant Karma* is a smart and funny book, and what emerges from its pages is a worldview that is at times absurd, at times insightful, and at its best a beautiful blur between the two. [T. J. Gerlach]

Carter Scholz. *The Amount to Carry*. Picador, 2003. 208 pp. $23.00.

Carter Scholz's *The Amount to Carry* contains twelve inventive stories that demonstrate the range and the limits of intelligence, as Scholz grounds his stories in math, science, and nature, with references as well to mythology, literature, and philosophy. The collection is epic in ambition and takes the reader from space stations and top-secret think tanks to boardinghouses, a country commune, sanitariums, artist studios, ancient caves, Kubla Khan's China, Mengele's South America, and Kafka's Prague, while exploring lay-ers of thought and reality. Yet some stories have a tedious, cold abstractness, focusing on only one or two extremely alienated characters, unbelievable situations, and obscure theories. Scholz also utilizes almost archaic En-glish words such as "charnelhouse," as well as lines from various lan-guages—Latin, Dutch, Greek, German—that will keep some readers scrambling for several dictionaries. It is startling to see such sentences as the one that tells of a character's use of an "ink compounded of his own blood and excrement" to write with a sharp tool on "his own body," which would seem to promise infection, a short-lived medical calamity—and ex-emplify a surprisingly faulty dramatic reach. However, very strong stories are here, especially the ones that strategically begin and close the collec-tion, among them "The Eve of the Last Apollo," about an astronaut, his shallow public career, his unhappy marriage, and his wife's leaving him for a commune's leader; "Blumfeld, an Elderly Bachelor," on the self-destructive late-life sexual awakening of an accountant; and "Mengele's Jew," which finds the Nazi war criminal imagining one last Jewish cage, a vision that calls forth moral judgment. (The last story involves Kafka, Wallace Stevens, and Charles Ives, and to say more would ruin a charming speculation.) Scholz's admirable ambition seems to be to remap known and unknown worlds. [Daniel Garrett]

Italo Calvino. *Hermit in Paris: Autobiographical Writings.* Trans. Martin McLaughlin. Pantheon, 2003. 255 pp. $23.00.

Known for fanciful narrative experiments like *Invisible Cities* and *If on a winter's night a traveler,* Italo Calvino is revealed in a less whimsical light in *Hermit in Paris,* a collection of autobiographical works spanning three decades and published here for the first time in English. Aspiring writers may despair of learning the secret behind the author's spare yet richly expressive prose style. Apparently, so did Calvino: in an interview published in 1985, he observes, "Every time I start writing something, it requires an effort of will, because I know that what awaits me is the labour and dissatisfaction of trying and trying again, correcting, rewriting." Other pieces deal with the author's youth, growing up with freethinker scientist parents at a time when fascism held sway in Italy. Calvino—who fought as part of the Italian resistance during the Second World War—eventually joined the Communist Party, only to have his ideals betrayed, first by Stalin, then by Khrushchev. After resigning from the party in 1957, Calvino expressed frustration with his dual commitments in a 1978 interview: "It is no accident that I spent many years of my life banging my head against a brick wall, trying to square the circle that was involved in living the life of literature and Communism at the same time." For American readers, the true centerpiece of this collection is not the title essay—a meditation on writing and place—but rather Calvino's American diary of 1959-60, when the author was visiting on a Ford Foundation scholarship. His wry and often withering observations take in everything from beatnik culture to the Cold War patriotism of Texas. The pieces in this collection present a portrait of the author as an ambivalent man, struggling to engage with the world in all its complacency and contradictions. [Pedro Ponce]

Carole Maso. *Beauty Is Convulsive: The Passion of Frida Kahlo.* Counterpoint, 2003. 170 pp. $24.00.

Amid the recent resurgence of interest in Frida Kahlo, Carole Maso's *Beauty Is Convulsive* offers an intimate tribute to the life and art of the Mexican painter. Maimed in a bus accident as a teenager, Kahlo began painting self-portraits during her lengthy convalescence. In her twenties she became a member of the Communist Party and married the famous muralist Diego Rivera; although they were fervently in love with one another, infidelity, illness, and infertility injured their lifelong relationship. *Beauty Is Convulsive* begins with the pain of Frida Kahlo, depicting the artist as a "misshapen angel," dreaming of "the way beauty keeps coming—the way color vibrates—convulsive—drawn / to the swirling / drawn / to the light." Through this series of devotional prose poems, Maso imagines a scintillating dialogue between two artists—Kahlo and herself—engaged in the process of "Arranging and rearranging. Outlining the shape of a woman and gently filling her in." Maso celebrates the artist's intense need to paint that emerges from "the spontaneous impulse of . . . feeling" and lovingly re-creates the physical eroticism of Kahlo's creative process. Yet while Maso's devotions express themselves in the voices of Kahlo's letters and lovers, her doctors and her critics, the radiant, fragmentary vision of Kahlo that Maso encounters upon this "elaborate stage" of identity is inherently personal. Maso repeatedly cites Rivera's description of Kahlo's art as "ascetic and tender, hard as steel and fire and delicate as a butterfly's wing, adorable as a beautiful smile and profound and cruel as life's bitterness." Without a doubt, one might apply these same words to Maso's precise and poetic prose, which brims with emotion, imagination, intelligence, and beauty. [Trey Strecker]

Rosmarie Waldrop. *Lavish Absence: Recalling and Rereading Edmond Jabès.* Foreword Richard Stamelman. Wesleyan Univ. Press, 2002. 205 pp. Paper: $17.95.

"Edmond Jabès does not write novels," Rosmarie Waldrop tells us. "Nor poems for that matter. He claims to write in a new genre, 'the book.' " Indeed, one of the things that makes Jabès an important literary figure is the way in which he seems to slip between genres: Jabès was writing hybrid genres well before the term was in vogue and does so in a way that seems at once necessary and aesthetically considered. In *Lavish Absence* Rosmarie Waldrop offers a critical book that is intergeneric as well—part commentary, part memoir, liberally sprinkled with Jabès's own words and writing—and which goes a long way toward revealing Jabès. Having translated Jabès's work into English for thirty years, Waldrop is in perhaps a unique position to do so. In addition to incisive analyses of particular notions in Jabès's work and intimate portraits of Jabès himself, Waldrop discusses the difficulties of translating a writer who is elliptical and interested in wordplay, offering examples of some of the difficulties a translator faces trying to render Jabès's economical and sparse, yet surprisingly double-voiced, French into an equally evocative English. "Readers who read Edmond Jabès in the English do not read Edmond Jabès," she indicates. "They do not read Rosmarie Waldrop either, but our dialogue and collaboration." Yet in both English and French, Jabès's meditations on authorship, nothingness, language, and on a God he doesn't believe in but that stands in for something else he can't quite pin down, remain highly original and quite moving. A wonderful introduction to both Jabès's work and Jabès the man, *Lavish Absence* is a provocative entry into Jabès's evocative world. [Brian Evenson]

Joseph Dewey, Steven G. Kellman, and Irving Malin, eds. *UnderWords: Perspectives on Don DeLillo's "Underworld."* Univ. of Delaware Press, 2002. 219 pp. $39.50.

The names of the editors suggest the background and experience that went into the compilation of this collection of critical essays and bibliographical information (reviews and articles to 2000 inclusive). Reflecting on the complexity of *Underworld,* Dewey notes that "the function of such a collection is to extend the round, to keep alive texts that promise to become defining works of their cultural moment." The essays might be divided into three categories: examinations of DeLillo's narrative methodology; the place of *Underworld* in relation to earlier masters, e.g., Eliot and Fitzgerald; and DeLillo's place in relation to his contemporaries, especially, of course, Thomas Pynchon. David Yetter examines the filmic characteristics of point of view in its shifting location and focus, "a technique that allows the reader to detect the whispers of the individual while simultaneously absorbing the clamor of the crowd." My own view, looking at the opening of this novel and of *Mao II* most notably, sees DeLillo as the Michael Cimino (*The Deer Hunter, Heaven's Gate*) of prose fiction, a genius at crowd scenes. Several of the essays turn to DeLillo's own commentary, "The Power of History," as a foundation: in "Sin and Atonement" Robert McMinn uses it in developing his sense of "how the sacred shades into the profane," one of both DeLillo and Pynchon's major interests. Cold War history, a postmodern view of history itself, shows up in Kathleen Fitzpatrick's use of J. H. Hexter's 1968 essay "The Rhetoric of History." Fitzpatrick notes, in regard to the novel, that "traces of the past . . . conceal as much as they reveal about the workings of history." All in all, these help to make for an interesting and helpful elaboration of DeLillo's text; whether necessary to "keep alive" *this* text, one doubts. Finally, while providing a valuable "Works Cited" section, this book, a scholarly collection, should have foot- or more specific endnotes. [Richard J. Murphy]

Nick Montfort and William Gillespie. *2002: A Palindrome Story in 2002 Words.* Illus. Shelley Jackson. Spineless, 2002. 24 pp. Paper: $16.00.

Frequent readers of *RCF* are more likely than most connoisseurs of contemporary fiction to be titillated by Oulipian fiction. The print arrival of *2002: A Palindrome Story* serves proof that the efforts of the Oulipo's progenitors have translated loud and clear to a new generation of experimentalists. Hallmark examples of Oulipian writing (which explores the nature of constraint, where artists operate under rigid, formalist rules) are Georges Perec's *Las Disparitions,* an entire novel composed without the letter *e,* and Doug Nufer's *Never Again,* wherein every word is used exactly once. In *2002* Montfort and Gillespie's formalist constraints are (1) exploring the palindrome as a narrative structuring device and (2) using a predetermined word count of 2002 words. That this experiment toes the lines of its dual constraints is in itself impressive; that *2002* actually is capable of delivering traceable characters (whose names, of course, are palindromes themselves: Bob, Anna, Otto), mood, and thematics is delightfully astonishing. Equally astonishing are Shelley Jackson's incredible pen and ink illustrations on vellum, tucked between the pages in this beautiful little edition (imagine City Lights's pocket books series from the 1960s, only smaller and with an actual, functioning aesthetic . . .). This also fails to mention the book's digital residence at www.spinelessbooks.com, where websurfers will find both a virtual bookstore and an electronic library on experimental writing in the computer age. Like the best works of experimental fiction (and I'm thinking beyond the Oulipo gang here, notably to John Barth's *Letters,* the cut-up trilogy of William Burroughs, Paul Auster's novella *Ghosts,* Raymond Federman's *Double or Nothing,* Gilbert Sorrentino's *Mulligan Stew,* and Ishmael Reed's *Mumbo Jumbo*), *2002*'s genius can be found *beyond* its experiment, insofar that experimental texts can teach us not only new ways to *read,* but new ways to *create* and to *mean.* [Trevor Dodge]

Books Received

Adonis. *If Only the Sea Could Sleep: Love Poems.* Trans. Kamal Boullata, Susan Einbinder, and Mirène Ghossein. Ed. Mirène Ghossein and Kamal Boullata. Green Integer, 2003. Paper: $11.95. (P)

Agee, Jonis. *Acts of Love on Indigo Road.* Coffee House, 2003. Paper: $16.95. (F)

Aldama, Frederick Luis. *Postethnic Narrative Criticism: Magico-realism in Oscar "Zeta" Acosta, Ana Castillo, Julie Dash, Hanif Kureishi, and Salman Rushdie.* Univ. of Texas Press, 2003. $30.00. (NF)

Alexie, Sherman. *Ten Little Indians.* Grove, 2003. $24.00. (F)

Allen, Stephanie. *A Place between Stations.* Univ. of Missouri Press, 2003. Paper: $15.95. (F)

Angelou, Maya. *A Song Sung up to Heaven.* Bantam, 2003. Paper: $13.00. (NF)

Arbogast, John. *Stepping off the Wheel.* Mochi, 2003. Paper: No price given. (F)

Atwood, Margaret. *Oryx and Crake.* Nan A. Talese/Doubleday, 2003. $26.00. (F)

Avrich, Jane. *The Winter without Milk.* Houghton Mifflin, 2003. Paper: $12.00. (F)

Ayers, Bill. *Fugitive Days.* Penguin, 2003. Paper: $14.00. (NF)

Aylett, Steve. *Dummyland.* Gollancz, 2002. Paper: £9.99. (F)

——. *Only an Alligator.* Gollancz, 2002. Paper: £5.99. (F)

——. *The Velocity Gospel.* Gollancz, 2002. Paper: £6.99. (F)

Barry, Sebastian. *Annie Dunne.* Penguin, 2003. Paper: $14.00. (F)

Bello, Antoine. *The Missing Piece.* Trans. Helen Stevenson. Harcourt, 2003. Paper: $14.00. (F)

Benjamin, Walter. *Selected Writings, Volume 3: 1935-1938.* Trans. Edmund Jephcott, Howard Eiland, et al. Ed. Howard Eiland and Michael W. Jennings. Belknap Press of Harvard Univ. Press, 2002. $39.95. (NF)

Benson, Stephen. *Cycles of Influence: Fiction, Folktale, Theory.* Wayne State Univ. Press, 2003. $39.95. (NF)

Berberova, Nina. *The Accompanist.* Trans. Marian Schwartz. New Directions, 2003. Paper: $11.95. (F)

Binding, Paul. *My Cousin the Writer.* Dewi Lewis Publishing, 2003. Paper: $13.95. (F)

Bishop, K. J. *The Etched City.* Prime, 2003. Paper: $16.95. (F)

Bök, Christian, ed. *Ground Works: Avant-Garde for Thee.* Intro. Margaret Atwood. Anansi, 2003. Paper: $22.95. (F)

Boyle, T. Coraghessan. *After the Plague.* Penguin, 2003. Paper: $14.00. (F)

——. *Drop City.* Viking, 2003. $25.95. (F)

Brodsky, Michael. *Detour.* Del Sol, 2003. $29.95. (F)

Brossard, Nicole. *The Blue Books: A Book, Turn of a Pang, and French Kiss, or, A Pang's Progress.* Trans. Susanne de Lotbinière-Harwood, Larry Shouldice, and Patricia Claxton. Intro. by the author. Coach House, 2003. Paper: $19.95. (F)

——. *Museum of Bone and Water.* Trans. Robert Majzels and Erin Mouré. Anansi, 2003. Paper: $17.95. (P)

Bryan, Mike. *The Afterword.* Pantheon, 2003. $16.00. (F)

Buckeye, Robert. *The Munch Case.* Amandla, 2003. Paper: $18.00. (F)

Budde, Rob. *The Dying Poem.* Coach House, 2002. Paper: $18.95. (F)

Bukowski, Charles. *Sifting through the Madness for the Word, the Line, the Way.* Ecco, 2003. $27.50. (P)

Buñuel, Luis. *The Exterminating Angel.* Trans. Chase Madar. Green Integer, 2003. Paper: $11.95. (F)

Burdett, John. *Bangkok 8.* Knopf, 2003. $24.00. (F)

Burroughs, William S. *Junky: The Definitive Text of "Junk."* 50th anniversary ed. Ed. and intro. Oliver Harris. Penguin, 2003. Paper: $14.00. (F)

Camilleri, Andrea. *The Terra-Cotta Dog.* Trans. Stephen Sartarelli. Penguin, 2003. Paper: $5.99. (F)

Carson, Tom. *Gilligan's Wake.* Picador, 2003. $25.00. (F)

Carter, Vincent O. *Such Sweet Thunder.* Steerforth, 2003. $25.95. (F)

Cavell, Benjamin. *Rumble, Young Man, Rumble.* Knopf, 2003. $22.00. (F)

Céline, Louis-Ferdinand. *Fable for Another Time.* Trans. and intro. Mary Hudson. Notes and preface Henri Godard. Univ. of Nebraska Press, 2003. Paper: $25.00. (F)

Chadwick, Cydney. *Under the Sun.* Illus. Meg Hitchcock. Obscure Publications, 2003. Paper: No price given. (F)

Charyn, Jerome. *Bronx Boy: A Memoir.* Dunne/St. Martin's, 2002. $23.95. (NF)

Christopher, Nicholas. *Franklin Flyer.* Delta, 2003. Paper: $13.95. (F)

Clanchy, John. *The Hard Word.* Univ. of Queensland Press, 2002. Paper: $27.00. (F)

Clark, Geoffrey. *Wedding in October.* Red Hen, 2002. Paper: $14.95. (F)

Claus, Hugo. *The Sorrow of Belgium.* Trans. Arnold J. Pomerans. Tusk Ivories, 2003. Paper: $17.95. (F)

Corrick, Martin. *The Navigation Log.* Random House, 2003. $24.95. (F)

Craig, Charmaine. *The Good Men: A Novel of Heresy.* Riverhead, 2003. Paper: $14.00. (F)

Crawford, Stanley. *The River in Winter: New and Selected Essays.* Univ. of New Mexico Press, 2003. $21.95. (NF)

Crocker, Daniel. *The Cornstalk Man.* Green Bean, 2003. Paper: $12.00. (F)

Crosthwaite, Luis Humberto, John William Byrd, and Bobby Byrd, eds. *Puro Border: Dispatches, Snapshots & Graffiti from La Frontera.* With Jessica Powers. Cinco Puntos, 2003. Paper: $18.95. (F, NF)

Crystal, David, and Ben Crystal. *Shakespeare's Words: A Glossary and Language Companion.* Preface Stanley Wells. Penguin, 2002. Paper: $18.00. (NF)

Cumyn, Alan. *Losing It.* St. Martin's, 2002. $24.95. (F)

Dalrymple, William. *City of Djinns.* Illus. Olivia Fraser. Penguin, 2003. Paper: $15.00. (NF)

Davies, Robertson. *For Your Eyes Alone: The Letters of Robertson Davies.* Ed. Judith Skelton Grant. Penguin, 2002. Paper: $16.00. (NF)

Davison, Philip. *McKenzie's Friend.* Penguin, 2003. Paper: $13.00. (F)

De Csipkay, Nicolette. *Black Umbrella Stories.* Illus. Francesca de Csipkay. Starcherone, 2003. Paper: $15.00. (F)

De Luca, Erri. *God's Mountain.* Trans. Michael Moore. Riverhead, 2003. Paper: $12.95. (F)

De Quierós, Eça. *The Crime of Father Amaro.* Trans. and intro. Margaret Jull Costa. New Directions, 2003. Paper: $14.95. (F)

——. *El crimen del Padre Amaro.* Trans. Nan Flanagan. Carcanet, 2003. Paper: £5.95. (F)

Dickey, James. *The One Voice of James Dickey: His Letters and Life, 1942-1969.* Ed. with commentary by Gordon Van Ness. Univ. of Missouri Press, 2003. $49.99. (NF)

Dillon, Millicent. *A Version of Love.* Norton, 2003. $23.95. (F)

Djebar, Assia. *Algerian White.* Trans. David Kelley and Marjolijn de Jager. Seven Stories, 2003. Paper: $13.95. (NF)

Dobie, Kathy. *The Only Girl in the Car.* Dial, 2003. $23.95. (NF)

Donovan, Gerard. *Schopenhauer's Telescope.* Counterpoint, 2003. $25.00. (F)

Dorfman, Ariel. *Exorcising Terror: The Incredible Unending Trial of General Augusto Pinochet.* Seven Stories, 2002. Paper: $11.95. (NF)

Duignan, Kate. *Breakwater*. Victoria Univ. Press, 2003. Paper: $12.95. (F)

Duncan, Pamela. *Plant Life*. Delacorte, 2003. $23.95. (F)

Ellenberg, Jordan. *The Grasshopper King*. Coffee House, 2003. Paper: $14.00. (F)

Enright, Anne. *The Pleasure of Eliza Lynch*. Atlantic, 2003. $23.00. (F)

Ensign, Robert Taylor. *Lean Down Your Ear upon the Earth, and Listen: Thomas Wolfe's Greener Modernism*. Univ. of South Carolina Press, 2003. $29.95. (NF)

Escalante, Beatriz. *Magdalena: A Fable of Immortality*. Trans. Jay Miskowiec. Intros. Julio Ortega and Gabriella de Beer. Aliform, 2002. Paper: $12.95. (F)

Evenson, Brian. *Understanding Robert Coover*. Univ. of South Carolina Press, 2003. $34.95. (NF)

Feal, Rosemary G., and Yvette E. Miller, eds. *Isabel Allende Today*. Latin American Literary Review Press, 2002. Paper: $15.95. (NF)

Feherty, David. *A Nasty Bit of Rough*. Penguin, 2003. Paper: $14.00. (F)

Feldman, Elliot. *Sitting Shiva*. Foxrock, 2002. Paper: $12.95. (F)

Fforde, Jasper. *The Eyre Affair*. Penguin, 2003. Paper: $14.00. (F)

Flisar, Evald. *My Father's Dreams*. Trans. by the author with Alan McConnell-Duff. Texture, 2003. Paper: $14.00. (F)

Flynt, Candace. *Mother Love*. Louisiana State Univ. Press, 2003. Paper: $17.95. (F)

Ford, Darnella. *Rising*. St. Martin's Griffin, 2003. Paper: $12.95. (F)

Furst, Joshua. *Short People*. Knopf, 2003. $23.00. (F)

Gadbow, Kate. *Pushed to Shore*. Sarabande, 2003. Paper: $13.95. (F)

Galloway, Janice. *Clara*. Simon & Schuster, 2003. $25.00. (F)

García, Cristina. *Monkey Hunting*. Knopf, 2003. $23.00. (F)

García Aguilar, Eduardo. *Luminous Cities*. Trans. Jay Miskowiec. Illus. Santiago Rebolledo. Aliform, 2002. Paper: $16.95. (F)

Garrett, George. *The Magic Striptease*. Louisiana State Univ. Press, 2003. Paper: $16.95. (F)

Gautreaux, Tim. *The Clearing*. Knopf, 2003. $24.00. (F)

Gay, Jackie, and Emma Hargrave, eds. *Her Majesty: 21 Stories by Women*. Tindal Street/Dufour, 2003. Paper: $15.95. (F)

Giardina, Denise. *Fallam's Secret*. Norton, 2003. $24.95. (F)

Gibbons, Reginald. *Sweetbitter*. Louisiana State Univ. Press, 2003. Paper: $18.95. (F)

Gillick, Liam. *Literally No Place*. Book Works, 2002. Paper: £9.95. (F)

Giono, Jean. *Two Riders of the Storm*. Trans. Alan Brown. Peter Owen/Dufour, 2002. Paper: $18.95. (F)

Gold, Charles H. *"Hatching Ruin" on Mark Twain's Road to Bankruptcy.* Univ. of Missouri Press, 2003. $29.95. (NF)

Goldbarth, Albert. *Pieces of Payne.* Graywolf, 2003. Paper: $15.00. (F)

Gonzalez, Ray. *Circling the Tortilla Dragon: Short-Short Fictions.* Creative Arts, 2002. Paper: $15.00. (F)

Grass, Günter. *Crabwalk.* Trans. Krishna Winston. Harcourt, 2003. $25.00. (F)

Greenberg, Alvin. *Time Lapse.* Tupelo, 2003. $22.95. (F)

Grimes, Tom. *WILL@epicqwest.com: A Medicated Memoir.* Ludlow, 2003. Paper: $12.95. (F)

Hall, Brian. *I Should Be Extremely Happy in Your Company: A Novel of Lewis and Clark.* Viking, 2003. $25.95. (F)

Hamsun, Knut. *Knut Hamsun Remembers America: Essays and Stories, 1885-1949.* Trans. and ed. Richard Nelson Current. Univ. of Missouri Press, 2003. $29.95. (F, NF)

Hansen, Brooks. *The Monsters of St. Helena.* Farrar, Straus & Giroux, 2003. $24.00. (F)

Haskell, John. *I Am Not Jackson Pollock.* Farrar, Straus & Giroux, 2003. $20.00. (F)

Hattenhauer, Darryl. *Shirley Jackson's American Gothic.* State Univ. of New York Press, 2003. Paper: $21.95. (NF)

Hemmingson, Michael. *My Dream Date (Rape) with Kathy Acker.* Eraserhead, 2002. Paper: $10.95. (F)

Herling, Gustaw. *The Noonday Cemetery and Other Stories.* Trans. Bill Johnston. New Directions, 2003. $25.95. (F)

Hollander, John. *Picture Window.* Knopf, 2003. $24.00. (P)

Houellebecq, Michel. *Platform.* Trans. Frank Wynne. Knopf, 2003. $25.00. (F)

Hugo, Ripley. *Writing for Her Life: The Novelist Mildred Walker.* Univ. of Nebraska Press, 2003. $29.95. (NF)

Hutchings, Kimberly. *Hegel and Feminist Philosophy.* Polity, 2003. Paper: £14.99. (NF)

Huxley, Aldous. *Complete Essays, Volume VI: 1956-1963.* Ed. Robert S. Baker and James Sexton. Ivan R. Dee, 2002. $35.00. (NF)

Hyder, Quarratulain. *River of Fire.* New Directions, 2003. Paper: $14.95. (F)

Iagnemma, Karl. *On the Nature of Human Romantic Interaction.* Dial, 2003. $22.95. (F)

Iggulden, Conn. *Emperor: The Gates of Rome.* Delacorte, 2002. $24.95. (F)

Jackson, Vanessa Furse. *What I Cannot Say to You.* Univ. of Missouri Press, 2003. Paper: $15.95. (F)

Jacobs, Laura. *Women about Town.* Penguin, 2003. Paper: $14.00. (F)

Jeppesen, Travis. *Victims.* Akashic, 2003. Paper: $13.95. (F)

Jonquet, Thierry. *Mygale.* Trans. Donald Nicholson-Smith. City Lights, 2003. Paper: $11.95. (F)

Judd, Alan. *Legacy.* Knopf, 2003. $24.00. (F)

Kapralov, Yuri. *Devil's Midnight.* Akashic, 2003. $22.95. (F)

Kennedy, A. L. *Indelible Acts.* Knopf, 2003. $23.00. (F)

Kennedy, William. *Roscoe.* Penguin, 2002. Paper: $14.00. (F)

Kerouac, Jack. *Book of Haikus.* Ed. and intro. Regina Weinreich. Penguin, 2003. Paper: $10.00. (P)

Kidd, Sue Monk. *The Secret Life of Bees.* Penguin, 2003. Paper: $14.00. (F)

King, Adele. *Rereading Camara Laye.* Univ. of Nebraska Press, 2003. $45.00. (NF)

King, Laurie R. *Keeping Watch.* Bantam, 2003. $23.95. (F)

Kirwan, Larry. *Liverpool Fantasy.* Thunder's Mouth, 2003. Paper: $14.95. (F)

Knight, Michael. *Goodnight, Nobody.* Atlantic, 2003. $23.00. (F)

Kona, Prakash. *Streets that Smell of Dying Roses.* Fugue State, 2003. Paper: $14.00. (F)

Krause, Richard. *Studies in Insignificance.* Livingston, 2003. $26.00. (F)

Laskas, Gretchen Moran. *The Midwife's Tale.* Dial, 2003. $23.95. (F)

Lê, Thi Diem Thúy. *The Gangster We Are All Looking For.* Knopf, 2003. $18.00. (F)

Le Clézio, J. M. G. *The Round and Other Cold Hard Facts.* Trans. C. Dickson. Univ. of Nebraska Press, 2003. Paper: $19.95. (F)

Levitsky, Rachel. *Under the Sun.* Futurepoem, 2003. Paper: $12.00. (P)

Long, J. J. *The Novels of Thomas Bernhard: Form and Its Function.* Camden House, 2001. $59.00. (NF)

Loy, Rosetta. *Hot Chocolate at Hanselmann's.* Trans. and intro. Gregory Conti. Univ. of Nebraska Press, 2003. Paper: $16.95. (F)

Lurie, Alison. *Boys and Girls Forever: Children's Classics from Cinderella to Harry Potter.* Penguin, 2003. Paper: $15.00. (NF)

Macdonald, D. R. *All the Men Are Sleeping.* Counterpoint, 2003. Paper: $14.00. (F)

Major, Clarence. *Such Was the Season.* Louisiana State Univ. Press, 2003. Paper: $15.95. (F)

Malladi, Amulya. *The Mango Season.* Simon & Schuster, 2003. $22.95. (F)

Maloney, Geoffrey. *Tales from the Crypto-System.* Prime, 2003. Paper: $17.95. (F)

Manchette, Jean-Patrick. *The Prone Gunman.* Trans. James Brook. City Lights, 2002. Paper: $11.95. (F)

Marías, Javier. *The Man of Feeling*. Trans. Margaret Jull Costa. New Directions, 2003. $22.95. (F)

Martin, Valerie. *Property*. Nan A. Talese/Doubleday, 2003. $23.95. (F)

Maso, Carole. *Aureole*. City Lights, 2003. Paper: $12.95. (F)

Mason, J. D. *And on the Eighth Day She Rested*. St. Martin's, 2003. Paper: $13.95. (F)

Mattessich, Stefan. *Lines of Flight: Discursive Time and Counter-cultural Desire in the Work of Thomas Pynchon*. Duke Univ. Press, 2002. Paper: $21.95. (NF)

Mazelis, Jo. *Diving Girls*. Parthian/Dufour, 2003. Paper: $13.95. (F)

Mazza, Cris. *Indigenous: Growing Up Californian*. City Lights, 2003. Paper: $16.95. (NF)

McCafferty, Kate. *Testimony of an Irish Slave Girl*. Penguin, 2003. Paper: $13.00. (F)

McCarthy, Susan Carol. *Lay That Trumpet in Our Hands*. Bantam, 2003. Paper: $12.95. (F)

McCrum, Robert, Robert MacNeil, and William Cran. *The Story of English*. 3rd rev. ed. Penguin, 2003. Paper: $16.00. (NF)

McElroy, Joseph. *A Smuggler's Bible*. Intro. Richard Howard. Overlook, 2003. Paper: $15.95. (F)

McMurtry, Larry. *The Wandering Hill: The Berrybender Narratives, Book 2*. Simon & Schuster, 2003. $25.95. (F)

Miles, Lisa A. *This Fantastic Struggle: The Life and Art of Esther Phillips*. Creative Arts, 2002. Paper: $18.00. (NF)

Montgomery, Arch. *Hank*. Bancroft, 2003. $19.95. (F)

Moskowitz, Faye. *Peace in the House: Tales from a Yiddish Kitchen*. Godine, 2002. $23.95. (F)

Nelson, Lee J. *The Boy in the Box*. Bridge Works, 2003. $23.95. (F)

Newman, Rafaël, ed. *Contemporary Jewish Writing in Switzerland: An Anthology*. Univ. of Nebraska Press, 2003. $60.00. (F)

Newman, Sandra. *The Only Good Thing Anyone Has Ever Done*. HarperCollins, 2003. $24.95. (F)

Oda, Makoto. *The Breaking Jewel*. Trans. Donald Keene. Columbia Univ. Press, 2003. Paper: $16.50. (F)

Olson, Toby. *Utah*. Green Integer, 2003. Paper: $12.95. (F)

Oropesa, Salvador A. *The Contemporáneos Group: Rewriting Mexico in the Thirties and Forties*. Univ. of Texas Press, 2003. $37.50. (NF)

Packer, ZZ. *Drinking Coffee Elsewhere*. Riverhead, 2003. $24.95. (F)

Pazzi, Roberto. *Conclave*. Trans. Oonagh Stransky. Steerforth, 2003. Paper: $14.95. (F)

Pearson, T. R. *Polar*. Penguin, 2003. Paper: $14.00. (F)

Pelevin, Victor. *Homo Zapiens*. Trans. Andrew Bromfield. Penguin, 2003. Paper: $14.00. (F)

——. *A Werewolf Problem in Central Russia and Other Stories.* Trans. Andrew Bromfield. New Directions, 2003. Paper: $12.95. (F)

Perez, Richard. *The Loser's Club.* Ludlow, 2003. Paper: $12.95. (F)

Pettigrew, Dawn Karima. *The Way We Make Sense.* Aunt Lute Books, 2002. Paper: $11.95. (F)

Poniatowska, Elena. *Here's to You, Jesusa!* Trans. Deanna Heikkinen. Penguin, 2002. Paper: $14.00. (F)

Powell, Anthony. *O, How the Wheel Becomes It!* Green Integer, 2002. Paper: $10.95. (F)

——. *Venusberg.* Green Integer, 2003. Paper: $10.95. (F)

Queneau, Raymond. *We Always Treat Women Too Well.* Trans. Barbara Wright. Intro. John Updike. New York Review Books, 2003. Paper: $12.95. (F)

——. *Witch Grass.* Trans. and intro. Barbara Wright. New York Review Books, 2003. Paper: $16.95. (F)

Rackman, Jeff. *The Rag & Bone Shop.* Penguin, 2002. Paper: $14.00. (F)

Randolph, Amy. *Cold Angel of Mercy.* Red Hen, 2002. Paper: $10.95. (P)

Ray, Francis. *Somebody's Knocking at My Door.* St. Martin's Griffin, 2003. Paper: $13.95. (F)

Rhode, William. *Paperback Original.* Riverhead, 2003. Paper: $14.00. (F)

Rimbaud, Jean-Nicholas-Arthur. *From Absinthe to Abyssinia: Selected Miscellaneous, Obscure, and Previously Untranslated Works.* Trans. Mark Spitzer. Creative Arts, 2002. Paper: $14.95. (NF, P)

Ríos, Julián. *Monstruary.* Trans. Edith Grossman. Northwestern Univ. Press, 2002. Paper: $19.95. (F)

Robbins, Tom. *Villa Incognito.* Bantam, 2003. $24.00. (F)

Roffey, Monique. *August Frost.* Atlantic, 2003. $24.00. (F)

Rosenstone, Robert A. *King of Odessa: A Novel of Isaac Babel.* Northwestern Univ. Press, 2003. $24.95. (F)

Ross, Ann B. *Miss Julia Throws a Wedding.* Penguin, 2003. Paper: $14.00. (F)

Roth, Joseph. *The Silent Prophet.* Trans. David le Vay. Peter Owen/Dufour, 2002. Paper: $18.95. (F)

Rowell, John. *The Music of Your Life.* Simon & Schuster, 2003. $24.00. (F)

Ruiz, Luis Manuel. *Only One Thing Missing.* Trans. Alfred Mac Adam. Grove, 2003. $24.00. (F)

Rush, Norman. *Mortals.* Knopf, 2003. $26.95. (F)

Salem, Ibtihal. *Children of the Waters.* Trans. Marilyn Booth. Univ. of Texas Press, 2002. Paper: $13.95. (F)

Salter, Mary Jo. *Open Shutters.* Knopf, 2003. $23.00. (P)

Sanchez, Thomas. *King Bongo: A Novel of Havana.* Knopf, 2003. $25.00. (F)

Sandor, Marjorie. *Portrait of My Mother, Who Posed Nude in Wartime.* Sarabande, 2003. Paper: $13.95. (F)

Sarvig, Ole. *The Sea below My Window.* Trans. Anni Whissen. Green Integer, 2003. Paper: $13.95. (F)

Schnitzler, Arthur. *Lieutenant Gustl.* Trans. Richard L. Simon. Green Integer, 2003. Paper: $9.95. (F)

Scholz, Carter. *Radiance.* Picador, 2003. Paper: $14.00. (F)

Scott, Anne. *Calpurnia.* Knopf, 2003. $24.00. (F)

Sebald, W. G. *On the Natural History of Destruction.* Trans. Anthea Bell. Random House, 2003. $23.95. (NF)

Shabtai, Yaakov. *Past Continuous.* Trans. Dalya Bilu. Tusk Ivories, 2003. Paper: $16.95. (F)

Shade, Eric. *Eyesores.* Univ. of Georgia Press, 2003. $24.95. (F)

Shapiro, Dani. *Family History.* Knopf, 2003. $23.00. (F)

Shelach, Oz. *Picnic Grounds: A Novel in Fragments.* City Lights, 2003. Paper: $11.95. (F)

Siegel, Lee. *Love and Other Games of Chance: A Novelty.* Viking, 2003. $27.95. (F)

Skemer, Arnold. *E.* Phrygian, 2003. Paper: $8.00. (F)

Smiley, Jane. *Good Faith.* Knopf, 2003. $26.00. (F)

Smith, Andrea. *Friday Nights at Honeybee's.* Dial, 2002. $22.95. (F)

Smith, April. *Good Morning, Killer.* Knopf, 2003. $24.00. (F)

Smock, Ann. *What Is There to Say?* Univ. of Nebraska Press, 2003. $45.00. (NF)

Sol, Adam. *Crowd of Sounds.* Anansi, 2003. Paper: $14.95. (P)

Spikes, Michael P. *Understanding Contemporary American Literary Theory.* Rev. ed. Univ. of South Carolina Press, 2003. Paper: $16.95. (NF)

Spinrad, Norman. *The Druid King.* Knopf, 2003. $24.95. (F)

Sporlender, Nicholas (Jeff VanderMeer). *The Exchange.* Illus. Louis Verden (Eric Schaller). Hoegbotton & Sons, 2001. Paper: $6.99. (F)

Stasiuk, Andrzej. *Tales of Galicia.* Trans. Margarita Nafpaktitis. Twisted Spoon, 2003. Paper: $14.00. (F)

Stegner, Wallace. *On Teaching and Writing Fiction.* Ed. and foreword Lynn Stegner. Penguin, 2002. Paper: $13.00. (NF)

Steinberg, Susan. *The End of Free Love.* FC2, 2003. Paper: $13.95. (F)

Stephenson, Gregory. *Understanding Robert Stone.* Univ. of South Carolina Press, 2002. $34.95. (NF)

Stoberock, Johanna. *City of Ghosts.* Norton, 2003. $23.95. (F)

Stow, Randolph. *To the Islands.* Univ. of Queensland Press, 2002. Paper: $17.95. (F)

Stralka, Stephen. *Not Too Happy about the Jumpsuit.* Hominoid, 2001. Paper: $3.00. (F)

Swift, Graham. *The Light of Day*. Knopf, 2003. $24.00. (F)

Thomas, Chantal. *Farewell, My Queen*. Trans. Moishe Black. Braziller, 2003. $22.50. (F)

Tolstaya, Tatyana. *The Slynx*. Trans. Jamey Gambrell. Houghton Mifflin, 2003. $24.00. (F)

Tomasula, Steve. *VAS: An Opera in Flatland*. Art and design Stephen Farrell. Barrytown/Station Hill, 2003. $34.00. (F)

Tonelli, Bill, ed. *The Italian American Reader: A Collection of Outstanding Fiction, Memoirs, Journalism, Essays, and Poetry*. Foreword Nick Tosches. Morrow, 2003. $27.95. (F, NF, P)

Troncoso, Sergio. *The Nature of Truth*. Northwestern Univ. Press, 2003. $22.95. (F)

Trujillo, Carla. *What Night Brings*. Curbstone, 2003. Paper: $15.95. (F)

Turner, Frederick. *1929*. Counterpoint, 2003. $25.00. (F)

Tytell, John. *Reading New York*. Knopf, 2003. $25.00. (NF)

VanderMeer, Jeff. *Veniss Underground*. Prime, 2003. Paper: $15.00. (F)

Vannatta, Dennis. *Lives of the Artists*. Livingston, 2003. Paper: $13.95. (F)

Vollmann, William T. *Argall*. Penguin, 2002. Paper: $18.00. (F)

Vreeland, Susan. *The Passion of Artemisia*. Penguin, 2003. Paper: $13.00. (F)

Weil, Simone. *Letter to a Priest*. Penguin, 2003. Paper: $12.00. (NF)

Whited, Lana A., ed. and intro. *The Ivory Tower and Harry Potter: Perspectives on a Literary Phenomenon*. Univ. of Missouri Press, 2002. $34.95. (NF)

Whiteford, Merry. *If Wishes Were Horses*. Dunne/St. Martin's, 2003. $23.95. (F)

Wright, Barbara. *Plain Language*. Touchstone, 2003. Paper: $13.00. (F)

Wright, C. D. *Steal Away: Selected and New Poems*. Copper Canyon, 2002. $25.00. (P)

Yancey, Richard. *A Burning in Homeland*. Simon & Schuster, 2003. $25.00. (F)

Yuknavitch, Lidia. *Real to Reel*. FC2, 2003. Paper: $13.95. (F)

Živković, Zoran. *The Library*. Trans. Alice Copple-Tošić. Polaris/Ministry of Whimsy, 2002. Paper: No price given. (F)

Zweig, Arnold. *The Case of Sergeant Grischa*. Trans. Eric Sutton. Tusk Ivories, 2003. Paper: $16.95. (F)

Contributors

JOSEPH DEWEY, Associate Professor of American Literature for the University of Pittsburgh, is the author of *In a Dark Time: The Apocalyptic Temper of the American Novel of the Nuclear Age* (1991), *Novels from Reagan's America* (1999), and *Understanding Richard Powers* (2002). He has also co-edited casebooks on Henry James and Don DeLillo's *Underworld.* He is currently completing a study on the fiction of DeLillo.

BRIAN EVENSON is the author of six books of fiction, including *Altmann's Tongue* and, most recently, *Dark Property,* and the author of *Understanding Robert Coover.* He is the Director of Creative Writing at the University of Denver and a senior editor at *Conjunctions* magazine. He has accepted a job at Brown University beginning in fall 2003.

JOANNA HOWARD has published fiction in *Quarterly West,* the *Chicago Review, Western Humanities Review, Third Bed, Conjunctions,* and other magazines. She teaches at the University of Denver.

Robert Creeley • Gertrude Stein
dous Huxley • Robert Coover • Jo
rth • David Markson • Flann O'Bri

www.dalkeyarchive.com

uis-Ferdinand Céline • Marguer
ung • Ishmael Reed • Camilo José C
Gilbert Sorrentino • Ann Quin
icholas Mosley • Douglas Woolf
aymond Queneau • Harry Mathews
kki Ducornet • José Lezama Lima
dan Higgins • Ben Marcus • Colem
owell • Jacques Roubaud • Dju
rnes • Felipe Alfau • Osman Lins
avid Antin • Susan Daitch • Vikt
klovsky • Henry Green • Curtis Wh
Anne Carson • John Hawkes • Fo
adox Ford • Janice Galloway • Mich

Your connection to literature.
DALKEY ARCHIVE PRESS

Bard FICTION PRIZE

Bard College invites submissions for its annual Fiction Prize for young writers.

The Bard Fiction Prize is awarded annually to a promising, emerging writer who is a United States citizen aged 39 years or younger at the time of application. In addition to a monetary award of $30,000, the winner receives an appointment as writer-in-residence at Bard College for one semester without the expectation that he or she teach traditional courses. The recipient will give at least one public lecture and will meet informally with students.

To apply, candidates should write a cover letter describing the project they plan to work on while at Bard and submit a C.V., along with three copies of the published book they feel best represents their work. No manuscripts will be accepted.

Applications for the 2003 prize must be received by July 15, 2003. For further information about the Bard Fiction Prize, call 845-758-7087, send an e-mail to bfp@bard.edu, or visit www.bard.edu/bfp. Applicants may also request information by writing to the Bard Fiction Prize, Bard College, Annandale-on-Hudson, NY 12504-5000.

Bard College PO Box 5000, Annandale-on-Hudson, NY 12504-5000

Dedicated to the promotion and advancement of the study and craft of translation, translators, and publishers of translated works since 1978. Annual conferences, newsletters, and the journal *Translation Review* and its supplement, *Annotated Books Received*, provide members of this professional association with the latest information in the field of translation.

American Literary Translators Association
The University of Texas at Dallas
Mail Station MC35, Box 830688
Richardson TX 75083-0688

972-883-2093
Fax: 972-883-6303

www.literarytranslators.org

PARTISAN REVIEW
SPRING 2003

A Tribute to William Phillips, Co-Founder and Editor-in-Chief

"Literary magazines, like writers, come out of a time and a place, out of some literary current or sensibility. Thus Partisan Review *was born in the thirties. . . . If it has not been restricted by its origins, if it has defied all the pressures of a time and country that have celebrated youth, novelty, and escape from traditions, I think it is mainly because of the continuity between the thirties and the following decades and because the traditions* Partisan Review *both inherited and helped form have continued to be pertinent.*"

William Phillips (1907–2002)

William Phillips, who co-founded *Partisan Review* in 1934, strongly believed that the present rises out of the past and reaches into the future. He ensured that the magazine would stay on top of new trends without going overboard, while at the same time remaining aware of the historical roots of these trends.

Read the spring 2003 issue of *Partisan Review,* and find out how luminaries such as Jules Chametzky, Morris Dickstein, Helen Frankenthaler, Allen Kurzweil, Edith Kurzweil, Doris Lessing, Steven Marcus, Czeslaw Milosz, Conor Cruise O'Brien, Jules Olitski, Cynthia Ozick, Norman Podhoretz, John Silber, Roger Straus, Rosanna Warren, and many others remember William Phillips.

Find *Partisan Review* at select newsstands, or subscribe online at:

www.partisanreview.org

River City -- Winter 2004

Now accepting submissions of poetry,
fiction, essays, and artwork for a
non-thematic issue.

Submission deadline: November 17, 2003

Subscriptions: 12.00 a year
(2 issues)
Single Issues: 7.00 per copy
Special rate: 24.00 for three
year subscription

Department of English
University of Memphis
Memphis, TN 38152
www.memphis.edu/~rivercity
(901) 678-4591
fax (901) 678-2226
rivercity@memphis.edu

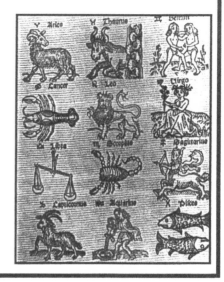

DELILLO FIEDLER GASS PYNCHON
University of Delaware Press
Collections on Contemporary Masters

UNDERWORDS
Perspectives on Don
DeLillo's *Underworld*

Edited by Joseph Dewey, Steven
G. Kellman, and Irving Malin

Essays by Jackson R. Bryer,
David Cowart, Kathleen
Fitzpatrick, Joanne Gass, Paul
Gleason, Donald J. Greiner,
Robert McMinn, Thomas Myers,
Ira Nadel, Carl Ostrowski,
Timothy L. Parrish, Marc Singer,
and David Yetter

$39.50

LESLIE FIEDLER
AND AMERICAN
CULTURE

Edited by Steven G. Kellman
and Irving Malin

Essays by John Barth, Robert
Boyers, James M. Cox, Joseph
Dewey, R.H.W. Dillard, Geoffrey
Green, Irving Feldman, Leslie
Fiedler, Susan Gubar, Jay L.
Halio, Brooke Horvath, David
Ketterer, R.W.B. Lewis, Sanford
Pinsker, Harold Schechter, Daniel
Schwarz, David R. Slavitt, Daniel
Walden, and Mark Royden
Winchell

$36.50

INTO *THE TUNNEL*
Readings of Gass's
Novel

Edited by Steven G. Kellman
and Irving Malin

Essays by Rebecca Goldstein,
Donald J. Greiner, Brooke
Horvath, Marcus Klein, Jerome
Klinkowitz, Paul Maliszewski,
James McCourt, Arthur Saltzman,
Susan Stewart, and Heide Ziegler

$35.00

PYNCHON AND
MASON & DIXON

Edited by Brooke Horvath and
Irving Malin

Essays by Jeff Baker, Joseph
Dewey, Bernard Duyfhuizen,
David Foreman, Donald J.
Greiner, Brian McHale, Clifford
S. Mead, Arthur Saltzman,
Thomas H. Schaub, David Seed,
and Victor Strandberg

$39.50

ORDER FROM ASSOCIATED UNIVERSITY PRESSES
2010 Eastpark Blvd., Cranbury, New Jersey 08512
PH 609-655-4770   FAX 609-655-8366   E-mail AUP440@ aol.com

*S*tudies in *T*wentieth *C*entury *L*iterature

Volume 27, No. 1 (Winter, 2003)

Contributors include:

Jennifer Forrest
    Pamela A. Genova
        Kimberly Healey
           Jutta Ittner
                Martha Kuhlman
                    Gerald M. Macklin
                        Anjali Prabhu

Volume 27, No. 2 (Summer, 2003)

Contributors include:

Susan Carvalho
    Laurie Corbin
        Malva E. Filer
           Scott Macdonald Frame
           Raphaël Lambert

Jill LeRoy-Frazier
    Eric P. Levy
        Laura McLary
           Caroline Rupprecht
           Gayle Zachmann

Silvia Sauter, Editor
Kansas State University
Eisenhower 104
Manhattan, KS 66506-1003
Submissions in: Spanish and Russian

Jordan Stump, Editor
University of Nebraska
PO Box 880318
Lincoln, NE 68588-0318
Submissions in: French and German

Please check our Web site for subscription and other information:
http://www.ksu.edu/stcl/index.html

Studies in American Fiction

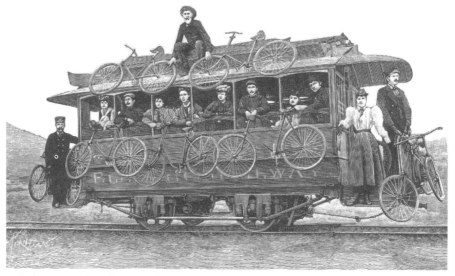

A journal of articles and reviews on the prose fiction of the United States. Published semiannually by the Department of English, Northeastern University.

Mary Loeffelholz, *Editor*

Recent numbers include: Beverly A. Hume, "Managing Madness in Gillman's 'The Yellow Wallpaper' "; Joseph Church, "Romantic Flight in Jewett's 'White Heron' "; Amy Blair, "Rewriting Heroines: Ruth Todd's 'Florence Grey,' Society Pages, and the Rhetorics of Success"; Claire Chantell, "The Limits of the Mother at Home in *The Wide, Wide World* and *The Lamplighter* "

Annual Subscriptions: Individual Subscribers: $10.00 / $13.00 outside the US
Institutional subscribers: $16.00 / $17.00 outside the US

Send subscriptions and inquiries to:
Studies in American Fiction, Department of English, Northeastern University, Boston, MA 02115-5000, 617-373.3687; or by email to **a.pikcilingis@neu.edu**

For a comprehensive source of **SAF** information, visit our web site:
www.casdn.neu.edu/~english/pubs/

the minnesota review

a journal of committed writing

Forthcoming:

n.s. 58-59

with a special section

The Legacies of Michael Sprinker

n.s. 60-61

with a special section

Smart Kids

Jeffrey J. Williams, Editor
the minnesota review
Department of English
107 Tate Hall
University of Missouri
Columbia, MO 65211

http://www.theminnesotareview.org

BRIDGE

Featured in Bridge 6:

Gus Van Sant, Richard Rorty, Greil Marcus, Bill Ayers, Alex Shakar, Stephan Fritsch, Ruth Root, Eduardo Kac, Brad Killam, Rick Moody, Charles Taylor, Ron Padgett and George Schneeman and essays on David Lynch.

Bridge 6 Includes:

The Bridge Short Film + Video Collection DVD with films by David Cronenberg, Miranda July, Harrell Fletcher, Chris Johanson, Kirsten Stoltman, Jim Trainor, Eric Fensler, Gabriel Fowler, Tom Palazzolo, Scott Roberts, Sterling Ruby, Emily Vey Duke and Cooper Battersby and many others.

www.bridgemagazine.org

FREDERICK BARTHELME
MARY ROBISON
ANGELA BALL
STEVEN BARTHELME
DAVID BERRY

Join us in south Mississippi,
where the workshops are thorough, sometimes strange, always friendly. Where most
of the jokes are funny. We have three dozen
writers working toward master's and doctoral
degrees in fiction and poetry. We have visi-
tors such as Rick Moody, Amy Hempel,
Lucie Brock-Broido, Dana Gioia, Padgett
Powell, Michael Waters,
Mary Gaitskill, Julia
Slavin, C. Michael Curtis
and others. Recent graduates
have won The Whiting Award,
The Transatlantic Award, The *Playboy* Fiction Contest, and
The Flannery O'Connor Award and have published widely. Five gradu-
ates are having books published this year. We edit and publish *Missis-sippi Review*, publish a student magazine, and manage to help our writ-
ers become better writers. It's a small program that gets good results.
For information contact Rie Fortenberry at rief@netdoor.com, check
www.centerforwriters.com, or write us in that old fashioned way.

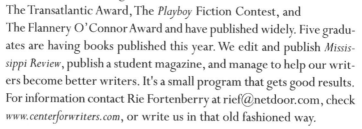

The Center for Writers

THE UNIVERSITY OF SOUTHERN MISSISSIPPI, BOX 5144, HATTIESBURG, MS 39406, (AA/EOE/ADAI)

Dalkey Archive Press

NEW RELEASES

Terra Nostra
by CARLOS FUENTES

La Bâtarde
by VIOLETTE LEDUC

The Celebration
by IVAN ÂNGELO

Inventing God
by NICHOLAS MOSLEY

Konfidenz
by ARIEL DORFMAN

Essays on Poetry
by RALPH J. MILLS, JR.

Terra Nostra

CARLOS FUENTES

Introduction by Jorge Volpi
Afterword by Milan Kundera
Translated by Margaret Sayers Peden

Latin American Literature Series
A Novel
$15.95 / paper
ISBN: 1-56478-287-5

One of the great masterpieces of modern Latin American fiction, *Terra Nostra* is concerned with nothing less than the history of Spain and of South America, with the Indian gods and with Christianity, with the birth, the passion, and the death of civilizations. Fuentes skillfully blends a wide range of literary forms, stories within stories, Mexican and Spanish myth, and famous literary characters in this novel that is both a historical epic and an apocalyptic vision of modern times. *Terra Nostra* is that most ambitious and rare of creations—a total work of art.

"Terra Nostra *is the spreading out of the novel, the exploration of its possibilities, the voyage to the edge of what only a novelist can see and say.*"
—*Milan Kundera*

"*The supreme example of a total literary creation, of the creative disruption of writing, of the cultural ransacking of the totality of the Spanish language.* Terra Nostra *is not only Carlos Fuentes's major work. It is also, beyond any doubt, one of the great monuments of the Spanish language novel.*"
—*Juan Goytisolo*

"*Written with a fervor that is both fierce and compassionate, this is a complex, powerful novel of huge scope.*" —Kirkus Reviews

—— *Now Available* ——

La Bâtarde

VIOLETTE LEDUC

Introduction by Deborah Levy
Foreword by Simone de Beauvoir
Translated by Derek Coltman

French Literature Series
Literature/Memoir
$15.95 / paper
ISBN: 1-56478-289-1

An obsessive and revealing self-portrait of a remarkable woman humiliated by the circumstances of her birth and by her physical appearance, *La Bâtarde* relates Violette Leduc's long search for her own identity through a series of agonizing and passionate love affairs with both men and women. When first published, *La Bâtarde* was compared to the work of Jean Genet for the frank depiction of sexual escapades and immoral behavior. A confession that contains portraits of several famous French authors, this book is more than just a scintillating memoir—like that of Henry Miller or Charles Bukowski, Leduc's brilliant writing style and attention to language transform this autobiography into a work of art.

"Whoever speaks to us from the depths of his loneliness speaks to us of ourselves. In La Bâtarde, *a woman is descending into the most secret part of herself and telling us about all she finds there with an unflinching sincerity, as though there were no one listening."* —Simone de Beauvoir

"Notoriety aside, Leduc is first and foremost a first-rate writer. Not someone who just tells a provocative story and is unafraid to reveal the most offensive parts of her personality and of her experience, but someone who is in love with words, struggles with them, wrestles with language, dies for adjectives, is tortured by her search for le mot juste.*"* —Women's Review of Books

—— *Now Available* ——

The Celebration

IVAN ÂNGELO

Translated by Thomas Colchie

Latin American Literature Series
A Novel
$13.50 / paper
ISBN: 1-56478-290-5

In the early morning of March 31, 1970 in Belo Horizonte, Brazil, the annual birthday celebration of a prominent and wealthy young artist is taking place, and a train docked in Plaza Station filled with starving, drought-stricken migrant workers seeking relief gets turned away by the authorities, sparking a riot. From these two seemingly unrelated events, Ivan Ângelo's remarkable novel connects and implicates the lives of a complex of characters, spanning three decades of tumultuous social and political history in twentieth-century Brazil. But with the central event—the celebration—missing, the reader is thrust into the middle of a puzzle, left to construct the story from the evidence that accrues in a range of comic, unnerving, misleading, and tragic episodes.

WINNER OF THE BRAZILIAN PUBLISHERS PRIZE

"Ângelo presents his events and characters through a variety of techniques and styles, like a juggler showing all his tricks."   —Washington Post

——— *Now Available* ———

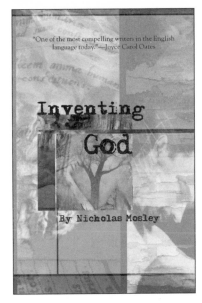

Inventing God

Nicholas Mosley

British Literature Series
A Novel
$14.50 / paper
ISBN: 1-56478-291-3

Set amid the current tension and violence of the Middle East, Nicholas Mosley's new novel features over a half-dozen characters searching for ways to quell society's self-destructive impulses. As the story develops, the actions and aspirations of these characters—which include a Muslim student working on the deadliest of biological weapons, a young Israeli girl trapped in a temple's ruins, and a middle-aged ex-television-guru who has mysteriously disappeared—create a moral and philosophical system illustrating the roles chance and coincidence play in our lives.

Concluding in September 2001, *Inventing God* is a fascinating and highly relevant new novel from a previous winner of the Whitbread Book of the Year award.

"One of the most compelling writers in the English language today."
—Joyce Carol Oates

"An astonishing piece of work with the potential to shift the way we view the world: surely a contender for the first great novel of the twenty-first century."
—Martin Bright, Observer (London)

"Mosley is the most serious and brilliant of Britain's novelists of ideas."
—Robert McFarlane, Times (London)

—— Now Available ——

Konfidenz

ARIEL DORFMAN

Introduction by Andrei Codrescu

Latin American Literature Series
A Novel
$13.50 / paper
ISBN: 1-56478-293-X

Told almost exclusively through dialogue, *Konfidenz* opens with a woman entering a hotel room and receiving a call from a mysterious stranger who seems to know everything about her and the reasons why she has fled her homeland. Over the next nine hours he tells her many disturbing things about her lover (who may be in great danger), the political situation in which they are enmeshed, and his fantasies of her. A terse political allegory that challenges our assumptions about character, the foundations of our knowledge, and the making of history, *Konfidenz* draws the reader into a postmodern mystery where nothing—including the text itself—is what it seems.

"With Konfidenz, *Dorfman steps confidently from the realm of Latin American storyteller into the arena of a world novelist of the first category.*"
—*Marie Arana,* Washington Post

"*Exhilarating for its finely tuned unfolding but somber in its conclusions,* Konfidenz *demands a fundamental reexamination of the nature of trust.*"
—Publishers Weekly *(starred review)*

——— *Now Available* ———

Essays on Poetry

RALPH J. MILLS, JR.

Introduction by Michael Anania

American Literature Series
Literary Criticism
$18.95 / paper
ISBN: 1-56478-294-8

$44.95 / cloth
ISBN: 1-56478-295-6

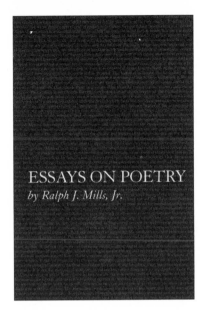

ESSAYS ON POETRY
by Ralph J. Mills, Jr.

Taken from throughout Mills's career, the essays collected in this volume delve into the work of such influential writers as Wallace Stevens, Denise Levertov, Samuel Beckett, Galway Kinnell, Edith Sitwell, Theodore Roethke, Karl Shapiro, Richard Wilbur, Isabella Gardner, James Wright, David Ignatow, Donald Hall, Robert Bly, Philip Levine, and Stanley Kunitz. Mills examines how the personal element informs the works of these writers and enables them "to speak to us, without impediment, from the deep center of a personal engagement with existence."

Ralph J. Mills, Jr. is a significant figure in contemporary poetry for his work as a poet, critic, and professor. His poetry collections include *Living with Distance, A Window in Air,* and *March Light,* which received the Carl Sandburg Award. He also edited the selected prose and letters of Theodore Roethke. From 1962 to 1965 he served as Assistant Professor and Associate Chairman of the Committee on Social Thought at the University of Chicago. He is professor emeritus of English at the University of Illinois at Chicago.

"Ralph Mills has the clearest of clear eyes, and knows exactly how to translate what is seen into what can be heard, so that we can share to an almost uncanny degree that crystalline vision."   —*Denise Levertov*

—— *Now Available* ——

ORDER FORM

Individuals may use this form to subscribe to the *Review of Contemporary Fiction*
or to order back issues of the *Review* or Dalkey titles at a 10-20% discount.

Title	ISBN	Quantity	Price

Subtotal_____

(10% for one book, 20% for two or more books) Less Discount_____

Subtotal_____

($4 domestic, $5 foreign) Plus postage_____

1 year individual subscription ($17 domestic, $20.50 foreign)_____

Total_____

Ship to _____

mail or fax this form to:

Dalkey Archive Press
ISU Campus Box 8905
Normal, IL 61790-8905
fax: 309.438.7422
tel: 309.438.7555

Credit card payment   ☐ Visa   ☐ Mastercard

Acct #_____   Exp. Date_____

Name on card_____   Phone Number_____

Please make checks (in U. S. dollars only) payable to *Dalkey Archive Press*